WISDOM CHRISTOLOGY IN THE FOURTH GOSPEL

Michael E. Willett

Mellen Research University Press
San Francisco

BT
198
.W467
1992

Library of Congress Cataloging-in-Publication Data

Willet, Michael E. (Michael Edward), 1955-
    Wisdom Christology in the fourth Gospel / Michael E. Willet.
       p.   cm.
    Revision of the author's thesis (Ph. D.)--Southern Baptist
Theological Seminary, 1985.
    Includes bibliographical references and indexes.
    ISBN 0-7734-9947-4
    1. Bible. N. T. John--Theology. 2. Jesus Christ--History of
doctrines--Early church, ca. 30-600. 3. Bible. N. T.--Relation to
the Old Testament. 4. Wisdom literature--Criticism, interpretation,
etc. 5. Wisdom (Biblical character) I. Title.
BT198.W467   1992
226.5' 06--dc20   92-36835
                                                                        CIP

Editorial Inquiries:

Mellen Research University Press
534 Pacific Avenue
San Francisco
CA 94133

Order Fulfillment:

The Edwin Mellen Press
P.O. Box 450
Lewiston, NY 14092
USA

Printed in the United States of America

TABLE OF CONTENTS

TABLE OF ABBREVIATIONS

AB	Anchor Bible
AJSL	American Journal of Semitic Languages and Literatures
AnBib	Analecta biblica
ATANT	Abhandlungen zur theologie des Alten und Neuen Testaments
ATR	Anglican Theological Review
AusBR	Australian Biblical Review
AWJEC	Aspects of Wisdom in Judaism and Early Christianity
BETL	Bibliotheca ephemeridum theologicarum lovaniensium
BETS	Bulletin of the Evangelical Theological Society
Bib	Biblica
b. Šabb.	Babylonian Talmud on Šabbat
BSR	Biblioteca di Scienze Religiose
BTB	Biblical Theology Bulletin
BZ	Biblische Zeitschrift
Cant. Rab.	Canticles Rabbah
CBQ	Catholic Biblical Quarterly
CCCT	Creation, Christ and Culture: Studies in Honour of T. F. Torrance
Cher.	Philo, De Cherubim
CIMCT Honor of	Current Issues in Biblical and Patristic Interpretation: Studies in Merrill Tenney
CINTI of Otto	Current Issues in New Testament Interpretation: Essays in Honor A. Piper

ConBT	Coniectanea biblica, New Testament
Conf.	Philo, De Confusione Linguarum
CSNT	Christ and Spirit in the New Testament: Studies in Honour of C. F.
D.	Moule
CurTM	Currents in Theology and Mission
CW	The Collected Works of Carl G. Jung
Deter.	Philo, Quod Deterius Potiori Insidiari Soleat
EBib	Études bibliques
Ebr.	Philo, De Ebrietate
EstBib	Estudios bíblicos
ETL	Ephemerides theologicae lovanienses
EvQ	Evangelical Quarterly
EvT	Evangelische Theologie
Exp	Explorations
ExpTim	Expository Times
Fug.	Philo, De Fuga et Inventione
Gig.	Philo, De Gigantibus
GTS	Gettysburg Theological Series
HBT	Horizons in Biblical Theology
HTR	Harvard Theological Review
ICC	International Critical Commentary
Immut.	Philo, Quod Deus Sit Immutabilis
Int	Interpretation
ITQ	Irish Theological Quarterly
IWST	Israelite Wisdom: Theological and Literary Essays in Honor of
Samuel	Terrien
JBL	Journal of Biblical Literature
JETS	Journal of the Evangelical Theological Society
JSNT	Journal for the Study of the New Testament
JSNTSS	Journal for the Study of the New Testament Supplement Series
JSOT	Journal for the Study of the Old Testament
JSS	Journal of Semitic Studies
JTS	Journal of Theological Studies
Leg. All.	Philo, Legum Allegoria

LTP	Laval théologique et philosophique
NCB	New Century Bible
NovT	Novum Testamentum
NovTSup	Novum Testamentum, Supplements
NRSV	New Revised Standard Version
NTS	New Testament Studies
Opif.	Philo, De Opificio Mundi
Post.	Philo, De Posteritate Caini
Praem.	Philo, De Praemis et Poenis
Qu. in Gen.	Philo, Questiones et Solutiones in Genesin
RAERG	Religions in Antiquity: Essays in Memory of Edwin Ramsdell Goodenough
RB	Revue biblique
RelSRev	Religious Studies Review
RevExp	Review and Expositor
Sacr.	Philo, De Sacrificiis Abelis et Caini
SAIW	Studies in Ancient Israelite Wisdom
SBL	Society of Biblical Literature
SBLDS	Society of Biblical Literature Dissertation Series
SBLMS	Society of Biblical Literature Monograph Series
SBLSBS	Society of Biblical Literature Sources for Biblical Study
SBLSP	Society of Biblical Literature Seminar Papers
SBT	Studies in Biblical Theology
Scr	Scripture
SE	Studia Evangelica
SIMSVD	Studia Instituti Missiologici Societatis Verbi Divini
Sipre Deut.	Sipre Deuteronomy
SJJNS	Studies in John Presented to Professor J. N. Sevenster
SJT	Scottish Journal of Theology
SM	Studia Missionalia
SNTS	Society for New Testament Studies
SNTSMS	Society for New Testament Studies Monograph Series
Somn.	Philo, De Somniis
Spec.	Philo, De Specialibus Legibus

TDNT	Theological Dictionary of the New Testament
Theo	Theology
TLZ	Theologische Literaturezeitung
TS	Theological Studies
TSK	Theologische Studien und Kritiken
TynBul	Tyndale Bulletin
VC	Vigiliae christianae
VT	Vetus Testamentum
WUNT	Wissenschaftliche Untersuchungen zum Neuen Testament
ZAW	Zeitschrift für die alttestamentliche Wissenschaft
ZNW	Zeitschrift für die neutestamentliche Wissenschaft
ZRGG	Zeitschrift für Religions- und Geistesgeschichte
ZTK	Zeitschrift für Theologie und Kirche

FOREWORD

The effort to understand the Gospel of John has repeatedly led scholars to probe the thought world of first-century Judaism and early Christianity for a context which makes the complexities of Johannine thought more intelligible. Each proposal has encountered difficulties. The development of gnosticism in the first century is difficult to trace. The Qumran scrolls and the rabbinic writings explain facets of Johannine thought, but not its core. By the same token, Philo's influence has been judged to be inadequate as an interpretive key to Johannine thought. But the Gospel of John was not composed in a vacuum. The question, therefore, remains: What influenced the peculiar development of this Gospel, and why is it so different from the other gospels?

The thesis that John was influenced by wisdom tradition is hardly new to Johannine studies. Nevertheless, the contribution of this dissertation is considerable. Building on the sturdy foundation of the work of Raymond E. Brown and James D. G. Dunn, among others, Willett demonstrates that by recognizing the influence of wisdom tradition on John one is able to provide a coherent explanation for many of the central features of the Gospel's thought. Methodically, the dissertation leads the reader through a survey of the development of wisdom speculation in biblical and early Judaism and evidences of its influence in the first century: in Torah speculation, Philo, and Apocalypticism.

The prologue of the Gospel has been the focus of most previous discussions of the formative influence of wisdom in John. Willett's procedure is exegetical and integrative. He analyzes the ways in which the prologue follows the pattern of hymns to Wisdom and develops themes drawn from the wisdom material:

preexistence, intimate relationship with God, connection with light and darkness, dwelling with the people, and the dynamics of acceptance and rejection.

The heart of the dissertation is the second chapter, which moves beyond the prologue to demonstrate the depth of the influence of wisdom motifs on John's characterization of Jesus. Again the method is analytical, thematic, and integrative. Six themes prominent in both the wisdom materials and John's portrait of Jesus are identified and discussed. These are not peripheral parallels. Rather, they form the grist of Johannine theology: preexistence, descent-ascent. revelation-hiddenness, acceptance-rejection, intimacy with disciples, and glory and life. The claim of preexistence functions both in the wisdom tradition and in the Gospel to substantiate the lofty claims made on behalf of Wisdom or Jesus respectively. The theme of descent follows on the emphasis on preexistence and relates the spatial dualism of the Gospel with its emphasis on the Son as one sent by the Father. Similarly, the intent to characterize the crucifixion, resurrection, and departure of Jesus as ascent explains John's use of such key terms as "going away," "lifting up," and "glorification." Wisdom is not the sole influence here, however, John combines themes related to three figures from the Hebrew scripture--the prophet, Wisdom, and the Son of Man--to furnish the fully developed descent-ascent schema. Willett also explores the related facets of John's presentation of Jesus as the revealer. The role of revealer presupposes intimacy with the revealed (the Father). In all three of the aspects of intimacy--will, knowledge, and love--John draws from parallel characterizations of Wisdom's intimacy with God. As the revealer, Jesus (like Wisdom) mediates intimacy with God. The "I am" sayings and the distinctive Johannine images such as light, bread, and water belong to John's "discourse of revelation." In instructive discussions, Willett demonstrates parallels to the Johannine material in the style of discourse, images, and themes of the depiction of Wisdom as revealer in the wisdom materials. Invariably, revelation leads to acceptance and rejection. The characterization of Jesus or Wisdom as the mediator of the revelation of God, therefore, logically leads to a soteriological dualism. Jesus, like Wisdom, sifts the hearers, and those who reject the revelation are in the end rejected. On the other hand, those who receive the revelation experience intimacy with the revealed. Just as Jesus gathers the disciples around him, so Wisdom gathers her children. Each creates a new community marked by intimacy, empowered by the revelation, and called to abide in the community and the teachings of its revealer. In turn, the new community sees the glory of the revealer and receives the promise of life. At each of these points, of course, there are connections with other motifs that play significant roles in the Gospel and in the wisdom material. The lucid analysis of the structure of Johannine thought and the extent to which each of these themes plays a similar role in the wisdom materials will be welcomed by all who are searching for the proper rubrics for understanding John's peculiar Christology. While carefully disclaiming that these themes are unique to the wisdom material, Willett concludes that the Gospel depicts Jesus as "Wisdom incarnate, the outreaching love of God enfleshed in a man."

The third chapter draws together the foregoing analysis by means of insightful syntheses of the implications of this work for understanding both John's Christology and the Johannine community.

This volume follows the direction of reliable guides in Johannine scholarship by positing the significance of Wisdom tradition as a formative factor in John's Christology. It therefore provides not only a useful compendium of recent scholarship, and analysis of leading Johannine themes, and references to the wisdom materials; it also offers a creative analysis of the conceptual framework of John's Christology. If not the end of the trail, therefore, this volume offers at least a refreshing vantage point that can serve as a benchmark by which to measure our progress along the way.

R. Alan Culpepper
Baylor University

This is a very competent piece of work which succeeds in demonstrating with a fair degree of probability that Wisdom christology is the basis of the Fourth Gospel's presentation of Jesus in the body of the Gospel as well as in the Prologue. The heart and strength of the thesis lies in Chapter 2 where Mr. Willett examines six prominent themes in the Gospel and demonstrates a significant similarity of content and emphasis with equivalent themes in the presentation of Wisdom in the Jewish wisdom tradition. Despite the lack of specific verbal links, the motif-parallels are sufficiently consistent and numerous for the thesis to be sustained. The contribution which the thesis makes to scholarship lies not in the basic assertion itself, but in thus demonstrating its plausibility for it in both breadth and depth.

James D. G. Dunn
University of Durham

PREFACE

This study is a thorough revision of a Ph.D. dissertation accepted in 1985 at the Southern Baptist Theological Seminary. A study such as this is, like a Gospel, a community document: although one person is responsible for its production, many people contribute. Those who have contributed significantly to this work include, first of all, members of my Committee of Instruction, who supervised the writing of the original dissertation. John B. Polhill, supervisor of the committee, has been friend, teacher, and constant supporter throughout my graduate and teaching career. R. Alan Culpepper has been both guide and fellow-pilgrim on the Gospel road. He first enticed me into "the Johannine school" through his course on the Gospel of John, my very first course as a Master of Divinity student in the fall of 1978, and his graduate seminar in the Fourth Gospel in the fall of 1981 allowed me to focus my interest in Johannine Christology. I have cherished his friendship and colleagueship since my graduation, and I am grateful to him for contributing to the dedicatory foreword for this work. E. Frank Tupper has continually encouraged me to build bridges between biblical exegesis and systematic theology. I first became intrigued with Wisdom Christology in his graduate seminar in contemporary Christology in the spring of 1982. Also playing an important role in this process was James D. G. Dunn of the University of Durham. I first sketched out the lines of argument for this dissertation in a paper for him, and he encouraged me to pursue the matter further. He also served as external reader for the original dissertation and made some valuable comments which I have tried to incorporate in this revision. I also appreciate his contributing to the dedicatory foreword.

Students in elective courses I have taught in the Gospel of John at Saint Paul School of Theology, Central Baptist Theological Seminary, and Howard University School of Divinity have encouraged me in developing the ideas contained in this study. Robert West, Editor-in-Chief of Mellen Research University Press, has been most patient and understanding through numerous delays, particularly involving my move from Kansas City to Washington, DC. The Research Center on Black Religious Bodies at Howard University School of Divinity graciously allowed me to use their printer, upon which the original copies of this work were produced. Joy Harman provided valuable assistance in helping compile the indexes. Finally, members of my home church Second Baptist Church in Liberty, Missouri have generously helped underwrite the publication costs of this study.

Space does not allow me to name teachers, colleagues, and friends who have contributed a piece of information, a word of encouragement, or a bit of humor. All, however, have been part of my community, and I hope that this study is worthy of them.

Michael E. Willett

Washington, DC
July 1992

INTRODUCTION

Out of his heart shall flow rivers of living water (John 7:38).

In the living water of Johannine Christology, "a child can wade and an elephant can swim."[1] The evangelist's picture of Jesus is both simple and complex, monolithic and multifaceted, comforting and challenging. Here is the Christ of the creeds and also the one who transcends all formulas. Jesus strides through the Gospel like a colossus. He is the preexistent Son who has come from above to reveal the Father. He works miraculous signs, delivers long discourses, and is finally lifted up in order to glorify the one who sent him.

When plunging into Johannine Christology, one is indeed navigating deep, turbulent waters. Questions arise: What tributaries flow into this sea? What accounts for the exalted picture of Jesus in the Gospel? Numerous suggestions for the proper matrix have been offered. Probably the most influential was that of Rudolf Bultmann, who argued that the evangelist was primarily influenced by a pre-Christian gnostic redeemer myth.[2] In recent years, however, scholars have recoiled from this idea and have turned toward Jewish motifs. A number have noted the similarity between the Johannine portrait of Jesus and the portrait of Wisdom in the biblical and early Jewish literature. Raymond Brown wrote, "In drawing [his]

---

[1]An anonymous quotation in Siegfried Schulz, Die Stunde der Botschaft: Einführing in der Theologie der vier Evangelisten (Hamburg: Furche, 1967), p. 297, cited by Robert Kysar, The Fourth Evangelist and His Gospel: An Examination of Contemporary Scholarship (Minneapolis: Augsburg Publishing House, 1975), p. 6.

[2]Rudolf Bultmann, The Gospel of John: A Commentary, trans. G. R. Beasley-Murray, et al. (Philadelphia: Westminster Press, 1971). For a current proponent of this view, cf. Siegfried Schulz, Das Evangelium nach Johannes (Göttingen: Vandenhoeck und Ruprecht, 1972). Kysar, Evangelist, p. 117, called this position "the Bultmann-Schulz thesis."

portrait of Jesus, the evangelist has capitalized on an identification of Jesus with personified Wisdom as described in the OT."[3]

Wisdom influence upon the Christology of the New Testament has received increasing attention in recent years. Eduard Schweizer demonstrated that the Pauline concept of preexistence and the sending formulae in the New Testament were influenced primarily by the Wisdom material.[4] James D. G. Dunn, drawing on Schweizer, made his chapter on Wisdom the hinge of his study of the New Testament roots of the incarnation.[5] Indeed, Dunn found the origins of the doctrine in the application of Wisdom categories to Christ.[6] Elisabeth Schüssler Fiorenza, in her feminist reconstruction of Christian origins, pointed out the importance of Wisdom Christology in the Palestinian Jesus movement and the early Christian missionary movement. She maintained that the earliest Christian theology was sophialogy because Jesus probably understood himself as the prophet and child of Sophia, and the early Christian missionary movement identified the risen Lord with the Sophia of God.[7] Elizabeth A. Johnson built on the work of all these scholars in order to recover the New Testament foundations for an inclusive Christology.[8]

Most of the attention concerning wisdom influence in the Gospels has focused on the synoptic Gospels. General treatments have been written by André

---

[3]Raymond E. Brown, The Gospel According to John, I-XII, AB 29 (Garden City, NY: Doubleday and Co., 1966), p. cxxii.

[4]Cf. Eduard Schweizer, "Zur Herkunft der Praexistenzvorstellung bei Paulus," in Neotestamentica: Deutsche und Englische Aufsätze 1951-1963 (Zürich/Stuttgart: Zwingli-Verlag, 1963), pp. 105-109; "Zum religionsgeschichtlichen Hintergrund der 'Sendungsformel' Gal 4,4f, Rom 8,3f, Joh 3,16f, 1 Joh 4,9," in Beiträge zur Theologie des Neuen Testaments (Zürich: Zwingli-Verlag, 1970), pp. 83-95. Cf. also "Aufnahme und Korrektur Jüdischer Sophiatheologie im Neuen Testament," in Neotestamentica, pp. 110-121. For other work on Wisdom in Paul, cf. André Feuillet, Le Christ Sagesse de Dieu d'après les Epîtres Pauliennes (Paris: J. Gabalda, 1966).

[5]James D. G. Dunn, Christology in the Making: A New Testament Inquiry into the Origins of the Doctrine of the Incarnation (Philadelphia: Westminster Press, 1980), cf. chap. VI: "The Wisdom of God," pp. 163-212.

[6]Ibid., p. 212.

[7]Elisabeth Schlüsser Fiorenza, In Memory of Her: A Feminist Theological Reconstruction of Christian Origins (New York: Crossroad, 1984), pp. 130-140, 188-192. Cf. also her "Wisdom Mythology and the Christological Hymns of the New Testament," in AWJEC, ed. Robert Wilken (Notre Dame: University of Notre Dame Press, 1971), pp. 17-41.

[8]Elizabeth A. Johnson, "Jesus the Wisdom of God: A Biblical Basis for Non-Androcentric Christology," ETL, 61 (1985), 261-294.

Feuillet, Felix Christ, David Smith, and James M. Robinson.[9] Furthermore, studies of Wisdom in Q have been pursued by Robinson, Richard Edwards, and John Kloppenborg.[10] These studies concluded that Q depicts Jesus as a child and prophet of Wisdom, although Feuillet and Christ went so far as to say that Q identifies Jesus and Wisdom. M. Jack Suggs, however, argued that Matthew was the first actually to identify the two through his editing of Q, and he has been followed by Fred W. Burnett and Celia Deutsch.[11]

Studies in the wisdom background of the Fourth Gospel have concentrated on the prologue. In the early part of this century J. Rendel Harris maintained that the prologue was originally a hymn to Sophia.[12] Before Bultmann came to his famous gnostic redeemer theory, he contended that the background was to be found in the Wisdom myth.[13] Rudolf Schnackenburg, Siegfried Schulz, Ernst Haenchen, C. H. Dodd, and Brown all included excurses in their commentaries

---

[9]André Feuillet, "Jésus et la Sagesse divine d'après les évangiles synoptiques," RB, 62 (1955), 161-196; Felix Christ, Jesus Sophia: Die Sophia-Christologie bei den Synoptikern, ATANT 57 (Zürich: Zwingli-Verlag, 1970); David W. Smith, Wisdom Christology in the Synoptic Gospels (Rome: Pontificia Studiorum Universitas A S. Thoma Aq. in Urbe, 1970); James M. Robinson, "Jesus as Sophos and Sophia: Wisdom Tradition and the Gospels," in AWJEC, pp. 1-16; "Very Goddess and Very Man: Jesus' Better Self," in Encountering Jesus: A Debate on Christology, ed. Stephen T. Davis (Atlanta: John Knox Press, 1988), pp. 111-122.

[10]James M. Robinson, "LOGOS SOPHON: On the Gattung of Q," in Trajectories through Early Christianity (Philadelphia: Fortress Press, 1971), pp. 71-113; Richard A. Edwards, A Theology of Q: Eschatology, Prophecy and Wisdom (Philadelphia: Fortress Press, 1976); John Kloppenborg, "Wisdom Christology in Q," LTP, 34 (1978), 129-147. Cf. also the latter's The Formation of Q: Trajectories in Ancient Wisdom Collections (Philadelphia: Fortress, 1987).

[11]M. Jack Suggs, Wisdom, Christology and Law in Matthew's Gospel (Cambridge, Mass.: Harvard University Press, 1970); Fred W. Burnett, The Testament of Jesus-Sophia: A Redaction-Critical Study of the Eschatological Discourse in Matthew (Washington: University Press of America, 1981); Celia Deutsch, Hidden Wisdom and the Easy Yoke: Wisdom, Torah, and Discipleship in Matthew 11:25-30, JSNTSS 18 (Sheffield: JSOT Press, 1987); and her "Wisdom in Matthew: Transformation of a Symbol," NovT, 32 (1990), 13-47. Marshall D. Johnson, "Reflections on a Wisdom Approach to Matthew's Christology," CBQ, 36 (1974), 44-64, however, objected to Suggs' position. A narrative-critical approach to the subject was offered by Frances Taylor Gench, "Wisdom in the Christology of Matthew" (Ph.D. dissertation, Union Theological Seminary, 1988), and a study from the perspective of reader-response criticism was pursued by Russell Pregeant, "The Wisdom Passages in Matthew's Story," SBLSP, ed. David J. Lull (Atlanta: Scholars Press, 1990), pp. 469-493.

[12]J. Rendel Harris, The Origin of the Prologue of St. John's Gospel (Cambridge: Cambridge University Press, 1917).

[13]Rudolf Bultmann, "The History of Religions Background of the Prologue to the Gospel of John," in The Interpretation of John, ed. John Ashton, Issues in Religion and Theology 9 (Philadelphia: Fortress Press, 1986), pp. 18-35. It was first published in ΕΥΧΑΡΙΣΤΗΡΙΟΝ: Festschrift für H. Gunkel (Göttingen: Vandenhoeck und Ruprecht, 1923), II, 3-26.

4

demonstrating that the closest parallels in thought are found in the Jewish wisdom literature.[14]

While the wisdom background of the prologue has held great fascination for commentators, the wisdom background of the whole Gospel has rarely caught their eye. A brief section in the introduction to Brown's commentary and a short article by Henry Moeller represent the most significant contributions in the field; both concluded that the Gospel portrays Jesus as Wisdom incarnate.[15] Dunn, building on Brown and on his own previous work on the incarnation, detected wisdom influence throughout the Gospel and discussed the implications for Johannine thought and the situation of the Johannine community.[16] George MacRae contended that in order to affirm the universality of Jesus the evangelist drew upon many religious backgrounds, but the primary background was wisdom.[17] In his study of the genre of the Gospels Charles Talbert noted the wisdom influence on the Fourth Gospel. He maintained that the Gospel tells the Jesus story in terms of the myth of a descending-ascending figure, which owed its origin to two streams in ancient Judaism, the wisdom tradition and angelology.[18] F.-M. Braun, in the second volume of his four-volume study of Johannine theology, argued that the wisdom themes are woven together with the prophetic themes to form the fabric of the

---

[14]Rudolf Schnackenburg, The Gospel According to St. John, trans. Kevin Smyth (New York: Crossroad, 1982), I, 481-493; Schulz, Evangelium, pp. 27-29; Ernst Haenchen, John 1: A Commentary on the Gospel of John Chapters 1-6, Hermeneia, trans. Robert W. Funk and ed. Robert W. Funk with Ulrich Busse (Philadelphia: Fortress Press, 1984), pp. 131-140; C. H. Dodd, The Interpretation of the Fourth Gospel (Cambridge: Cambridge University Press, 1953), pp. 263-285. Dunn, Christology, pp. 239-245, restricted his study of the wisdom influence in the Gospel to the prologue.

[15]Brown, Gospel, pp. cxxii-cxxiv; Henry R. Moeller, "Wisdom Motifs and John's Gospel," BETS, 6 (1963), 93-98.

[16]James D. G. Dunn, "Let John Be John: A Gospel for Its Time" in Das Evangelium und Evangelien: Vorträge vom Tübinger Symposium 1982, ed. Peter Stuhlmacher (Tübingen: Mohr-Siebeck, 1983), pp. 330-337.

[17]George W. MacRae, "The Fourth Evangelist and Religionsgeschichte," CBQ, 32 (1970), 13-24.

[18]Charles H. Talbert, What is a Gospel? The Genre of the Canonical Gospels (Philadelphia: Fortress Press, 1977), cf. chap. 3: "Mythical Structure--2," pp. 53-90, which built on his article, "The Myth of a Descending-Ascending Redeemer in Mediterranean Antiquity," NTS, 22 (1976), 418-439. Talbert, however, gave greater attention to angelology and to the merger of these two streams. Wisdom was treated in Talbert, Gospel, pp. 56-57, angelology pp. 57-61, and the merger pp. 61-65.

Gospel's Christology.[19] Studies on individual chapters, such as those on chapter 6 by Feuillet and Peder Borgen, have isolated the wisdom background.[20]

This brief survey of research in Wisdom Christology in the New Testament in general and in the Fourth Gospel in particular has revealed a number of gaps. The vast majority of studies on wisdom influence in the Gospel has focused on the prologue. Studies on the rest of the Gospel have either treated the wisdom themes in summary fashion or investigated specific passages. No monograph or extended article has combined the concern for breadth with that of depth, that is, discussion of the wisdom themes in the presentation of Jesus throughout the Gospel and detailed exegesis of the relevant passages. Furthermore, Dunn's brief sketch in his article has drawn out the implications of wisdom influence for Johannine theology and the situation of the Johannine community. The present work attempts to fill these gaps. It will be argued that the evangelist's portrait of Jesus is heavily influenced by wisdom themes from the biblical and early Jewish literature. The Gospel presents Jesus as the Wisdom of God incarnate.

It is first necessary to discuss a few matters of definition and style which will be used throughout this study. Gospel will refer to the Fourth Gospel, the Gospel of John. Evangelist will refer to the author of the Gospel, with no further attempt at identification. Capitalized Wisdom will refer to the preexistent Wisdom figure, while lower-case wisdom will refer to that body of literature which includes Proverbs, Job, Ecclesiastes, Sirach, and the Wisdom of Solomon. Baruch will be added for the purposes of this investigation. The New Revised Standard Version of the Bible will be used unless otherwise noted.

The course which this study will follow will now be set out. Chapter 1 will summarize contemporary scholarship in two areas: first, Wisdom in biblical and

[19]F.-M. Braun, Jean le Théologien: Les grandes traditions d'Israel et l'accord des Ecritures selon le Quatrième Evangile (Paris: J. Gabalda, 1964), pp. 49-152. Cf. also his "Saint Jean, la Sagesse et l'historie," in Neotestamentica et Patristica: Freundsgabe für Oscar Cullmann, NovTSup, VI (Leiden: E. J. Brill, 1962), pp. 123-133.

[20]André Feuillet, "The Principle [sic] Biblical Themes in the Discourse on the Bread of Life," in Johannine Studies, trans. Thomas Crane (Staten Island, NY: Alba House, 1964), pp. 53-128; Peder Borgen, Bread from Heaven: An Exegetical Study of the Concept of Manna in the Gospel of John and the Writings of Philo, NovTSup, X (Leiden: E. J. Brill, 1965).

Unfortunately, not available to me was the forthcoming work by Martin Scott, Sophia and the Johannine Jesus, JSNTSS 71 (Sheffield: JSOT Press, 1992). This study explores the relationship between Wisdom and the Johannine Jesus, and then considers the effect of Wisdom on the portrayal of women in the Gospel.

early Jewish literature and second, the transformation of Wisdom in the Johannine prologue. The consideration of Wisdom in biblical and early Jewish literature will begin with a survey of the pictures of Wisdom in the relevant material, which will include Job 28, Proverbs 1-9, Sirach, Baruch 3:9-4:4, Wisdom of Solomon, Philo, the Similitudes of Enoch, and the Tannaitic literature. The place and function of Wisdom will then be examined, including the literary category to which Wisdom belongs and the function which she exercised in Jewish thought. Attention will then turn to the transformation of Wisdom in the Johannine prologue. The Wisdom parallels to the prologue will first be set out, and then the function of Wisdom in the prologue will be discussed.

The heart of the study will be chapter 2. It will be shown that the same colors which were used to paint Wisdom in the biblical and early Jewish literature were also used to paint the portrait of Jesus in the Gospel. The six themes to be probed include preexistence, descent-ascent, revelation-hiddenness, acceptance-rejection, intimacy with disciples, and glory and life. First, the place and function of preexistence in the portraits of Wisdom and of Jesus will be plumbed. Second, the discussion of the descent-ascent schema will give attention to the spatial dualism, the sending motif, and the ascent motif of both the Gospel and the Wisdom material. Third, the treatment of the revelation-hiddenness theme will include discussion of the intimacy Jesus-Wisdom has with God, the revelation which each brings, the images and sayings which communicate that revelation, and the paradoxical hiddenness of the revealer. Fourth, examination of the acceptance-rejection theme will entail consideration of the division in humanity which results from the appearance of the revealer and the rejection which the revealer meets. Fifth, the intimacy which the disciples enjoy with Jesus-Wisdom will be explored. Finally, attention will be given to the glory and life which the disciples receive.

Chapter 3 will discuss the place and function of Wisdom in the Gospel and in the Johannine community. Attention will first be given to the literary function of Wisdom in the Gospel. The transformation of Wisdom in the Gospel will be considered, as well as the relationship between the Gospel prologue and narrative on the one hand and between the Gospel and Jewish thought on the other. The socio-historical function of Wisdom in the Johannine community will then be discussed. The community's character as a wisdom school, its setting in hellenistic Jewish

Christianity, the place of Wisdom in community history, and the role of women in the community will be considered.

Chapter 4 will be the conclusion of the study. The findings will first be summarized, and then suggestions for further research will be offered.

This study is part of a larger project in the Gospel. Recently my interests have turned to the psychological interpretation of the Gospel, using the analytical psychology of Carl G. Jung.[21] I am therefore contemplating a monograph on a Jungian interpretation of the Gospel, with special attention to how psychological criticism interfaces with reader-response criticism. In this current work, however, little reference is made to Jungian psychology or reader-response criticism.

Thus is charted this voyage into the rough waters of Johannine Christology. There will be many rapids, falls, and eddies. Yet the threat of danger is outweighed by the prospect of discovery.

---

[21]Cf. my "Jung and John," Exp, 7 (1988), 77-92, and "Again, a Symbolic Reading of the Fourth Gospel," paper presented to the New Testament Section of the Central States SBL meeting, Columbia, MO, March 26, 1990.

Chapter 1

WISDOM IN BIBLICAL AND EARLY JEWISH LITERATURE AND
ITS TRANSFORMATION IN THE JOHANNINE PROLOGUE

Before setting off onto new paths, it is first necessary to survey territory
which has already been explored. This chapter will summarize previous scholarship in two areas. First, the picture of Wisdom in biblical and early Jewish literature will be explored. Second, Wisdom in the prologue of the Gospel of John will
be discussed. The intent of this chapter is not to push scholarship in new directions
in this area but to see exactly where previous paths have led.

Wisdom in Biblical and Early Jewish Literature

Out of the sea of moral maxims emerges a preexistent heavenly figure
named Wisdom, holding life in her right hand and riches in her left hand, summoning people to fellowship with God. One of the most perplexing phenomena in research in biblical scholarship is the appearance of Wisdom. How did these didactic
sentences beget Wisdom? A number of scholars have noted this "untimely birth."[1]
This section will pursue two tasks. First, it will trace the pictures of Wisdom presented in biblical, Second Temple, and Tannaitic texts. Then it will examine the
place and function of Wisdom in the Judaism of this period.

---

[1]Robert Hamerton-Kelly, "The Idea of Pre-existence in Early Judaism: A Study in the
Background of New Testament Theology" (Th. D. dissertation, Union Theological Seminary in the
City of New York, 1966), p. 95, called it "one of the most intractable problems of the history of
religions." Roland E. Murphy, "Wisdom--Theses and Hypotheses," in IWST, ed. J. Gammie, et
al. (Missoula, MT: Scholars Press, 1978), p. 38, noted the distance at which Wisdom stands
from the didactic sentences that go under the name of wisdom.

Pictures of Wisdom

The picture of Wisdom is not a still photograph but a moving picture, consisting of a series of snapshots scattered throughout biblical and early Jewish literature. Attention will be given to the snapshots which appear in eight different pieces of literature: Job, Proverbs, Sirach, Baruch, Wisdom of Solomon, Philo, the Similitudes of Enoch, and the Tannaitic Literature. The presentation of Wisdom in each will be summarized.[2]

Job 28. The figure of Wisdom appears in Job, a book which wrestles with the question of human suffering.[3] Wisdom, then, becomes an element in theodicy. She appears in the poem or hymn in chapter 28 as the hidden object of God's action. John Ashton, in his article on wisdom influence in the Johannine prologue, contended that the most important general feature of the wisdom tradition is the combination of two types of wisdom, which he called "the accessible" and "the remote." He distinguished the two in this way: "Available wisdom, while it may be taught, is essentially a matter of experience. Remote wisdom, if it is to be brought within man's grasp, has to be revealed."[4] Ashton continued that Job 28 is "the most outstanding account of remote wisdom."[5] This note of the hiddenness of wisdom is sounded strongly in the refrain (vv. 12-14 and 20-22): "Where shall wisdom be found? . . . It is hidden from the eyes of all living" (vv. 12a, 21a). Wisdom, that is, the knowledge of the reasons for innocent suffering, is not available to humanity.

Although Wisdom is hidden from humanity and therefore priceless (vv. 15-19), God understands the "way" to her (v. 23, cf. v. 13).[6] God's possession of Wisdom is then traced back to creation (vv. 25-26). Verse 27 is the key verse of the poem and also the most difficult: "Then he saw it and declared it: he

---

[2]For a similar brief survey, cf. Celia Deutsch, "Wisdom in Matthew: Transformation of a Symbol," NovT, 32 (1990), pp. 17-31. Also cf. p. 18 n. 38 for a listing of more complete surveys.

[3]Job is variously dated between the sixth and third centuries B.C.E. Cf. Marvin H. Pope, Job, AB 15 (Garden City, NY: Doubleday and Co., 1973), p. xl. Chapter 28 is often considered an interpolation, though it has perhaps been written by the author of the book. Cf. R. Gordis, The Book of God and Man (Chicago: University of Chicago Press, 1965), pp. 100-102.

[4]John Ashton, "The Transformation of Wisdom: A Study of the Prologue of John's Gospel," NTS, 32 (1986), 164.

[5]Ibid., p. 163.

[6]This point was made previously in the book of Job, in which God is said to be the possessor of Wisdom; cf. 11:6; 12:13, 16.

established it, and searched it out."[7] In the process of God's ordering the universe, the principle of order was found. Norman Habel noted that Wisdom is "the deep and mysterious principle behind all other laws, principles and designs of the cosmos."[8] Similarly, Gerhard von Rad called Wisdom the "'meaning' implanted by God in creation."[9] God asks rhetorically in Job 38:36-37: "Who has put wisdom in the clouds, or given understanding to the mists? Who can number the clouds by wisdom?" Wisdom is the ability to understand the workings of the world, to plumb the depths of the universe. Such knowledge is unattainable for humanity; it is the exclusive possession of God. God alone understands the divine mystery of creation.

The conclusion of the poem (v. 28), which is often taken as a gloss by a redactor,[10] mitigates somewhat the stress in the poem on the inaccessibility of wisdom. Here God speaks: "Truly, the fear of the Lord, that is wisdom; and to depart from evil is understanding." A tension, then, is set up in Job 28: Wisdom is hidden from humanity, but it is available through the fear of the Lord. The emphasis, however, is on the hiddenness. Wisdom, the ability to understand the place of innocent suffering in the moral order of the universe, is essentially inaccessible to humanity.

Proverbs. Proverbs 1-9 continues where Job 28:28 left off: Wisdom is available to all through the fear of the Lord.[11] God remains the sole possessor of Wisdom, but God gives her to the upright (2:6-7). In order to press home this

---

[7]Cf. P. P. Zerafa, The Wisdom of God in the Book of Job (Rome: Herder, 1978), p. 165.

[8]Norman Habel, "Of Things Beyond Me: Wisdom in the Book of Job," CurTM, 10 (1983), 165. He went on to show how this meaning is basic to the meaning of wisdom in Job.

[9]Gerhard von Rad, Wisdom in Israel (Nashville: Abingdon Press, 1972), p. 148.

[10]Cf. Zerafa, Wisdom, p. 155. Habel, "Things," p. 153, noted how v. 28 fits into the literary design of the poet; the terms used to define wisdom are employed to characterize Job in 1:1.

[11]Prov. 1-9 is usually dated in the post-exilic period, e.g. Claudia Camp, Wisdom and the Feminine in the Book of Proverbs, Bible and Literature Series 11 (Decatur, GA: Almond, 1985), pp. 75f; R. B. Scott, Proverbs, Ecclesiastes, AB 18 (Garden City, NY: Doubleday & Co., 1965), p. xxxvii; R. N. Whybray, Wisdom in Proverbs (London: SCM Press, 1965), p. 106. A few scholars, however, have placed this material in the pre-exilic era, e.g. Christa Kayatz, Studien zu Proverbien 1-9 (Neukirchen-Vluyn: Neukirchener, 1966), p. 135; Bernhard Lang, Wisdom in the Book of Proverbs: A Hebrew Goddess Redefined (New York, 1986), p. 4ff. Camp, Wisdom, p. 76, suggested that personified Wisdom might have been conceived as early as the reign of Solomon.

availability, Wisdom is personified and given a number of roles, including prophet, teacher, lover, witness of creation, and householder. Of particular interest are the speeches of Wisdom in 1:20-33 and 8:1-36, in which she appears as street preacher calling to people openly (1:20-21; 8:1-3).[12] Her message is to the simple (1:22; 8:5). She speaks as a prophet, calling for decision and pronouncing judgment on a decision already made.[13] Her message, however, goes beyond the prophetic "Thus saith the Lord"; Wisdom says, "I will pour out my thoughts to you" (1:23); "I will speak noble things" (8:6).[14] The concentration here is not on the word of the Lord but the words of Wisdom. Wisdom is here claiming divine authority for herself and her message.[15] She also speaks as a teacher, summoning people to take her instruction, knowledge, advice, and insight (8:10, 14, 33).

The speech in 1:20-33 is primarily an oracle of judgment upon those who have rejected Wisdom; she promises to be inaccessible to them (v. 28). A positive note, however, is sounded more clearly in 8:1-36, for this speech is invitation rather than judgment. The benefits which Wisdom has to offer--understanding, strength, and wealth--are fully available (cf. vv. 4-21). She promises love and honor (vv. 17-18; cf. also 4:6-9). The authority of her teaching is supported by her claim to preexistence in verses 22-31. Wisdom was present at the beginning; she was begotten (v. 22),[16] established (v. 23), and brought forth (v. 24).[17] She was a witness to creation (vv. 24-29); she was God's little child[18] and delight (v. 30). Wisdom is not here an instrument of creation (as in 3:19), but a witness to creation.

---

[12]Lang, Wisdom, p. 31, contended that the reason that Wisdom makes her appearance in the public places such as the streets, squares, and city gate is that "Wisdom must demonstrate her usefulness in the arena of public life." He also suggested that the public square and the city gate were places where schools, teachers, and classes were found.

[13]For parallels to prophetic literature, cf. Deutsch, "Wisdom," p. 18 n. 41 and the literature which she cited there.

[14]Lang, Wisdom, pp. 57-59, noted that the "I" speech was a common literary style used for kings and gods in the ancient Near East.

[15]Christa Kayatz, Studien, pp. 24-25, noted the tendency in Prov. 1:20-33 to transfer to Wisdom motifs which elsewhere are associated with Yahweh, so that Wisdom is brought into the closest relationship with Yahweh and endowed with his authority.

[16]The verb can also be translated "acquired." Cf. Bruce Vawter, "Proverbs 8:22: Wisdom and Creation," JBL, 99 (1980), 208-210; Scott, Proverbs, pp. 71-72. For the translation "begot," cf. Whybray, Proverbs, p. 101; Lang, Wisdom, p. 54.

[17]Camp, Wisdom, p. 263, pointed out that God is here depicted as the mother of Wisdom. Deutsch, "Wisdom," p. 20, contended that God is described as both father and mother.

[18]Lang, Wisdom, pp. 65-66, listed the possible translations: infant, confidant, master builder, and counselor; because of contextual factors he chose "infant."

As a joyful child, she delights in God's ordering the world. Such delight in the cosmic order is also available to people through Wisdom (cf. vv. 32-36). There is, then, a tension in Proverbs between the inaccessibility and availability of Wisdom.

Another role which Wisdom fulfills is that of householder, as seen in 9:1-6. In her seven-pillared house,[19] she has prepared a meal of bread, meat and wine and invites people to participate in the banquet, which is interpreted as a metaphor for accepting her teaching. Set in contrast to Wisdom here, however, is the "foolish woman" or Folly (9:13-18; cf. also 2:16-19; 5:3, 20; 6:24; 7:10-27). Both own houses (9:1, 14; cf. also 2:18); both call from the high places to those who pass by (9:3, 14); both call to the simple (vv. 4, 16); both offer bread and drink (vv. 5, 17). Wisdom's invitation, however, is far superior, for she has servants, who call from the "highest" places (v. 3), and she offers wine (v. 5) while Folly offers only stolen water (v. 17). Primarily, though, Wisdom offers her guests life (v. 6), while in Folly's house death awaits (v. 18). Indeed, just as life is an important theme in the portrayal of Wisdom in Proverbs 1-9 (cf. 3:16, 18; 4:13, 23), death is consistently associated with Folly (cf. 2:18; 5:5; 7:27). Through the contrast with Folly, Wisdom and her teaching is made much more desirable.

Wisdom is personified, then, in various roles--prophet, teacher, lover, witness to creation, householder--in order to underline the importance of the teaching given in Proverbs. Wisdom goes out seeking those who would come to her house and learn from her in order to possess understanding, insight, and life. Wisdom is able to bestow these gifts because she preexisted creation, thus grounding her teaching in the primeval order of the universe. She is available yet inaccessible, both human and divine.

Sirach. Sirach, a document generally dated in the early second century B.C.E., is "the first to elaborate a true theology of Wisdom in Israel."[20] Sirach accomplishes this purpose by bringing Wisdom into conjunction with the fear of the Lord and the Law. To this formula is added the Law or the commandments. Sirach 19:20 expresses it well: "The whole of wisdom is fear of the Lord, and in all wisdom there is the fulfillment of the Law" (cf. also 1:14-20; 1:26; 15:1; 21:11).

---

[19]Lang, Wisdom, pp. 90-93, maintained that this house with seven pillars denotes "an unusually spacious and elegant construction" (p. 92), for four pillars were standard for an ancient Israelite urban dwelling.

[20]Edmond Jacob, "Wisdom and Religion in Sirach," in Gammie, IWST, p. 254.

Wisdom, the fear of the Lord, and the Law are defined in terms of one another, and each reaches its fulfillment in the others. Wisdom is concretized in the Law, and the Law is given a cosmic framework.[21] While Wisdom remains transcendent and hidden (cf. 1:1-10), the primary emphasis falls on the availability of Wisdom in the Law.[22]

In Sirach Wisdom is mother (4:11; 15:2) and wife (15:2) of the faithful. Yet she is also right reason; the one who meditates on Wisdom is also the one who reasons intelligently (14:21). Wisdom assumes divine authority and takes the place of God; relationship with her determines one's relationship with God (cf. 4:14). She is teacher, putting the prospective follower through a period of testing. She invites people to take on her fetters, collar, bonds, and yoke, but to those who persevere she grants joy, revelation, and rest (6:18-31; cf. also 4:11-19; 51:23-30). Other benefits which Wisdom bestows, which are similar to those in Proverbs 1-9, include life (1:12; 4:12), joy (1:12; 4:12; 6:28), judgment over the nations (4:15a), security (4:15b), wealth (1:17), peace (1:18), and, for the first time, glory (1:11; 4:13; 15:27). Bread and water are also symbols for her benefits (15:3; cf. Prov. 9:5).

Wisdom is also preexistent, as seen clearly in Sirach 1:1-10 and 24:1-34. In Sirach 1:1-10, as in Job 28 and Proverbs 8, Wisdom is said to belong solely to God and is with God from the beginning of creation. Wisdom here, however, is indisputably the first created being (cf. vv. 4, 9). Furthermore, Wisdom is diffused throughout all creation and given to those who love God (vv. 9b-10). Sirach 24 traces Wisdom's course from her creation before eternity (v. 9) to her presence in all creation (vv. 3-6) to her dwelling in Israel (vv. 8, 10-12). Furthermore,

---

[21]George W. E. Nickelsburg, Jewish Literature Between the Bible and the Mishnah (Philadelphia: Fortress Press, 1981) pointed out that Sirach is the earliest datable book that discusses the relationship of Wisdom and the Law in detail and in theory. James L. Crenshaw, Old Testament Wisdom: An Introduction (Atlanta: John Knox Press, 1981), p. 153, maintained that Sirach subordinated Wisdom to the Law and the fear of the Lord. J. Coert Rylaarsdam, Revelation in Jewish Wisdom Literature (Chicago: University of Chicago Press, 1946), p. 31, reflected on the theological meaning of this development: "The surrender of the Jewish wisdom movement to the Law, beginning with Ben Sira, results ultimately in a shift from reliance upon human reason to a dependence upon divine grace and transcendent faith." He, however, seemed to be importing terminology from Christian theology, esp. Pauline thought, into the discussion of wisdom. A better expression is found in von Rad, Wisdom, p. 245, when he said that Sirach was "endeavoring to legitimatize and to interpret the Torah from the realm of understanding characteristic of Wisdom."

[22]Cf. Ashton, "Transformation," p. 166-167.

Wisdom is explicitly identified with the Law (v. 23). A tension is set up between universalism and particularism.[23] Wisdom has a possession in every people and nation (v. 6), yet she has taken up residence in Israel. The Wisdom scattered through all creation has now taken historical form in the Law. Harmut Gese wrote, "Wisdom becomes revelation. . . . Up to Sirach, one has talked of Wisdom only as the order of creation, but now the saving history of revelation is joined to it."[24] Wisdom, therefore, gains a history. Although Wisdom is now revealed in the Law, this revelation does not mean that Wisdom is fully comprehensible. Neither the first man (referring to the Genesis narrative) nor the last man has known her perfectly (v. 28). She is more complex than the sea and the abyss, returning to the theme of the inscrutability of Wisdom in Sirach 1:2-3 and Job 28:12-22.

Wisdom is depicted in various roles in Sirach, much as in Proverbs 1-9. She was present in creation but she is now present in the form of the Law. Wisdom therefore enters salvation history and becomes revelation, that is, written revelation in the Law. Because Wisdom is now concretized in the Law, she creates a school of instruction which the faithful can enter. It is, however, a rigorous discipline to undertake. Yet those who complete it receive life, joy, and peace.

Baruch. The poem or hymn in Baruch 3:9-4:4 echoes Job 28 and Sirach 24.[25] The passage gives the reason for the Israelites' punishment in exile: "You have forsaken the fountain of wisdom" (3:12), which is identified with the Law (4:1). It attempts to answer questions of theodicy: Why does Israel suffer? Wisdom, then, becomes, as in Job, a way in which to explain human suffering. In Job, however, the Wisdom needed to understand the reasons for suffering are hidden from humanity. In Baruch, however, suffering is explained as the result of the rejection of Wisdom, as known in the Law.

The theme of the inaccessibility of Wisdom is prominent, as in Job 28:12-22. A connection is also drawn between Wisdom and creation, as in Job 28:23-26 and Proverbs 8:23-31. As in Sirach 24, God gave Wisdom to Israel (3:29-37) in the form of the Law (4:1). Life, blessing, and God's pleasure are available to those

---

[23]Cf. J. Wood, The Wisdom Literature: An Introduction (London: Duckworth, 1967), pp. 75-77; and Rylaarsdam, Revelation, p. 38.

[24]Harmut Gese, "Wisdom, Son of Man, and the Origins of Christology: The Consistent Development of Biblical Theology," trans. U. Mauser, HBT, 3 (1981), 35.

[25]Because of this dependence, the hymn has usually been dated in the early second century B.C.E., but the book itself has been dated as late as after 70 C.E.

who accept Wisdom, a note also sounded in Proverbs. A tension, then, is evident between the remoteness and the availability of Wisdom. Furthermore, Baruch does not have the developed feminine imagery seen in Proverbs or Sirach.[26]

Wisdom of Solomon. Wisdom of Solomon contains the fullest picture of Wisdom in the biblical and early Jewish literature.[27] She is given a place in creation and redemption; she is both creator and savior. Throughout history, God has been dealing with the people of God through Wisdom, from the beginning of time when she was "the fashioner of all things" (7:22a, cf. also 8:5, 6; 9:2), through salvation history when she protected Adam, Noah, Abraham, Lot, Jacob, and Joseph (chap. 10), to the present when "she passes into holy souls, making them friends of God and prophets" (7:27). A connection between creation and Wisdom, present in Job 28, Proverbs 8, and Sirach, is drawn as well, so that Wisdom is a participant in creation. She is "the fashioner of all things" (7:22a), "the active cause of all things" (8:5), and the "fashioner of what exists" (8:6); she formed humanity (9:2). Her specific role in creation, however, is left undefined. On the other hand, her role in salvation is demonstrated in two ways. First, Wisdom was operative in salvation history, rescuing and protecting the early heroes of Israel's faith. Chapter 10 gives historical illustrations of how "people . . . were saved by Wisdom" (9:18). In six stanzas, each beginning with αὕτη, salvation history is recounted from Adam to Moses. The leading actor, however, is not God but Wisdom. She is the one who saved (10:4), rescued (10:6, 9), protected (10:1, 12), and delivered (10:1, 13). Wisdom was a savior in Israel's past, and she continues to be a savior in the present. She makes the faithful "friends of God" (7:14, 27). As "the fashioner of all things" (7:22a), she can do all things and she renews all things (7:27). The author, then, binds together creation and redemption, placing the emphasis on redemption. Wisdom is not only a cosmological principle but also a soteriological principle which God uses to bring people to Godself.

In order to bestow salvation, Wisdom goes in search of the faithful. She is a "seeking savior" (cf. esp. 6:12-16). Wisdom no longer calls people to come to her, as in Proverbs, but she goes in search of disciples so that she might reveal her-

---

[26]Cf. Deutsch, "Wisdom," p. 25.

[27] Wisdom of Solomon is usually dated in the late first century B.C.E. to the early first century C.E. David Winston, Wisdom of Solomon, AB 43 (Garden City, NY: Doubleday and Co., 1979), pp. 22-24, contended for a date in the reign of Caligula (37-41 C.E.).

self to them. In so doing, she reveals God, for she is "an initiate in the knowledge of God" (8:4). Wisdom is identified as closely as possible with God, as shown in 7:25-26, in which a fivefold succession of metaphors--breath, emanation, reflection, mirror, and image--states emphatically that Wisdom perfectly expresses God's power, glory, light, working, and goodness. To the faithful Wisdom gives understanding and knowledge (6:15; 7:17), and the ability to judge rightly. As King Solomon, the author attributes his judgment to Wisdom (8:9-15; 9:11-12). Wisdom of Solomon 6:12-11:1 is dominated by Solomon's desire and prayer for Wisdom (7:1-22a; 8:2-9:18). He wants her for his bride (8:2, 9-12), so that she might be his teacher (8:6-7; 9:11; cf. also 6:17-20). Wisdom also bestows immortality (6:18-19; 8:13, 17), yet in this life Wisdom gives wealth (7:11, 13-14; 8:18), joy (8:16), glory (8:10), and all good things (7:11).

In order to possess Wisdom, it is necessary to ask God for her (7:7; 9:1-4, 10), for Wisdom is with God (9:9) and sits by God's throne (9:4). God then gave Wisdom (8:21, 9:4) or sent her (9:10) to be with the faithful. Wisdom coalesces with the Spirit and the Word. The three are almost interchangeable, although the focus remains on Wisdom. Wisdom is characterized as a spirit (1:6; 7:7, 22b). Similar functions are postulated of Wisdom and the Spirit: both are active in the creation and regulation of the world (Wisdom, 7:24, 27; 8:1; 9:2; Spirit, 1:7; 7:23; 12:1). The two stand parallel in 9:17. Furthermore, functions that were previously assigned to the Spirit, such as prophecy and royal power, are now gifts of Wisdom (6:9, 24; 7:27; 8:13-17; 9:12).[28] In 9:1-3 both the Word and Wisdom are instruments of creation (cf. Prov. 3:19). The Word is responsible for all things,[29] and Wisdom is responsible for humanity: its creation, its dominion over the world (recalling Gen. 1:26-28), and its moral reasoning.

In summary, Wisdom becomes a savior figure in Wisdom of Solomon. Burton Mack noted that the cosmological aspect of Wisdom has prepared for her soteriological function.[30] Her salvation is intellectual, spiritual, and physical; Wisdom grants understanding, immortality, and deliverance from danger. Though

---

[28]Rylaarsdam, Revelation, p. 117, concluded that this process "assured to Divine Wisdom the same capacity of contemporaneity that was enjoyed by the Spirit."

[29]Although Wisdom also fashions and effects all things (7:22; 8:5).

[30]Burton Mack, Logos und Sophia: Untersuchungen zur Weisheitstheologie im hellenistichen Judentum (Göttingen: Vandenhoeck und Ruprecht, 1973), p. 72.

indissolubly linked with creation, Wisdom is ushered into the realm of redemption. The fashioner of all things renews all things. Creation and redemption are parts of one cosmic event in which Wisdom is the leading actor. Furthermore, since Wisdom is identified with the Word or the Spirit which God gives, she is less accessible than in Sirach; a tension is retained between availability and hiddenness.

Philo. Philo of Alexandria, who lived from 25-20 B.C.E. to 45-50 C.E, used the word σοφία over 200 times in his writings.[31] Jean Laporte noted that the theme of preexistent Wisdom is very rich in Philo.[32] As with nearly all the literature surveyed up to this point, she is brought into connection with creation; she is "that through which the world came into existence" (Fug. 109) or "was brought into completion" (Deter. 16, 54). Wisdom is not the instrument of creation, for that role is reserved for the Logos, but she is the "mother and nurse of all" (Ebr. 31). Wisdom is God's consort by whom God begat the world (Fug. 108-112). Wisdom is the mother of humanity, and God is the father (Leg. All. II,49; Deter. 54).

Wisdom is also called the daughter of God and the spouse of humanity (Praem. 49-59). She is the divine source of virtue, often symbolized by a woman in the Old Testament such as Sarah, Rebekah, Sipporah, and Hannah.[33] Wisdom is brought into intimate connection with humanity. She may abide with humanity, as she did with Moses (Gig. 11). She is the perfect or royal way which leads to God (Immut. 30). The branches of human knowledge are the principles of Wisdom (Immut. 20). She is the fountain from which the individual sciences are watered (Fug. 109), and in the wise person, she is the "art of arts" (Ebr. 22).

Wisdom, however, did not receive from Philo the elaborate treatment which he bestowed upon the Logos.[34] The Logos seems to take Wisdom's place in Philo's thought. A number of scholars have pointed to the similarity between the

---

[31]Ulrich Wilckens, "σοφία," TDNT, ed. Gerhard Friedrich and trans. G. W. Bromiley (Grand Rapids: Wm. B. Eerdmans, 1971), VII, 500.

[32]Jean Laporte, "Philo in the Tradition of Biblical Wisdom Literature," AWJEC, ed. R. L. Wilcken (Notre Dame: University of Notre Dame Press, 1975), p. 114.

[33]Cf. Laporte, "Philo," p. 117.

[34]James Drummond, Philo Judaeus: The Jewish-Alexandrian Philosophy in its Development and Completion (London: Williams and Norgate, 1888), II, 209. His discussion of the relation between the Logos and Wisdom is probably the most extensive.

Logos in Philo and Wisdom in the Wisdom of Solomon.[35] The Logos penetrates all things, even the human mind (Deter. 90; Gig. 27; Leg. All. I, 37-38; cf. Wis. 7:24). The Logos is the image of God (Opif. 17; Wis. 7:26); he is at the side of (παρά) God (Immut. 31; cf. Wis. 9:9 where Wisdom is said to be with, μέτα, God). The Logos is the ὄργανον, the instrument through which creation came to be (Cher. 127), the seal by which everything received its shape (Fug. 12); through the Logos the universe was formed (Sacr. 8; cf. Wis. 7:22a; 8:6; 9:2). Like Wisdom, the Logos is concerned with redemption as well as creation. He draws humanity to himself (Sacr. 8; cf. Wis. 6:12-16). Those who place themselves under the Logos become sons of God (Conf. 145-147; Spec. I, 318; cf. Wis. 7:27). The Logos is light (Conf. 60-63) and the model of light (Somn. I, 75; cf. Wis. 7:26, 29).

What is the relationship between the Logos and Wisdom in the writings of Philo? There are places in which the two are identified (Leg. All. I, 19; Deter. 31), and Wisdom is an alternative name for the Logos (Leg. All. I, 65), yet there are also passages in which the two are distinguished from one another: in one passage Wisdom is the fountain of the Logos (Somn. II, 37), in another the Logos is the fountain of Wisdom (Fug. 97), and a third says that God is the Father of all things, Wisdom is the Mother, and the Logos is their Son (Fug. 109). W. Schencke maintained that the alternation between the Logos and Wisdom was a compromise between Greek philosophy and the language of the Hebrew scriptures. Logos was the common expression of the idea from the philosophical viewpoint, but when a biblical passage alluded to a female person Philo used the feminine σοφία in his allegorical exegesis.[36] James Drummond suggested that Wisdom is used almost invariably in relation to humanity because of her more distinct personal associations, and because she expresses "a moral soundness and acquired knowledge" not necessarily present in the Logos.[37] Ultimately, then, Wisdom has no real place or

---

[35]Winston, Wisdom, p. 38; H. A. Wolfson, Philo (Cambridge: Harvard University Press, 1947), I, 287-289; Edwin R. Goodenough, By Light, Light: The Mystic Gospel of Hellenistic Judaism (Amsterdam: Philo Press, 1969), p. 277.

[36]W. Schencke, Die Chokma (Sophia) in der jüdischen Hypostasenspekulation (Kristiana: Jacob Dybwad, 1913), p. 68. There are passages, however, in which Wisdom is represented by masculine persons or images (cf. Quod. Det. 9; Leg. All. I, 14).

[37]Drummond, Philo, II, 211.

function in Philo's thought, for she has been eclipsed by the Logos, the instrument of God in creation and redemption. Wisdom is "hidden" in the Logos.

Similitudes of Enoch. The way of Wisdom passed into apocalyptic literature.[38] She appears in two passages in the Similitudes of Enoch: 1 Enoch 42, which depicts Wisdom's departure from and return to heaven, and 1 Enoch 48-50, the central section concerning the work of the Son of Man.[39] First Enoch 42 concerns Wisdom's search for a place to dwell. Verse 1 summarizes Wisdom's path: she could not find a place to dwell, but she did find a place in the heavens (cf. Sir. 24:4-7, where the sequence is reversed). It is implied that she is rejected (cf. Prov. 1:24-33; Bar. 3:12). Because of her inability to find a dwelling place, Wisdom returned to the heavens, where she was established (v. 2; cf. Sir. 24:10, where Wisdom was established in Zion). Wisdom withdraws from earth completely (cf. Prov. 1:24-33, in which Wisdom withdraws from those who have rejected her). Just as she goes out to humanity in order to dwell with them, she now returns to heaven after finding no place to dwell. Then, only Iniquity finds a place to dwell among humanity (v. 3).

In the heart of the central section concerning the work of the Son of Man (chaps. 48-50), Wisdom plays a key role. In 1 Enoch 48:1 numerous fountains of Wisdom surround the fountain of righteousness. Those who are thirsty drink from the fountains and are filled with Wisdom, thus ensuring their place among the righteous. The preexistent Son of Man, who was named before creation (v. 3; cf. also v. 6), revealed Wisdom to the righteous (48:7). The spirit of Wisdom dwells in him (49:3), through which he exercises judgment and knows the secret things, which have their source in God (49:4-5). Wisdom, then, becomes a possession of the Son of Man, who is preexistent and exercises judgment. This picture of the Son of Man as preexistent judge is probably influenced both by the picture of

---

[38]Cf. von Rad, Wisdom, pp. 271-283, for the contention that apocalypticism grew out of wisdom.

[39]The dating of the Similitudes has been a controversial subject; dates range from the second century B.C.E. to 270 C.E. Cf. M. A. Knibb, "The Date of the Parables of Enoch: A Critical Review," NTS, 25 (1978-79), 345-359; Christopher L. Mearns, "Dating the Similitudes of Enoch," NTS, 25 (1978-79), 360-369; E. Isaac, "1 Ethiopic Apocalypse of) Enoch: A New Translation and Introduction," in The Old Testament Pseudepigrapha, ed. James Charlesworth (Garden City, NY: Doubleday, 1983), I, 7, who noted that the consensus of scholars at the SNTS Pseudepigrapha Seminars in 1977 and 1978 was that the Similitudes were from the first century C. E.

preexistent Wisdom and the Danielic figure of the Son of Man (Dan. 7:13-14).[40] As in Philo, Wisdom is eclipsed, but this time by the Son of Man.

The Similitudes of Enoch, then, present two different pictures of Wisdom, one in which she is established in heaven after finding no place in heaven to dwell, and the other in which she becomes a possession of the Son of Man. In the first she is completely hidden from humanity, but in the second she is available only through the Son of Man.

Tannaitic Literature. C. K. Barrett pointed out that in speculative Judaism wisdom had two successors: rabbinic Judaism and Philo.[41] In the Tannaitic literature wisdom took the form of Torah speculation.[42] The identification of Wisdom and the Law (Sir. 24:23; Bar. 4:1) led to the Law being endowed with qualities associated with Wisdom.[43] Just as Wisdom was preexistent, so too the Law was claimed by the rabbis to be preexistent, often using Proverbs 8:22-31 as a basis. Sipre Deuteronomy 11:10, a text attributed to the school of Rabbi Ishmael (c. 100 C.E.) reads, "The Law, because it was more highly prized than everything, was created before everything." Genesis Rabbah c. 8, a Palestinian work of the fifth century but drawing on earlier material, says that the Law is 2000 years older than creation. Seven things were created before the world, headed by the Law (Sipre Deut. 32:6). The Law was not only present at creation; it was also an instrument in it. Rabbi Akiba (d. 132 C.E.) called the Law "the precious instrument with which the world was created" ('Abot 3:15). In Genesis Rabbah Rabbi Oshayah wrote, "The Holy One looked into the Torah and then created the world."[44] In a rare appearance of Wisdom, the Fragmentary Targum on Genesis 1:1 interprets "in the beginning God created" as "through Wisdom God created."

The rabbis took over many of the images which the wisdom writers used in speaking of the benefits Wisdom bestows. The Law gives life. The Law is often

---

[40]Gese, "Wisdom," p. 40.

[41]C. K. Barrett, The Gospel According to St. John: An Introduction with Commentary and Notes on the Greek Text (2d ed.; Philadelphia: Westminster Press, 1978), p. 153.

[42]Emphasis here will be placed on the earliest Tannaitic period 10-220 C.E.

[43]Cf. M. Maher, "Some Aspects of Torah in Judaism," ITQ, 38 (1971), 310-325, for an excellent discussion of this topic. Much of the following material is indebted to this article. Cf. also Hamerton-Kelly, "Pre-existence," p. 128-129; Martin Hengel, Judaism and Hellenism (London: SCM Press, 1975), I, 169-175.

[44]George Foot Moore, Judaism in the First Century of the Christian Era: The Age of the Tannaim (Cambridge, MA: Harvard University Press, 1927), I, 267.

associated with the tree of life. For example, Neofiti, a second or third century C.E. document which may represent the Palestinian Targum of the first century B.C.E., reads: "The Law is the tree of life for all who study it. ᾽Abot 2:8 attributes a saying to Hillel summing up Proverbs 3:1f in the words "more Torah, more life." Light, a popular image in speaking about Wisdom, was also used in describing the Law. In the Targumim the word light is occasionally replaced by Law. For example, where Isaiah 2:5 reads, "Let us walk in the light of Yahweh," the Targum on it reads, "Let us walk in the study of the Law." Deuteronomy Rabbah 7:3, a tenth-century document though containing earlier material, asserts, "Just as oil gives light to the world, so too do the words of the Torah give light to the world." The image of water (cf. Sir. 24:24f) is also applied to the Law. Canticles Rabbah 1:2, dated in the seventh or eighth century, reads, "As water refreshes the body, so does the Torah refresh the soul." The themes of water and life are connected in Sipre Deuteronomy 84a: "As water gives life to the world, so do the words of the Torah give life to the world." A favorite form of this image is that the Law is a well of living water, as in the Targum to the Canticles 74:15, where the targumist refers to the abundant waters that irrigate Israel "because [the Israelites] are occupied with the words of the Torah which are compared to a well of living water." The Law is also compared to bread and wine (cf. Prov. 9:5; Sir. 15:3). The words of Isaiah 3:1 about "the whole stay of bread and the whole stay of water" are interpreted as the Law (b. Šabb. 120a, a fifth-century document). In Genesis Rabbah c. 70 the proselyte may find in Israel the "bread of the Torah." And the Law is compared to wine: as wine rejoices the heart temporally, so the Torah rejoices the heart spiritually (cf. Cant. Rab. 1:2).

It is now necessary to put these snapshots end to end and summarize the various pictures of Wisdom in the biblical and early Jewish literature. In Job 28 she is the order of creation, which is hidden from humanity. In Proverbs 1-9 she becomes accessible to persons, personified as teacher, lover, savior, and prophet, who gives life and understanding to persons. Sirach and Baruch identify Wisdom with the Law, giving her a history and making her completely available. The Tannaitic literature continues this identification but transfers the characteristics of Wisdom to the Law. Similarly, Philo gives to the Logos most of her traits formerly associated with Wisdom. And the Similitudes of Enoch depict Wisdom both as established in heaven and as a possession of the Son of Man.

Place and Function of Wisdom

The above discussion leaves a number of questions unanswered: What is Wisdom? In what literary category should she be placed? What role did she exercise in the religious thought and practice of the day? This section will summarize the various answers which scholars have given to these questions, looking first at the various ways in which Wisdom has been categorized in contemporary scholarship and then at the function which she played in biblical and early Judaism.

Literary Category. Scholars have conceptualized Wisdom in a number of ways: hypostasis, personification, myth, metaphor, and symbol. Up until recently, discussion about Wisdom has involved the question of whether she was conceived as a hypostasis or personification. Helmer Ringgren argued that Wisdom was a hypostasis, accepting the definition by W. O. E. Oesterley and G. H. Box that a hypostasis was "a quasi-personification of certain attributes of God, occupying an intermediate position between personalities and absolute beings."[45] A number of scholars, however, have challenged the proposition that Wisdom was a hypostasis.[46] Some have preferred to speak of Wisdom as a personification, which R. N. Whybray defined as "a representation in personal terms of something which is not a person," which has as its main purpose to express in a vivid way the characteristics inherent in the thing personified.[47] Most who placed Wisdom in this category said that she was a personification of an attribute of Yahweh. For example, J. Marböck characterized Wisdom as "a poetic personification for God's intimate activity and for his personal summons."[48] Gerhard von Rad, however,

---

[45]W. O. E. Oesterley and G. H. Box, The Religion and Worship of the Synagogue (London: Sir Isaac Pitman and Sons, 1911), p. 169, in Helmer Ringgren, Word and Wisdom: Studies in the Hypostatization of Divine Qualities and Functions in the Ancient Near East. (Lund: H. Ohlssons Bokr, 1947), p. 8. For other definitions of hypostasis, cf. also James Barr, "Hypostatization of Linguistic Phaenomena in Modern Theological Interpretation," JSS, 7 (1962), 93; and G. Pfeiffer, Ursprung und Wesen der Hypostasenvorstellungen im Judentum (Stuttgart: Calver, 1967), p. 15.

[46]Cf. von Rad, Wisdom, p. 147 n. 3; Camp, Wisdom, pp. 34-36, 49-50. Lang, Wisdom, p. 140, said that Wisdom becomes a hypostasis only in Sirach and Wisdom of Solomon but not in Proverbs.

[47]Whybray, Wisdom, p. 80.

[48]J. Marböck, Weisheit in Wandel: Untersuchungen zur Weisheitstheologie bei Ben Sira (Bonn: Peter Hanstein Verlag, 1971), p. 130. Cf. also H. J. Wicks, The Doctrine of God in Jewish Apocryphal and Apocalyptic Literature (London: Hunter and Longhurst, 1915, reissued 1971), p. 85, who called Wisdom "a periphrasis for God in action."

contended that Wisdom was the "self-revelation of the orders of creation."[49] Bernhard Lang distinguished between "poetic personification" and "mythological personification," and maintained that Wisdom has a mythological background, but in Proverbs she becomes a personification of the poetic type.[50] Specifically, she represents "the wisdom teaching with its moral injunctions."[51]

Burton Mack, however, eschewed the language of hypostasis and personification; rather, he preferred to speak of a wisdom myth and mythology.[52] He criticized those scholars such as Rudolf Bultmann who reconstructed a unified wisdom myth by piecing together fragmented motifs in the extant literature. He acknowledged that mythic language has been borrowed from Egyptian myths of goddesses such as Maat or Isis, but he contended that this language has been worked into new configurations, creating a "wisdom mytho-logy," which was an early form of Jewish theology. Elisabeth Schüssler Fiorenza similarly made a distinction between "the basic Wisdom myth" of Isis or Maat and the appropriation of that myth through "reflective mythology," as seen in Sirach 24, Proverbs 1-9, and Wisdom of Solomon.[53]

Other scholars have understood Wisdom as a symbol or metaphor. Norman Habel pioneered such an approach in his analysis of the main motifs in Proverbs 1-9.[54] Adopting Paul Ricoeur's definition of symbol as "a double [or multiple] meaning linguistic expression that requires an interpretation,"[55] Habel considered "the way" as the "nuclear symbol" of Proverbs 1-9.[56] Claudia Camp, in her study

---

[49]von Rad, Wisdom, p. 317.

[50]Lang, Wisdom, pp. 132-136. For his distinction between "poetic personification" and "mythological personification," Lang was dependent on W. Porscher, "Personifikation," Der kleine Pauly: Lexicon der Antike, vol. 4 (Munich: Druckenmuller, 1972), pp. 661-663.

[51]Lang, Wisdom, p. 135. There have been scholars who have disagreed with the characterization of Wisdom as a personification. Cf. Wood, Wisdom, p. 97, 156, who pointed out that a personification tends to be simple and limited to one attribute, while Wisdom goes beyond literary personification and should be called an "entity." Such a term, however, seems quite vague.

[52]Burton Mack, "Wisdom Myth and Mytho-logy," Interpretation, 24 (1970), 46-60. He was pursuing concerns first addressed in his earlier work Logos.

[53]Elisabeth Schüssler Fiorenza, "Wisdom Christology and Christological Hymns," in Wilken, AWJEC, pp. 28-33.

[54]Norman Habel, "The Symbolism of Wisdom in Proverbs 1-9," Int, 26 (1972), 131-157.

[55]Paul Ricoeur, Freud and Philosophy: An Essay in Interpretation, trans. D. Savage (New Haven: Yale University Press, 1970), p. 9, quoted in Habel, "Symbolism," p. 132.

[56]Habel, "Symbolism," pp. 133-135. He listed three zones in which this nuclear symbol operates: personal human experience, Yahwistic religion, and cosmological reflection.

of Proverbs 1-9, understood Wisdom not only as a personification and symbol, but also as a metaphor. The metaphor results from the interaction of the word "wisdom" (the tenor or the lesser known term) and the implicit word "woman" (the vehicle or the better known term).[57] The vehicle of this metaphor, woman, is understood through an investigation of the female imagery in the Hebrew Bible, such as woman as wife and mother, love, harlot and adulteress, and wise woman.[58] The personification is a special kind of metaphor in which the abstract, general subject is aligned with a metaphorical, concrete predicate. In this way, Camp contended, personified Wisdom literarily unites the general and the particular, while theologically uniting the human and the divine.[59] The religious symbol, viewed from the perspective of Clifford Geertz's model of religion as a cultural system, functions to synthesize a people's ethos (i.e. lifestyle and moral and aesthetic preferences) and world view (i.e. the framework of their beliefs about the nature of reality).[60] Wisdom in Proverbs, Camp concluded, functioned as such a symbol in the early post-exilic era of ancient Israel.[61]

Building on Camp's study, Celia Deutsch also analyzed Wisdom as metaphor and symbol in her work on Wisdom in Matthew.[62] She distinguished between a "steno-symbol," which has a one-to-one correspondence to that which it represents, and a "tensive symbol," which has a multiplicity of meanings.[63] Through repeated use of the symbol, Wisdom became the subject of certain "stories" or myth. Deutsch wrote, "[W]hen cast in traditional forms, myth and symbol make access to new meaning available to the entire community for which

---

[57]Camp, Wisdom, p. 72-74.

[58]Ibid., pp. 79-147.

[59]Ibid., pp. 212-222.

[60]Ibid., p. 228-231. Cf. Clifford Geertz, The Interpretation of Cultures: Selected Essays (New York: Basic Books, 1977), esp. "Religion as a Cultural System," pp. 87-125.

[61]Camp, Wisdom, p. 290.

[62]Deutsch, "Wisdom," p. 15; "Jesus as Wisdom: Metaphor and Social Structure in Matthew's Gospel," paper presented to the Israelite and Christian Wisdom section of the Annual Meeting of the Society of Biblical Literature, Kansas City, MO, November 25, 1992, p. 2. I am indebted to Prof. Deutsch for graciously sharing copies of both her paper and article with me. Cf. also her Hidden Wisdom and the Easy Yoke: Wisdom, Torah and Discipleship in Matthew 11.25-30, JSNTSS 18 (Sheffield: JSOT Press, 1987).

[63]She was at this point dependent on Norman Perrin, Jesus and the Language of the Kingdom: Symbol and Metaphor in New Testament Interpretation (Philadelphia: Fortress, 1976), pp. 29-30, who himself was dependent on Ricoeur and Philip Wheelwright. Cf. the latter's Metaphor and Reality (Bloomington, IN: University of Indiana Press, 1962).

those forms are familiar."[64] She summarized, "Lady Wisdom is a symbol and the myth of Wisdom becomes . . . a vehicle for reflection on issues of cosmogony, theodicy and revelation prevalent in the Second Temple era. The tensive nature of the symbol allows it to be transformed according to the needs of the community."[65] Deutsch, then, was attentive to the social nature of the Wisdom symbol. Following Peter Berger, she stated, "Religious symbols, then, serve to maintain socially constructed reality. They emerge from the social structures of the collective and legitimate them."[66]

This method of looking at Wisdom as a myth, symbol, and metaphor seems to hold promise, for it enables us to see that the Wisdom material does not represent discursive thought which speaks to the mind but expressive thought which addresses the emotions and imagination. It is important, however, to consider the form in which the symbol or myth is communicated. Many of the Wisdom passages which have been surveyed are poems or hymns (e.g. Job 28:1-28; Prov. 1:20-33; 8:1-36; Sir. 1:1-10; 24:1-34; Wis. 7:22b-8:1; Bar. 3:9-4:4; 1 Enoch 42:1-2). Poetry engages the emotions in ways which prose does not. Furthermore, it builds up community, as a people claims a hymn or poem as its song. Wisdom, then, derives her power, not only because she is a symbol, but also because she often speaks or is spoken of in poetic form.

Function. How, then, did the Wisdom function in Israel as a symbol? This question has been addressed both in terms of early Jewish theology and in terms of the social settings out of which it arose. A number of scholars have spoken about Wisdom as a unifying principle in the Israelite theology. For example, R. N. Whybray maintained that Wisdom reconciled the wisdom tradition and the main Israelite religious tradition.[67] The former emphasized "creation theology,"[68] while the latter emphasized the mighty works of God as demonstrated in salvation history. The latter held the ascendance, and the sages realized that in order to maintain

---

[64]Ibid., p. 16.
[65]Ibid.
[66]Deutsch, "Jesus as Wisdom," p. 5. Cf. Peter Berger, The Sacred Canopy: Elements of a Sociological Theory of Religion (Garden City, NY: Doubleday, 1969), pp. 34, 42; Geertz, Interpretation, pp. 89f.
[67]Whybray, Wisdom, p. 11.
[68]A phrase made famous by Walther Zimmerli. Cf. his "The Place and Limit of the Wisdom in the Framework of the Old Testament Theology," in SAIW, ed. James L. Crenshaw (New York: KTAV, 1976), pp. 314-328.

their place in the Jewish religion, they would have to reconcile themselves some-how to the mainstream. Wisdom, then, was brought into connection with the fear of the Lord (Job 28:28; Prov. 1:7, 29; 8:13; 9:10; Sir. 1:11-14, 16, 18; 15:1; 19:20); she was identified with the Mosaic Law (Bar. 4:1; Sir. 24:23); and she was accorded responsibility for the saving acts in Israel's history (Wis. 10:1-11:1). The Wisdom of the sages was also the Wisdom active in salvation history. Whybray contended that in order to bridge the gap between the wisdom tradition and the main Israelite religious tradition, the sages emphasized that all Wisdom comes from God.[69]

Other scholars have suggested that Wisdom served not only as a figure of reconciliation between two trends within the Hebrew religious tradition, but also as a figure of reconciliation within the Jewish doctrine of God. W. Bousset and H. Gressmann wrote, "The trend towards the transcendent and the abstract in the Jew-ish belief in God" favored the origin of "middle-beings" which interposed them-selves "between God, who had become remote from the world, and man."[70] These "middle-beings" included angels, the spirit, the Word, and finally Wisdom. They were "personifications of the divine activity and power."[71] Wisdom assumed more importance than the others. She was endowed with human characteristics in order to picture God's personal invitation to humanity. Gerhard von Rad expressed well such an approach: "Wisdom does not turn towards man in the shape of an 'It', teaching, guidance, salvation, or the like, but of a person, a summoning 'I'. So Wisdom is truly the form in which Yahweh makes himself present and in which he wishes to sought by man."[72] Commenting on Wisdom of Solomon, James Reese wrote that the Wisdom figure becomes "a means of preserving the absolute tran-scendence of the unique God of revelation while at the same time offering in attrac-

---

[69]Whybray, Wisdom, p. 104. Cf. also James L Crenshaw, "Prolegomenon," in Crenshaw, SAIW, p. 25.

[70]W. Bousset and H. Gressmann, Die Religion des Jüdentums in späthellenistischen Zeitalter (Tübingen: Mohr-Siebeck, 1926), pp. 319, 342, in Hengel, Judaism, I, 155. Cf. also Hans Heinrich Schmid, Wesen und Geschichte der Weisheit, Beihefte zur ZAW 101 (Berlin: Topelmann, 1966), pp. 154, 158; and the response to Schmid in Camp, Wisdom, pp. 158-160.

[71]O. S. Rankin, Israel's Wisdom Literature: Its Bearing on Theology and the History of Religion (Edinburgh: T. & T. Clark, rpt. 1954), p. 229.

[72]Gerhard von Rad, Old Testament Theology, trans. D. M. G. Stalker (New York: Harper & Brothers, 1962), I, 444.

28

tive imagery the possibility of intimate communion with Him."[73] Wisdom, therefore, was the way to reconcile God's transcendence and immanence. Wisdom is the instrument through which God relates to creation. She is "God Himself in his work in and regarding the world."[74]

Still others have contended that the introduction of Wisdom not only met a threat within Judaism but also a threat from outside, first, in the form of a foreign cult. Numerous scholars contended that the picture of Wisdom was influenced by neighboring cults. For example, Gustav Boström suggested that the "foreign woman" in Proverbs was the goddess Astarte, and Wisdom was created to lure the Israelites away from the wiles of the foreign goddess.[75] In a somewhat different vein, Lang argued that Wisdom originally was the divine patroness of the Israelite school system, but in a monotheistic context, she was redefined as a personification of school wisdom.[76] Scholars have also maintained that the presentation of Wisdom in Sirach 24 and Wisdom of Solomon has been shaped by the Isis aretalogies. In his study of Sirach 24, Hans Conzelmann called Isis "the mother of Wisdom."[77] Concerning Wisdom of Solomon, John Kloppenborg wrote, "The peculiar configuration of Sophia's characteristics is a result of and a response to the immediate and powerful challenge to Judaism presented by another feminine figure, savior and revealer, a goddess linked to the pursuit of Wisdom and one associated with the throne: Isis."[78] He continued that this borrowing from the Isis cult provided religious identity and structure to the Jewish people under attack, and it laid the basis for communication with the worshipers of Isis.[79]

---

[73]James M. Reese, Hellenistic Influence on the Book of Wisdom and Its Consequences (Rome: Biblical Institute Press, 1970), pp. 41-42.

[74]Peter Dalbert, Die Theologie der hellenistisch-jüdischen Missionsliteratur unter Ausschluss von Philo und Josephus (Hamburg: H. Riech, 1954), pp. 72-90, in Reese, Hellenistic Influence, p. 42.

[75]Gustav Boström, Proverbienstudien: Die Weisheit und das fremde Weib in Spruche 1-9 (Lund: C. W. K. Gleerup, 1935), pp. 163-164. Cf. also Rankin, Wisdom Literature, pp. 259-264. For a response to Boström, cf. Camp, Wisdom, pp. 26-28, as well as the literature cited on p. 293 n. 4.

[76]Lang, Wisdom, pp. 6-7, 129-136.

[77]Hans Conzelmann, "The Mother of Wisdom," in The Future of Our Religious Past: Essays in Honor of Rudolf Bultmann, ed. James M. Robinson (London: SCM Press, 1971), pp. 230-246. Cf. also Hengel, Judaism, I, 158.

[78]John Kloppenborg, "Isis and Sophia in the Book of Wisdom," HTR, 75 (1982), 57-82. Cf. also Reese, Hellenistic Influence, pp. 36-50; Mack, Logos, pp. 90-96.

[79]Kloppenborg, "Isis," p. 67.

Scholars have also pointed to another "foreign woman" which shaped the presentation of Wisdom: hellenistic thought. Sirach and the Wisdom of Solomon represent two different responses to this threat, the former identifying Wisdom and the Law and the latter attempting to communicate Wisdom in the philosophical parlance of the day. According to Johannes Fichtner, Israel's Wisdom could only survive against the onslaught of Hellenism if she was brought into connection with the Law, Israel's prize possession.[80] Wisdom defined in terms of the Law was not merely a theological development; it was a "quest for survival."[81] The response of the Wisdom of Solomon, however, was different. Rather than fighting Greek philosophy, the author embraced it, finding Wisdom to be, according to David Winston, "the perfect bridge between the exclusive nationalist tradition of Israel and the universalist philosophical tradition [i.e. Middle Platonism] which appealed so strongly to the Jewish youth of Roman Alexandria."[82] Similarly, F.W. Dillistone noted that the wisdom literature formed a bridge between the transcendence of Hebrew thought and the immanence of Greek philosophy.[83] In the latter, the author of Wisdom of Solomon found the divine rational principle which corresponded to Wisdom.[84] Wisdom, then, received a cosmic, speculative cast, becoming an emanation from God, an associate in all God's works from creation to redemption. In this view, then, Wisdom served as a figure of reconciliation between Jewish and hellenistic thought.

Some, however, have considered such a "theological" approach overly speculative and have attempted to locate the concrete social setting out of which Wisdom arose. Mack pointed to the post-exilic era in Israel, after the defeat of Jerusalem and the destruction of the kingdom. During this time of turmoil, the Wisdom myth was employed theologically to address the question of theodicy and to affirm the purposes of God.[85] Camp sought to describe this setting even more

---

[80]Johannes Fichtner, Die altorientalische Weisheit in ihrer israelitisch-jüdischen Ausprägung (Giessen: A. Topelmann, 1933), pp. 127-128, in Hengel, Judaism, I, 162.

[81]The title of the chap. on Sir. in Crenshaw, OT Wisdom, p. 153.

[82]Winston, Wisdom of Solomon, p. 37.

[83]F. W. Dillistone, "Wisdom, Word, and Spirit: Revelation in the Wisdom Literature," Int, 2 (1948), 284.

[84]Cf. Ringgren, Word and Wisdom, p. 119, who maintained that the author of the Wisdom of Solomon found in the Wisdom figure the Israelite equivalent to νοῦς and λόγος of Greek philosophy.

[85]Mack, "Wisdom Myth," pp. 57-58.

specifically. Taking her cue from Geertz, she attempted to plumb the ethos and world-view of post-exilic Israel in order to determine how Wisdom functioned as a religious symbol in Proverbs.[86] She maintained that Israel had become a community of families rather than a nation ruled by a king, and thus Wisdom legitimated the heightened role which women made to society. Furthermore, Wisdom as counselor, lover, and administrator of divine justice fulfilled the roles formerly performed by the king. Deutsch, in commenting on the whole wisdom movement, noted that the possession of Wisdom legitimated the authority of the sage, who was male in the vast majority of cases.[87] Therefore, the Wisdom metaphor "conveys to a male audience the nature of the quest for wisdom as intimate, engaging the depths of human affectivity. And, it implies that intimacy with Wisdom will also bring the person into intimacy with God."[88]

Mack, Camp, and Deutsch were correct to point to the concrete social setting in which the Wisdom myth, symbol, or metaphor was employed. It is also necessary, however, to note again the poetic or hymnic form in which the symbol appears. The Wisdom poems or hymns would have engaged the emotions of the community members in order that they might affirm the presence of God in the difficult circumstances in which they found themselves. Furthermore, these hymns or poems would have bound the community together in solidarity. Questions of theodicy were answered in song!

In summary, Wisdom functioned as a myth, symbol, and metaphor in Israel, responding theologically to new situations in Israel's history, first in the aftermath of the return from exile and then in the cultural diversity of the hellenistic world. Wisdom, then, emerged as a response to crisis. In the post-exilic and hellenistic periods, Israel attempted to confess their faith and maintain community identity through Wisdom. When chaos characterized Israel's experience, Wisdom was the hidden order in creation. When God seemed far off, Wisdom mediated the divine. Wisdom provided solidarity within Israel and interpreted the new situations

---

[86]Camp, Wisdom, pp. 227-282.

[87]She did note exceptions: the women sages behind the early strata of Prov. 1-9, the Therapeutae, and Beruriah the wife of Rabbi Meir. Cf. Deutsch, "Jesus as Wisdom," pp. 6-7.

[88]Ibid., p. 7.

in which it found itself. She was the product of the Hebrew imagination in order to conceptualize God's work in the world and Israel's place within that world.[89]

This first major section of this chapter has traced the way of Wisdom from Job to the Tannaitic literature, from a Wisdom hidden from humanity to one fully available in the Law. Wisdom functioned as a myth, symbol, and metaphor in order to address the varied situations in which Israel found itself, both in the post-exilic and the hellenistic eras. Through Wisdom, Israel was able to make her way in the world.

The Transformation of Wisdom in the Johannine Prologue

Wisdom also makes her way into the New Testament; she takes her stand at the gates of the Gospel, the prologue (John 1:1-18). Wisdom, however, is transformed in the light of the Christ event; she is now the Word who has become flesh in Jesus of Nazareth. Yet the prologue's description of this preexistent, creative, redemptive Word is continuous with the Wisdom material's description of Wisdom. The consideration of Wisdom in the Johannine prologue will include two sections: the wisdom parallels will first be isolated, and the place and function of Wisdom in the prologue will then be probed.

Wisdom Parallels

Wisdom is one of numerous candidates which have been proposed for the precursor to the Johannine Word. T. E. Pollard wrote, "For a long time it was widely assumed that the Fourth Gospel was the most 'hellenistic' writing in the New Testament, with little or no contact with the Palestine in which the Gospel events took place."[90] Scholars, therefore, looked for the background to the Word in three areas in the hellenistic milieu: (1) Greek philosophy, in which both Heraclitus and the Stoics spoke of the Logos as a cosmic principle which gives order to

---

[89]Gordon D. Kaufman, The Theological Imagination: Constructing the Concept of God (Philadelphia: Westminster Press, 1981), p. 11, wrote, "Theology is (and always has been) essentially a constructive work of the human imagination, an expression of the imagination's activity helping to provide orientation for human life through a symbolical picture of the world roundabout and of the human place within that world." This is exactly what the wisdom tradition has done in developing the picture of Wisdom.

[90]T. E. Pollard, Johannine Christology and the Early Church, SNTSMS 13 (Cambridge: Cambridge University Press, 1970), p. 7.

the universe;[91] (2) Philo, in whose writings the Logos appears over 1400 times;[92] (3) gnosticism, which was said, principally by Rudolf Bultmann, to contain a "gnostic redeemer myth."[93]

In recent years, however, studies in the prologue have turned away from hellenistic parallels and looked to Jewish motifs. M. E. Boismard's statement in 1957 is still true: "Today we are recognizing more and more that St. John for the main lines of his thought is indebted to the great streams that traversed and gave life

---

[91]Cf. A. Dyroff, "Zum Prolog des Johannesevangeliums," in Pisciculi, ed. Theodor Klauser (Munster: Aschendorff, 1939), pp. 86-93; Bernhard Jendorff, Der Logosbegriff, Europaiische Hochschriften, 20/19 (Frankfurt: Lang, 1976). Jendorff maintained that the evangelist intended to imitate Heraclitus. Cf. also William Inge, Christian Mysticism (London: Charles Scribner's Sons, 1899), p. 47 n. 1, who believed that the evangelist was "referring deliberately" to Heraclitus.

[92]Cf. also A. W. Argyle, "Philo and the Fourth Gospel," ExpTim, 63 (1951-52), 385-386, who regarded the Word as the Philonic Logos baptized into the Christian faith. C. H. Dodd, The Interpretation of the Fourth Gospel (Cambridge: Cambridge University Press, 1953, pp. 276-278, provided a helpful list of parallels and concluded that the evangelist was influenced by hellenistic Jewish thought similar to Philo. Cf. also Robert McL. Wilson, "Philo and the Fourth Gospel," ExpTim, 65 (1953-54), 47, who wrote of "a common theological background and climate of thought." Most recently, cf. Thomas H. Tobin, "The Prologue of John and Hellenistic Jewish Speculation," CBQ 52 (1990), 252-269, who argued a position similar to Dodd's.

[93]Cf. Rudolf Bultmann, The Gospel of John: A Commentary, trans. G. R. Beasley-Murray, et al. (Philadelphia: Westminster Press, 1971), pp. 25-29. Siegfried Schulz, Das Evangelium nach Johannes (Göttingen: Vandenhoeck und Ruprecht, 1972), pp. 27-29, moderated Bultmann's proposal and maintained that the absolute personification of the Word stemmed from a hellenistic gnosticism where the concept of a fully personalized mediator was well-known. Carsten Colpe, Die Religionsgeschichtliche Schule: Darstellung und Kritik ihres Bildes vom gnostischen Erlösermythus (Göttingen: Vandenhoeck und Ruprecht, 1961) presented the first major refutation of Bultmann's proposal, arguing that it was an abstraction from later sources. Rudolf Schnackenburg, The Gospel According to St. John, trans. Kevin Smyth (New York: Crossroad, 1982), I, 488-493, offered an extensive rebuttal of the Bultmann-Schulz proposal, concluding that the wisdom literature offers better parallels with the prologue and that the absolute use of λόγος is better explained from hellenistic Judaism. Erich Fascher, "Christologie und Gnosis im vierten Evangelium," TLZ, 93 (1968), 726, similarly argued that one cannot postulate a gnostic milieu for the prologue.

Recent research in the Nag Hammadi texts has focused on the parallels between Trimorphic Protennoia and the prologue. Cf. Craig A. Evans, "On the Prologue of John and the Trimorphic Protennoia," NTS, 27 (1981), 395-401; James M. Robinson, "Sethians and Johannine Thought: The Trimorphic Protennoia and the Prologue of the Gospel of John," in The Rediscovery of Gnosticism, Vol. II, Sethian Gnosticism, ed. Bentley Layton (Leiden: E. J. Brill, 1981), pp. 642-643. No scholar has maintained that the prologue was dependent upon this gnostic tractate, but most postulate a similar sapiential background. Cf. the comments of Carsten Colpe, Robert McL. Wilson, and James M. Robinson in "Discussion: Session 2," in Layton, Rediscovery, pp. 662-670.

to the Hebrew scripture."[94] The four streams into which scholars have dipped include Hebrew scripture's use of the Word of the Lord,[95] Torah speculation,[96] the Targumic use of Memra,[97] and wisdom. The consensus of contemporary scholarship, however, is well-expressed by Rudolf Schnackenburg: "The closest parallels in thought are to be found in Jewish Wisdom speculation."[98] Indeed, in discussing other possible backgrounds to the Word, scholars pointed out that Philo, gnosticism, Torah speculation and the prologue all share a common background in the wisdom literature.[99] Therefore, Wisdom themes and specific parallels will be discussed in this section.

Most scholars agree that a hymn lies behind this passage, though there is no clear agreement as to what constituted the original hymn.[100] A number of scholars

---

[94]M. E. Boismard, St. John's Prologue, trans. Carisbrooke Dominicans (London: Blackfriars Publications, 1957), p. 82. Cf. also Robert Kysar, The Fourth Evangelist and His Gospel: An Examination of Contemporary Scholarship (Minneapolis: Augsburg Publishing House, 1975), p. 107

[95]A number of scholars have contended that the Word of the Lord has influenced the presentation of the Johannine Word. Cf. Boismard, Prologue, p. 100; André Feuillet, Le Prologue du Quatrième Evangile (Paris: Brouwer, 1968), pp. 224-225, 239-242. Few, however, have seen it as the sole source. Cf., however, P. Hugolinus Langhamer, "Zur Herkunft des Logostitels im Johannesprolog," BZ, 9 (1965), 91-94, who argued that the personification of the Word is simply the evangelist's unique addition to or interpretation of the Old Testament-Jewish themes.

[96]Barrett, Gospel, p. 54, contended that Torah speculation was "of first importance for the understanding of John." Cf. also Boismard, Prologue, pp. 97-98.

[97]Cf. C. T. R. Hayward, "The Holy Name of the God of Moses and the Prologue of St. John's Gospel," NTS, 25 (1978-79), 17-18.

[98]Schnackenburg, Gospel, I, 481. Raymond E. Brown, The Gospel According to John, I-XII, AB 29 (Garden City, NY: Doubleday and Co., 1966), p. 523, similarly stated, "In the OT presentation of Wisdom, there are good parallels for almost every detail of the Prologue's description of the Word." Cf. Dodd, Interpretation, pp. 274-275, who provided a helpful chart isolating the wisdom parallels in the Prologue.

[99]Cf. Brown, Gospel, p. 520, who made this point in regard to Philo. Tobin, "Prologue," pp. 253-255, agreed that the hymn is rooted in Jewish wisdom speculation, but he noted that there were elements which could not be explained from the wisdom tradition, such as the use of λόγος, its role in creation, the contrast between light and darkness, and the incarnation. He argued that the most likely thought-world of the hymn was "the speculative biblical interpretations of Hellenistic Judaism represented by a figure such as Philo of Alexandria" (p. 256). Concerning gnosticism, cf. p. 32 n. 93 above. Robinson in "Discussion," p. 666, affirmed a trajectory from the wisdom literature to gnosticism on which lay the Prologue and the Trimorphic Protennoia.

[100]Cf. Brown, Gospel, pp. 19-23; Schnackenburg, Gospel, I, 224-229, and "Logos-Hymnus und johanneischer Prolog," BZ, 1 (1957), 69-109; Serafin de Ausejo, "¿ Es un himno a Cristo el prologo de San Juan?" EstBib, 15 (1956), 223-277, 381-427; Bultmann, Gospel, pp. 14-18. Barrett, Gospel, p. 151 and The Prologue of St. John's Gospel (London: Athlone Press, 1971), p. 27; rpt. New Testament Essays (London: SPCK), p. 48, however, considered it a prose introduction to the Gospel. Cf. also W. Eltester, "Der Logos und sein Prophet," in Apophoreta:

have suggested that the Wisdom hymns offer a parallel in general literary form to the hymn to the Word.[101] In its present form, the prologue may be divided into three christological sections, omitting the references to John the Baptist: verses 1-5, the Word in the beginning; verse 9-13, the Word in the world; and verses 14, 16-18, the Word in the community.[102] The hymn to the Word, then, consists of three stanzas. A spiral-like structure can be noted: each section deals with the Word, his coming into the world, and his benefits for believers.[103] The Word's incarnation possessed glory, grace, and truth only because he was with God and was God in the beginning. The community knew that this Word was God only because they experienced his benefits.

---

festschrift für E. Haenchen (Berlin: Töpelmann, 1964), pp. 109-134; Peder Borgen, "Logos was the True Light: Contributions to the Interpretation of the Prologue of John," NovT, 14 (1972), 115-130. More recently, cf. G. Rochais, "La formation du prologue (Jn 1, 1-18)," ScEs 37 (1985), 5-9, who listed the various suggestions of scholars as to which verses constituted the original hymn.

[101]Brown, Gospel, p. 522; Eldon Jay Epp, "Wisdom, Torah, Word: The Johannine Prologue and the Purpose of the Fourth Gospel," in CIMCT, ed. G. F. Hawthorne (Grand Rapids: Wm. B. Eerdmans, 1975), p. 130; Boismard, Prologue, pp. 73-76; Harmut Gese, "The Prologue to John's Gospel," in Essays on Biblical Theology, trans. Keith Crim (Minneapolis: Augsburg Publishing House, 1981), p. 190; Robert Hamerton-Kelly, Pre-existence, Wisdom, and the Son of Man (Cambridge: Cambridge University Press, 1973), p. 209. C. Spicq, "Le Siracide et la structure litteraire du prologue de saint Jean," in Memorial Lagrange (Paris: J. Gabalda, 1940), pp. 183-195, however, went too far when he wrote that the evangelist drew directly on the model and structure of the book of Sirach.

[102]A similar structure was noted by Schnackenburg, Gospel, I, 227, and Herman Ridderbos, "The Structure and Scope of the Prologue to the Gospel of John," NovT, 8 (1966), 189-201. Cf. also Joachim Jeremias, "The Revealing Word," in The Central Message of the New Testament (Philadelphia: Fortress Press, 1981), pp. 72-72; Barrett, Gospel, p. 149; and Barnabas Lindars, The Gospel of John, NCB (Grand Rapids: Wm. B. Eerdmans, 1972), pp. 77-79, who postulated four divisions by adding vv. 6-8 as a separate division.

[103]As the prologue progresses, these points are brought into sharper focus. The Word shone in the darkness (v. 5) through his coming into the world (v. 9), which was his being in the flesh (v. 14). He gave humanity life and light (v. 4), power to become children of God (v. 12), and glory, grace, and truth (vv. 14, 16-17). The perspective narrows from all creation (v. 3) to the world of humanity (v. 4, 10) to "his own" (v. 11) to the new "his own," the community of believers (vv. 12, 14, 16-17). The prologue is a community document, which begins from the community's own experience of the Word and moves out to the boundaries of existence. Furthermore, the two verses in which ὁ λόγος appears, vv. 1 and 14, form the foci around which the prologue's spiral revolves. They highlight the two stages of the Word's existence: "with God" and "among us," "was God" and "became flesh." They are like the two poles of an electrical field, both standing in tension with yet generating power from one another.

The first stanza (vv. 1-5), which speaks of the Word's relationship with God (vv. 1-2), to creation (v. 3), to humanity (v. 4), and to evil (v. 5),[104] is replete with wisdom parallels. The first two verses affirm the intimate relationship between God and the Word. Like God, the Word was in the beginning (ἐν ἀρχῇ; cf. Gen. 1:1 LXX); that is, the Word was preexistent.[105] Indeed, this claim that the Word preexisted creation serves as the foundation for the following claims that the Word is able to give life and light (John 1:4-5), power to become children of God (vv. 12-13), and glory, grace and truth (vv.14, 16). A refrain running throughout the Wisdom material is the preexistence of Wisdom. Job 28, Proverbs 8, and Wisdom of Solomon all affirm the presence of Wisdom at the creation of the world (cf. Job 28:26-27; Prov. 8:22-31; Wis. 6:22; 9:9). In Proverbs 8:22-23 Wisdom testifies that she was created "at the beginning of God's work," set up "before the beginning of the earth." In Wisdom of Solomon her course is traced "from the beginning of creation" (Wis. 6:22). Furthermore, preexistence functions in much the same way as in the prologue, for claims made about Wisdom are grounded in the prior claim that she existed before creation. For example, Wisdom's statements concerning her preexistence in Proverbs 8:22-31 are bounded on either side by her words about the benefits she bestows, such as instruction, life, and joy. Wisdom's preexistence, though, was limited, for she was the first created being (Prov. 8:22; Sir. 1:4, 9; 24:9). The Word, however, simply "was" in the beginning (John 1:1-2). The imperfect ἦν of verses 1 and 2 contrasts with the aorist ἐγένετο of verse 3: All things became, but the Word already was.

---

[104]Cf. Ed L. Miller, "The Logic of the Logos Hymn," NTS, 29 (1983), 555. One might add that each relationship builds upon the previous one mentioned. Because the Word was with God, he was able to bring about creation; the one who brought about creation also effected redemption; and redemption resulted in the defeat of the forces of evil. Yet there is also movement in the opposite direction. Because believers experienced life and victory over evil, they inferred that this same power must be the original creative principle, and this principle can only belong to God, indeed be God. The theological stream flows back and forth.

[105]Numerous commentators point out that this statement about preexistence is not temporal but qualitative. Cf. Brown, Gospel, p. 4; Jeremias, "Revealing Word," p. 78; Gerhard Delling, "ἀρχή," TDNT, ed. Gerhard Kittel and trans. G. W. Bromiley (Grand Rapids: Wm. B. Eerdmans, 1964), I, 482. Bultmann, Gospel, p. 32, expressed the idea well: "In the person and work of Jesus, one does not encounter anything that has its origin in the world or in time; the encounter is with the reality that lies beyond the world and time."

The Word was not alone in the beginning but was πρὸς τὸν θεόν (vv. 1b, 2), usually rendered as "with God," "toward God," or "in God's presence."[106] Wisdom is also said to be with (μετά) God forever (Sir. 1:1; cf. also Wis. 9:9). She was beside (παρά) God at creation (Prov. 8:30 LXX). The Word was preexistent, the Word was in God's presence, and θεὸς ἦν ὁ λόγος (John 1:1c). A literal translation reads, "The Word was God."[107] Encounter with the Word is an encounter with God. Oscar Cullmann wrote, "The Word is God in his revelation."[108] Wisdom too reveals God, as expressed primarily in Wisdom of Solomon 7:25-26: "For she is a breath of the power of God, and a pure emanation of the glory of the Almighty. . . . For she is a reflection of eternal light, a spotless mirror of the working of God, and an image of his goodness."

The Word enjoyed an intimate relationship with God, and because of that relationship exercised a creative relationship with the world. "All things came to be through him" (John 1:3a); creation was accomplished through the Word, echoing the story of creation in Genesis 1. Wisdom also played a role in creation. Though such a role is debatable in Proverbs (3:19; 8:30?), it comes to the fore in the Wisdom of Solomon, for there she is "the fashioner of all things" (Wis. 7:22a; cf. 8:5, 6). Wisdom of Solomon 9:1-2 is particularly significant, for "wisdom" and "word" appear in parallel as instruments of God in creation: "O God of my ancestors and Lord of mercy, who has made all things by your word (ἐν λόγῳ σου), and by your wisdom (τῇ σοφίᾳ σου) have formed humankind. . ."

---

[106]Much has been written as to whether this phrase means accompaniment ("with God") or relationship ("toward God"). Brown, Gospel, p. 5, noting the sense of preexistent accompaniment in 17:5, attempted to combine the two alternatives with his translation "in God's presence."

[107]Some have recoiled from this rendering, preferring to read, "The Word was divine." Cf. R. H. Strachan, The Fourth Gospel: Its Significance and Environment, 3d ed. (London: SCM Press, 1941), p.99; Ernst Haenchen, "Probleme des johannesichen Prologs," ZTK, 6 (1963), 313; and John 1: A Commentary on the Gospel of John Chapters 1-6, Hermeneia, trans. Robert W. Funk and ed. Robert W. Funk with Ulrich Busse (Philadelphia: Fortress Press, 1984), pp. 109-111; the translations by Goodspeed and Moffatt. For the present translation, however, cf. Bruce Metzger, "On the Translation of John 1:1," ExpTim, 63 (1951-52), 125-126.

[108]Oscar Cullmann, The Christology of the New Testament, trans. Shirley Guthrie and Charles A. M. Hall, rev. ed. (Philadelphia: Westminster Press, 1963), p. 265. Cf. also Bultmann, Gospel, pp. 35-36.

The creative Word also brings about the new creation: "What has come into being in him was life" (John 1:4a).[109] The reference is not to natural life but eternal life (cf. 3:16; 10:10; 11:25). Verse 4a, then, refers to special creation in the Word. The Word brought forth all things; the Word also brought forth life to those who believe in him. The focus is narrowed from creation to the new creation. John Ashton contended that verse 4 is an allusion to the tradition represented by Wisdom of Solomon 10, which accords a role to Wisdom in salvation history. He therefore argued that "what has come into being in him" refers to "the special events of God's intervention on behalf of his people."[110]

Just as life is given by the Word, life is also the primary gift bestowed by Wisdom. Following her claim to preexistence in Proverbs 8:22-31, she says, "For whoever finds me finds life and obtains favor from the Lord" (v. 35). Roland Murphy called life the message of wisdom "summed up in one word"[111] and the "kerygma of wisdom."[112] This life is first the good life here and now, including long life and prosperity. In Wisdom of Solomon, however, this perspective changes a bit: immortality is the gift of Wisdom (Wis. 6:18-19; 8:13). Furthermore, creation and redemption, joined in the activity of the Word, are also joined in the activity of Wisdom, for she both formed and saved humanity (9:2, 18).

The life which the Word bestowed was also the light of humanity, light which is not overcome by the darkness (John 1:4b-5). It is the light which shines

---

[109]It is better to take ὅ γέγονεν with v. 4. This reading was the only one known to the writers of the first three centuries and was changed because it was interpreted in a semi-Arian sense. Furthermore, the poetry of the Prologue demands it. Cf. Brown, Gospel, p. 14; Bruce F. Vawter, "What came to be in him was life, Jn 1, 3b-4a," CBQ, 25 (1963), 401-406; F. W. Schlatter, "The Problem of Jn 1:3b-4a," CBQ, 34 (1972), 54-58; Kurt Aland, "Eine Untersuchung zu John 1.3-4: über die Bedeutung eines Punktes," ZNW, 59 (1968), 174-209; Bultmann, Gospel, p. 39. For those who took ὅ γέγονεν with v. 3, cf. Barrett, Gospel, p. 157; Schnackenburg, Gospel, I, 240; Bruce Metzger, A Textual Commentary on the Greek New Testament: A Companion Volume to the United Bible Societies' Greek New Testament (London: United Bible Societies, 1971), p. 196.

[110]Ashton, "Transformation," p. 173.

[111]Roland E. Murphy, "Israel's Wisdom: A Biblical Model of Salvation," SM, 30 (1981), 25.

[112]Roland E. Murphy, Wisdom Literature and Psalms, Interpreting Biblical Texts (Nashville: Abingdon Press, 1983), p. 29.

upon every person (cf. v. 9b). As Bultmann noted, the light is revelation.[113] As light, the Word reveals God. This same image illumines the Wisdom material. Wisdom is radiant and unfailing (Wis. 6:12); her instruction is like light (Sir. 24:27, 32); she offers light for the eyes (Bar. 3:14); she is the reflection of eternal light (Wis. 7:26). While the path of the righteous is like the light of dawn, the way of the wicked is like deep darkness (Prov. 4:18-19). Wisdom is superior to the light because light is succeeded by night, but against Wisdom evil does not prevail (Wis. 7:29-30), a striking parallel to the prologue's statement that the darkness does not overcome the light of the Word (John 1:5).

Verses 9-13 form the second major christological section, depicting the Word in the world. While verses 4-5 contain a hint that the Word was in the world granting life and light, the present section makes it clearer: he came into the world (v. 9c); he was in the world (v. 10a).[114] His presence resulted in a division in humanity between those who rejected the Word (vv. 10c, 11b) and those who accepted (v. 12a), the latter group being empowered to become children of God (vv. 12-13). The second stanza, then, continues to describe the Word's various relationships, with the world (v. 10), with "his own" (v. 11), and with the new "his own" (vv. 12-13).

This stanza also evidences wisdom influence. The Word "was the true light . . . coming into the world" (v. 9ac). Just as the Word came from preexistence with God into world history, Wisdom too came into the world. She came from her dwelling in the high places to make her dwelling in Israel (Sir. 24:4, 8). She was

---

[113]Bultmann, Gospel, p. 43. He interpreted it existentially as the "illumined condition of existence" (p. 41), "the light of self-understanding" (p. 47). Barrett, Gospel, p. 161, connected it with judgment: "The light shines upon every man for judgment to reveal who he is."

[114]Vv. 9-10 present a number of exegetical problems. For example, do they refer to the work of the preexistent Word throughout history or to the moment of incarnation? In other words, does this section refer to the Logos asarkos or the Logos ensarkos? The vocabulary of this section is that used of Jesus in the Gospel: he came into the world (3:19; 6:14; 11:27; 12:46; 16:28); the world did not know him (7:7); his own people, the Jews, did not receive him (5:43); some, however, believed in his name (20:31); they were not born of flesh (3:5-6); his death brought together the children of God (11:52). Verses 9-13, then, refer to the incarnate Word, Jesus Christ. As mentioned above, the prologue is arranged in a spiral, where a reference to the incarnation is implicit in the first section, clearer in the second, and explicit in the third.

A distinction, however, is sometimes made between the original hymn and the prologue in the Gospel as it now stands. For example, Tobin, "Prologue," p. 253, suggested that the first reference in the original hymn to the incarnate Word appears in v. 14, but when the hymn was integrated into the Gospel and the references to John the Baptist were added, the incarnation was seen as taking place in v. 10. Cf. the literature he cited in p. 253 n. 5.

sent from God's throne to be with Solomon (Wis. 9:10). The prologue continues, "And the world was made through him" (John 1:10b); the focus is narrowed from "all things" (v. 3) to humanity. Similarly, God formed humanity by Wisdom (Wis. 9:2a). Though the Word was the source of the world's being, the world did not know him (John 1:10c). Robert Hamerton-Kelly noted that knowledge is a central category in the wisdom tradition.[115] Baruch 3:9 reads, "Hear the commandments of life, O Israel; give ear and learn wisdom (γνῶναι θρόνησιν)."[116] The rejection of Wisdom is also a familiar theme in wisdom literature. Wisdom's speech in Proverbs 1:20-33 is a speech of judgment because humanity has refused to listen to her (v. 24) and has hated her (ἐμίσησαν σοφίαν, v. 29 LXX). Baruch 3:9-4:4 laments Israel's rejection of Wisdom: they have forsaken her (3:12) and have not understood (οὐκ ἔγνωσαν) her paths (3:20; cf. also 3:31).

The Word came into his own (τὰ ἴδια, i. e. Israel), but his own people (οἱ ἴδιοι, i.e. the Jews) did not receive him (John 1:11).[117] Just as verse 10b represents a narrowing down of verse 3a, verse 11 represents a narrowing down of verse 10. The Word was not only in the world, he was in his own place, Israel; not only did the world not accept him, his own people, the Jews, did not accept him. Like the Word, Wisdom too came into "her own" (v. 11a), the people of Israel. Sirach 24:8, 10-12 says that God gave Wisdom a place for her tent in Israel and was there so established (v. 8; cf. also Bar. 3:36).

Although the Word's "own" rejected him, he created a new "his own." While most did not accept (παρέλαβον, John 1:11) the Word, some did receive (ἔλαβον, v. 12) him and became children of God. Similarly, those who stand with Wisdom stand in a special relationship with God. Wisdom makes her disciples friends of God (Wis. 7:14, 27); those who serve her serve God, and God in turn loves those who love her (Sir. 4:14). Parallels to the concept of children of God appear in the wisdom literature. The author of Proverbs and of Sirach speak to the reader as "my child" (Prov. 2:1; 3:1, 11; 4:1, 20; 5:1, 7, 20; 6:1, 3, 20; 7:1, 24; Sir. 2:1; 3:1, 17; 4:1; 6:32; 10:28). Wisdom is also referred to as a mother (Wis.

---

[115]Hamerton-Kelly, Pre-existence, p. 211 n. 3.

[116]Schnackenburg, Gospel, I, 257 n. 129, listed a number of references from the wisdom literature for this concept of knowing.

[117]Cf. John W. Pryor, "Jesus and Israel in the Fourth Gospel--John 1:11," NovT 32 (1990), 201-218, for a comprehensive discussion of this verse.

7:12; Sir. 15:2) who has sons (Sir. 4:11; cf. Luke 7:35). The wise man is known as a son of God (Sir. 4:10; Wis. 2:13, 16, 18; 5:5).[118]

In the third stanza, the Word in the community (John 1:14-18), the evangelist employs explicitly Christian language.[119] Verse 14a, "and the Word became flesh and lived among us," is often called the climax of the prologue,[120] but it is important to see that it reformulates verses 9-11; it states how the Word came into the world. Yet it states it "in the most paradoxical terms."[121] The Word became (ἐγένετο) flesh at a particular point in time, in contrast to the beginning, when the Word simply was (ἦν). At that time he was with God (πρὸς τὸν θεόν), but then he was among us (ἐν ἡμῖν). The greatest paradox, however, is that the Word became flesh. It is at this point that the prologue goes beyond the Wisdom material, for though it is said that Wisdom "passes into holy souls" (Wis. 7:27), nowhere does Wisdom actually become a human being. The personification of Wisdom is different, then, from the incarnation of the Word. Yet the language used to describe the incarnation does contain echoes from the Wisdom material. In verse 14a the Word is said to have lived or dwelt (ἐσκήνωσεν) "among us," that is, in the midst of those who have believed in his name (v. 12). Similarly, Wisdom after dwelling (κατεσκήνωσα) in high places, made her dwelling (σκήνην) in Israel (Sir. 24:4, 8). In the form of the Law, "she appeared upon earth and lived with humankind" (Bar. 3:37-4:1).

In the dwelling of the Word, the community saw his glory (John 1:14b).[122] Wisdom is an emanation of God's glory (Wis. 7:26); her branches are

---

[118]Cf. Gese, "Prologue," p. 218; R. Alan Culpepper, "The Pivot of John's Prologue," NTS, 29 (1980), 19-20. It is interesting to note that while the wisdom literature refers to sons, the Gospel speaks of children in contrast to the Son.

[119]Haenchen, Gospel, p. 164. He was not correct, however, in maintaining that wisdom motifs stand behind the first half of the original hymn (vv. 1-5, 9-11) but not the second half; cf. p. 139. Cf. also John Painter, "Christology and the History of the Johannine Community in the Prologue of the Fourth Gospel," NTS, 30 (1984), 465-468, who argued that a sectarian Jewish hymn in praise of Wisdom underlies vv. 1-14c and a hellenistic Christian community added vv. 14d-18.

[120]Cf. esp. Schnackenburg, Gospel, I, 266: "This is something new (καί . . .) and unique, which took place only once, a real event (ἐγένετο)."

[121]Barrett, Prologue, p. 27.

[122]Bultmann, Gospel, p. 63, maintained that the paradox of the prologue--indeed, the entire Gospel--is that the glory is seen in the flesh. But Ernst Käsemann, "The Structure and Purpose of the Prologue to John's Gospel," in New Testament Questions of Today (London: SCM Press, 1969), pp. 159-161, argued that the paradox was not in the Word becoming flesh but in the presence of God on earth. His view of Johannine Christology was further developed in The

glorious (δόξης, Sir. 24:16); Solomon has glory because of Wisdom (Wis. 8:10), and will be guarded with her glory (Wis. 9:11). The Word's glory was as the glory of a father's only son (μονογενοῦς, John 1:14c; cf. also v. 18). The term μονογενής connotes not "only-begotten," but "unique in kind."[123] In the list of the twenty-two attributes of Wisdom in Wisdom of Solomon 7:22, she is described as μονογένες, "unique."[124] Furthermore, the kind of intimacy which is expressed here and in verse 18 between parent and child is also present in Proverbs 8:30-31, where Wisdom is God's "darling child, rejoicing before him always."

The Word in his incarnate state was "full of grace and truth" (John 1:14c). Similarly, Wisdom's branches are not only glorious but also graceful (χάριτος, Sir. 24:16). According to Ignace de la Potterie, the Johannine concept of truth is rooted in the wisdom literature, for there truth is used as a synonym of wisdom (cf. Prov. 23:23; Sir. 4:28; Wis. 3:9).[125]

The grace and truth in Jesus Christ is set side by side with the law of Moses (John 1:17). A synthetical parallelism is set up: grace and truth, already found in the Law, are found in plenitude in Jesus.[126] Wisdom was identified with the Law

---

Testament of Jesus, trans. Gerhard Krodel (Philadelphia: Fortress Press, 1968), in which he labeled it "naive docetism" (p. 26).

[123]Cf. Dale Moody, "God's Only Son: The Translation of John 3:16 in the Revised Standard Version," JBL, 72 (1953), 213-219; Paul Winter, "," ZRGG, 5 (1953), 335-363; Th. C. de Kruijf, "The Glory of the Only Son (John 1:14)," SJJNS, NovTSup XXIV (Leiden: E. J. Brill, 1970), pp. 11-123. For an attempt to rehabilitate the translation of "only-begotten," cf. John V. Dahms, The Johannine Use of Monogenes Reconsidered," NTS, 29 (1983), 222-232.

[124]Cf. J. Rendel Harris, The Origin of the Prologue of St. John's Gospel (Cambridge: Cambridge University Press, 1917), p. 13.

[125]Ignace de la Potterie, "L'arrière-fond de theme johannique de verité," in SE, ed. Kurt Aland, et al. (Berlin: Akademie-Verlag, 1959), I, 277-294.

[126]Others, however, have seen an antithetical parallelism: grace and truth are not found in the Law but only in Jesus. For a thorough discussion of this issue, cf. Severino Pancaro, The Law in the Fourth Gospel: The Torah and the Gospel, Moses and Jesus, Judaism and Christianity According to John, NovTSup XLII (Leiden: E. J. Brill, 1975), pp. 534-546. He maintained that the two are antithetical parallels. Bultmann, Gospel, p. 79, saw here the Pauline contrast between grace and law, and Painter, "Christology," p. 466, argued that the hymn was edited by a "'Hellenist' Christian community where the Pauline Law/Grace antithesis was known and accepted."

On the other hand, it can be argued that v. 17 contains a synthetical parallelism. The Law is not denigrated, for it said to be God's gift (ἐδόθη). Yet the Law is not exalted, for grace and truth is not attributed to it. His purpose in setting "the law through Moses" side by side with "grace and truth through Jesus Christ" is to show the exceeding worth of the latter in comparison to the former. Schnackenburg, Gospel, I, 277, captured the thought: "The previous legal system has been surpassed by the reality of the grace of Jesus Christ." Cf. also Dodd, Interpretation, p.

in Baruch (3:36-4:1), Sirach (24:8-12), and the Tannaitic literature. In other words, the presence of God is encountered in the Law. The prologue, however, says that that presence is encountered in Jesus Christ. Through him, grace and truth came (ἐγένετο); in him the Word became (ἐγένετο) flesh. The manifestation of God on earth is not in the form of a book but a person. Indeed, the thought here is more like that of the Wisdom of Solomon, who associates Wisdom with the king (Wis. 6:21-9:18) and with the luminaries of Israel's past, such as Adam, Abraham, and Moses (10:1-11:4).

The prologue ends in the same way it begins, with a reference to the intimacy of the Word with God and an affirmation of the Word as God. The difference, however, is that here at the end this intimacy is opened up to believers. "No one has ever seen God. It is God the only Son, who is close to the Father's heart, who has made him known" (μονογενὴς θεός ὁ ὢν εἰς τὸν κόλπον ἐκεῖνος ἐξηγήσατο, John 1:18).[127] The connection which the prologue makes between seeing and making known also appears in the Wisdom material. Job 28:27 says that at creation God saw and declared (ἐξηγήσατο, LXX) Wisdom. Sirach 43:31a reads: "Who has seen [God] and can describe (ἐκδιηγήσεται) him?" The answer is given two verses later: "For the Lord has made all things, and to the godly he has granted wisdom" (Sir. 43:33).

In summary, then, the hymn to the Word takes up much of the arrangement and many of the notes from the wisdom score. Like Wisdom, the Word is the pre-existent revealer of God and the instrument of God in creation; the Word enters into history and is rejected but grants life, light, glory, grace, truth, and intimacy with God to those who accept the Word. The prologue's rendering of the Word has been shaped by the picture of Wisdom in the biblical and early Jewish literature.

It is important to note, however, the differences between the prologue and the Wisdom material, the Word and Wisdom. The Word was not only with God but was God. Those who accept the Word are not only friends of God but children of God. Primarily, though, Word has become a human being, Jesus of Nazareth.

84, who claimed that the difference was between shadow and substance rather than direct opposition.

[127]The reading μονογενὴς θεός is preferred because it has strong manuscript evidence and it is the more difficult reading. Cf. Metzger, Textual Commentary, p. 198. Schnackenburg, Gospel, I, 279-280, and Bultmann, Gospel, pp. 81-82 n. 2, preferred μονογενὴς υἱός. Boismard, Prologue, p. 66, preferred simply μονογενής.

In other words, an incarnation has occurred. In the biblical and early Jewish literature Wisdom is a metaphor or personification. In the prologue, however, the
metaphorical has given way to the historical, a personification to a person.[128]
Baruch and Sirach gave concrete expression to Wisdom by identifying her with he
Law. The Wisdom of Solomon attributed vitality to Wisdom by characterizing her
as a spirit. The prologue preserves both vitality and tangibility by identifying the
Word with Jesus Christ. He is the one whom Wisdom-Word became.

One question, though, has perplexed scholars: Why does the prologue
speak about the Word rather than Wisdom? A number of explanations have been
offered. Some have contended that since Jesus was male, a masculine noun (ὁ
λόγος rather than ἡ σοφία) was needed to express the incarnation.[129] Others,
however, have contended that the absolute use of the Word is influenced by the
Word of the Lord in Hebrew scripture,[130] while still others have seen evidence of
hellenistic thought informed by Stoicism, such as one finds in the writings of
Philo.[131] A few scholars have pointed to the Christian sphere, in which the
preaching of the good news of Jesus Christ was known as "the word" (Mark 4:13-
20 par.). It was a logical progression, then, to call Christ himself "the Word."
Such a progression is anticipated in the body of the Gospel, where Jesus not only
speaks truth but is truth (John 14:6), not gives the bread of heaven but is this bread
(6:35). It is a short step for the prologue to say that Jesus not only spoke the Word
but was the Word.[132]

The Function of Wisdom in the Prologue

In the prologue Wisdom has become the Word, which has been incarnated
in Jesus of Nazareth. How, then, does this transformation of Wisdom into the

---

[128]This point was made strongly by James D. G. Dunn, Christology in the Making: A
New Testament Inquiry into the Origins of the Doctrine of the Incarnation (Philadelphia:
Westminster Press, 1980), p. 243-244.

[129]Brown, Gospel, p. 523; Lindars, Gospel, p. 83. A. Grillmeier, Christ in Christian
Tradition: From the Apostolic Age to Chalcedon (451), trans. J. S. Bowden (New York: Sheed
and Ward, 1965), p. 31, suggested that the feminine form would lend itself to gnostic speculation.

[130]Cf. Gese, "Prologue," pp. 198-199.

[131]Cf. Schnackenburg, Gospel, I, 493; Tobin, "Prologue," pp. 255-262.

[132]Cf. Edwin C. Hoskyns, The Fourth Gospel, ed. F. N. Davey (London: Faber and
Faber, Ltd., 1940), pp. 162-163; also Barrett, Gospel, pp. 154-155; Lindars, Gospel, p. 83.
Schnackenburg, Gospel, I, 483-484, disagreed.

44

Word function in the prologue and in the community which produced it? Two studies have given attention to this question, and they will be briefly summarized.

In his article on the transformation of Wisdom in the prologue, John Ashton set forth a double hypothesis: the prologue originated as a hymn in praise of Wisdom, and it is also a hymn to the Incarnate Word.[133] Ashton contended that one must take into consideration this "double interest" of the passage if one is to understand the climactic statement of verse 14, which Ashton regarded as part of the original hymn. Ashton maintained that the central insight of the prologue was "the identification of Jesus Christ, revered and worshipped by Christians alone, with the figure of Wisdom. This stems from the realisation, expressed throughout the hymn, that the history of Wisdom has been re-enacted by Christ: the divine plan seen at work throughout the history of Israel has taken flesh in him."[134]

Ashton suggested that the prologue presents the reader not with history or metaphor but with myth, which he defined in the following way: "the expression in story-form of a deeply held religious conviction concerning man's relation to the deity, the cosmos (or part of it) or human institutions. . . . In general it helps man to locate himself, to know where he belongs vis-a-vis God, the universe and his fellow human beings."[135] The myth presented in the prologue, Ashton continued, attempts to make sense of the community's rejection by the synagogue through the use of the tradition of Wisdom, especially that part of the tradition which depicts the rejection of Wisdom by her own people. The heavenly figure Wisdom is now identified with the historical individual Jesus of Nazareth, locating the community in relationship to God and to the synagogue.

Warren Carter, in his article on the relationship between the prologue and the Gospel, also attempted to understand the prologue in terms of the community's polemic with the synagogue.[136] "Both the community and the synagogue claimed

<hr/>

[133]Ashton, "Transformation."
[134]Ibid., p. 170.
[135]Ibid., p. 180. Ashton rejected Schüssler Fiorenza's suggested term "reflective mythology" (cf. above p. 21), for it "seems to imply a deliberate distancing from the religious experience, and . . . it fails to do justice to the properly religious involvement of the Prologue or the other christological hymns to which Fiorenza wishes to apply it" (p. 180). Cf. also Robert Kysar, John the Maverick Gospel (Atlanta: John Knox Press, 1976), pp. 30-31, who called the prologue "prime Christ myth."
[136]Warren Carter, "The Prologue and John's Gospel: Function, Symbol, and the Definitive Word," JSNT 39 (1990), 35-58.

to possess the revelation of divine wisdom, and came into irreconcilable conflict over the key question of where wisdom was to be found. . . . One solution, offered by Jamnia and the local synagogue, claimed Moses' revelation in Torah as the dwelling place of Wisdom. John's community offered another, Jesus."[137] Against the synagogue's accusation that the Johannine community compromised the Jewish belief in one God, wisdom is used to uphold monotheism, for, like Wisdom, Jesus is the revelation of God.[138]

Carter also addressed the question of how the prologue as a poetic unit functioned for the Johannine community. He turned to Geertz's view of communities as symbol-making entities, which attempt to make sense of their experience through the use of symbols. "Symbols . . . express the perceived nature of reality, and dramatize the positive and negative values of experience, drawing together in a comprehensive worldview the community's values, as well as the forces opposing their realization."[139] The prologue, then, asserts that the community's understanding of experience is grounded in divine reality. Because the community has accepted the divine claim of Jesus and society has rejected it, their belief is legitimated. The prologue is one symbolic unit in the Johannine "cluster of sacred symbols" which expresses "the essential understanding and experience of the community--rejected by the surrounding society, yet unique and special in perceiving the divine act."[140]

Ashton and Carter have both made important contributions to understanding the literary and social function of the prologue, particularly in relationship to the transformation of the Wisdom symbol. They both attempted to situate the prologue in the social setting of the community's polemic with the synagogue, and they both brought new perspectives to bear, Ashton through looking as the prologue as myth and Carter through considering it as a symbolic unit. Carter has particularly opened up new avenues of research through his use of Geertz's work on symbols.

Some refinement in their proposals, however, is called for. While Ashton's "double reading" on the prologue is helpful, it is questionable to assert that this pas-

---

[137]Ibid., p. 47.

[138]Ibid., p. 48.

[139]Ibid., p. 49. Cf. Clifford Geertz, "Ethos, Worldview and the Analysis of Sacred Symbols," The Interpretation of Cultures: Selected Essays (New York: Basic Books, 1977), pp. 126-141.

[140]Carter, "Prologue," p. 50.

sage was originally a hymn to Wisdom. It seems preferable to call it a hymn in praise of the Incarnate Word using wisdom categories. Although Ashton's definition of myth is illuminating, it needs to be supplemented by work in this area from the social sciences. Carter takes an important step through his use of Geertz. Carter's discussion of symbols, though quite stimulating, is very brief and needs further explication. One possible direction might be to explore the individual symbols that make up the prologue's "symbolic world," such as Word, life, light, glory, and grace. It seems that many of these symbols are taken over from the Wisdom material and derive their energy from the transformation of the Wisdom symbol into the Word.

It might be further asked whether Carter has adequately addressed the question which he posed for himself: How did the prologue as a poetic unit function in the community? Carter's answer was that the prologue simply represents a different literary form from the Gospel narrative, with different expressions and metaphors. It seems, though, that there is something unique about the poetic form of the prologue which gives it its power. It was noted above that the Wisdom poems or hymns engaged the emotions of the Israelites in difficult circumstances and bound the community together in solidarity.[141] The Johannine community too found itself in a difficult situation, struggling with its identity in the aftermath of excommunication from the synagogue. The hymn to the Word, then, summoned the emotions of the community to affirm that Wisdom was now found in Jesus of Nazareth. Questions of theodicy were again answered in song! The power of the prologue, then, derives not only from its form but also its content, both of which are grounded in the wisdom tradition. The hymn to the Word took over its symbols and the arrangement of those symbols in poetry from the Wisdom material.

The transformation of the Wisdom symbol in the Johannine prologue performed an important function in the community setting out of which the Gospel arose. Chapter 3 will give further attention to this matter, particularly in regard to the relationship between the prologue and the narrative.[142] Suffice it to say at this point that the prologue, through its appropriation of symbols from the wisdom tradition, helped the community cope with the crisis of excommunication from the

[141]Cf. above, p. 30.
[142]Cf. below, pp. 129-131.

synagogue. The community grounded its identity in divine reality, which has always been reaching out to humanity but has always been rejected.

This chapter has surveyed contemporary scholarship in Wisdom in biblical and early Jewish literature and in the transformation of Wisdom in the Johannine prologue. The pictures of Wisdom were first traced through the relevant material, and Wisdom was seen as the preexistent agent of God, who was present at creation and who brings humanity into intimacy with God. Wisdom functioned as a myth, metaphor, and symbol, often expressed in poetic form. She emerged in times of crisis in order to affirm the presence of God and build up community. The prologue of the Gospel of John takes over many of the themes from the Wisdom material. Like Wisdom, the Word participated in creation and redemption, bringing life, light, and glory. Also like Wisdom, the Word is a symbol and myth, placed in the form of a hymn, engaging the community's emotions so that in crisis they might affirm that Wisdom, the presence of God, was now experienced in Jesus.

Chapter 2

WISDOM THEMES IN THE JOHANNINE
PORTRAIT OF JESUS

Wisdom's influence upon the Gospel is not restricted to the prologue. Rather, Wisdom is a "kindly spirit" (Wis. 1:6a) that breathes life into the whole of the Gospel. This chapter will attempt to isolate wisdom themes in the Johannine portrait of Jesus. Six such themes will be probed: preexistence, descent-ascent, revelation-hiddenness, acceptance-rejection, intimacy with disciples, and glory and life. These themes were selected based on their prominence in the Gospel and in the Wisdom material.[1] Each theme will be traced through the Gospel, and it will then be demonstrated that the Gospel's presentation of this theme is informed by the Wisdom material of biblical and early Jewish literature. It is not the intention of this chapter to prove that all six are exclusively wisdom themes, for they appear in other types of biblical literature. The primary concern is to show a plausible milieu out of which Johannine Christology emerged; the interest is in the complex of ideas which depicts Wisdom and in another setting Christ.

---

[1]These themes parallel those set out by William Loader in his book The Christology of the Fourth Gospel, BET 23 (Frankfurt am Main: Peter Lang, 1989), p. 76. He lists 14 elements of the structure of Johannine Christology: (1) The Father (2) sends and authorizes the Son, (3) who knows the Father, (4) comes from the Father, (5) makes the Father known, (6) brings light and life and truth, (7) completes his Father's work, (8) returns to the Father, (9) exalted, glorified, ascended, (10) sends the disciples (11) and sends the Spirit (12) to enable greater understanding, (13) to equip for mission, (14) and to build up the community of faith. Cf. also his "The Central Structure of Johannine Christology," NTS, 30 (1984), 188-216.

Preexistence

In the beginning was the Word, and the Word was with God, and the Word was God. He was in the beginning with God (John 1:1-2).

The strongest claim for the preexistence of Christ in the Gospel, indeed, in the entire New Testament, is found in the prologue, yet this conception underlies the Gospel's picture of Jesus. The references to preexistence, though only occasional, buttress the Gospel's christological statements. William Loader wrote that the Gospel "assumes the pre-existence of the Son and uses it throughout as a basis for asserting the Son's authority to speak and act in a way that confronts the world and offers life in relationship with himself and with the Father."[2] Aside from the prologue, the references to preexistence appear in 1:30, 8:58, and 17:5, 24.[3] A brief glance will show how each of these passages functions in the Gospel.

In 1:30 the Gospel places a claim for Jesus' preexistence on the lips of John the Baptist: "This is he of whom I said, 'After me comes a man who ranks ahead of me, because he was before me.'"[4] John goes on to narrate the baptism of Jesus as an event in the past.[5] The words here are framed by two titles of Jesus: the Lamb of God (1:29) and the Son of God (1:34). The claim to preexistence sup-

---

[2]Loader, Christology, p. 154. He was responding to Rudolf Bultmann, who said that preexistence plays no part in Johannine christology. Cf. his The Gospel of John: A Commentary, trans. G. R. Beasley-Murray, et al. (Philadelphia: Westminster Press, 1971), pp. 254-255.

[3]Bultmann, Gospel, p. 76, added 6:62 to this list, although the reference to "the Son of man ascending to where he was before" does not necessarily imply preexistence. Cf. his discussion of the verse on p. 445, which does not mention preexistence. Similarly, Robert G. Hamerton-Kelly, Pre-existence, Wisdom, and the Son of Man: A Study of the Idea of Pre-existence in the New Testament, SNTSMS 21 (Cambridge: Cambridge University Press, 1973), pp. 197-242, considered the Son of man sayings along with the prologue and chap. 17 in his study of the preexistence in the Gospel. The distinguishing characteristic of the Son of man, however, is not that he is preexistent but that he descends and ascends.

[4]C. H. Dodd, Historical Tradition in the Fourth Gospel (Cambridge: Cambridge University Press, 1963), p. 274, suggested the translation: "There is a man in my following who has precedence of me, because he is and always has been essentially my superior." This rendering, which seems rather forced, obscures the reference to preexistence. Furthermore, it presents Jesus following John as a disciple (pp. 273-274). Raymond E. Brown, The Gospel According to John, I-XII, AB 29 (Garden City, NY: Doubleday and Co., 1966), p. 56, admitted this latter possibility but contended that the synoptic parallels support a reference to Jesus following John chronologically in ministry.

[5]The synoptic Gospels all narrate the event itself. Cf. Matt. 3:13-17; Mark 1:9-11; Luke 3:21-22.

ports the claim that Jesus is uniquely qualified to be both God's remedy for sin and the perfect revelation of God.[6]

John's statement in 1:30 also appears in the prologue (1:15) as his witness to the Word become flesh (Ἰωάννης μαρτυρεῖ περὶ αὐτοῦ). Throughout the Gospel, John functions as witness.[7] Here he is a witness to Jesus' preexistence. Indeed, John is the only character other than Jesus himself to refer to it. He uses preexistence as an argument for the preeminence of Jesus. Jesus is superior because he existed first. Oscar Cullmann maintained that this verse is a polemic against the Baptist sectarians, who claimed that because John came before Jesus he was superior to Jesus. Priority in time means priority in dignity.[8] The Gospel agrees with this principle and shows that in fact Jesus was before John. The ἦν of 1:30c recalls the ἦν of 1:1. There it refers to the timeless existence of the Word, in contrast to the temporal beginning of all things (ἐγένετο, v. 3). The contrast here is between Jesus' preexistence and earthly ministry: he became superior to John (ἔμπροσθεν γέγονεν) in his earthly ministry because he was before him (πρῶτος ἦν) in preexistence.

A similar argument is set forth in 8:58. This saying of Jesus occurs in the context of his discussions with the Jews. Raymond Brown noted that 8:58 forms an inclusion with 8:12, in which Jesus says, "I am the light of the world."[9] The discussion with "the Jews who had believed in him" (8:31-59) centers around the theme of Abraham. Verses 31-47 address the question of whether or not these Jews are children of Abraham; verses 48-59 refer to Jesus' superiority to Abraham. Just as superiority to John is grounded in preexistence, so also superiority to Abraham is grounded in preexistence. Furthermore, Jesus' discussion with the Jews contains a number of high christological statements: Jesus' word results in freedom

---

[6]R. Alan Culpepper, Anatomy of the Fourth Gospel: A Study in Literary Design, Foundations and Facets (Philadelphia: Fortress Press, 1983), p. 88: "Jesus' task is to reveal the Father by bearing witness to the truth . . . and take away the sin of the world."

[7]This view of John as solely a witness is unique to the Gospel. For a comparison of the evangelists' respective views of John, cf. Walter Wink, John the Baptist in the Gospel Tradition, SNTSMS 7 (Cambridge: Cambridge University Press, 1968).

[8]Oscar Cullmann, "Ο ΟΠΙΣΩ ΜΟΥ ΕΡΧΟΜΕΝΟΣ," The Early Church, ed. A. J. B. Higgins (London: SCM Press, 1956), pp. 177-184.

[9]Brown, Gospel, I-XII, p. 367; Bultmann, Gospel, p. 327 n. 4, however, disagreed, for he contended that this verse has nothing to do with the "I am" sayings because it has no substantive.

and life (vv. 32, 51); he came forth from God (v. 42); he enjoys intimacy with his Father (vv. 38, 55); he is greater than Abraham (v. 53). These statements come to a climax at 8:58: "Jesus said to them, 'Very truly, I tell you, before Abraham was, I am.'" Again preexistence serves as the basis for the high christological statements.

Just as John confessed that Jesus preexisted him, Jesus now claims to pre-exist Abraham. The beginning is pushed back further: Jesus not only preexisted a contemporary prophet; he preexisted the father of the Hebrew people. Yet these statements are to be read in light of the prologue, in which the Word preexisted all things (1:1-3). Again the Gospel uses the contrast between εἰμί and γίνομαι. Here Abraham's becoming is contrasted with the eternal existence of the Word. The verb tense, however, distinguishes this text from others; a present εἰμί appears in 8:58, while an imperfect ἦν appears in 1:1-2 and 1:30. The Gospel places Jesus in the eternal present, where temporal references are meaningless. The Word takes up within himself past, present, and future; eternity confronts humanity in Jesus. The import of the statement, though, is not metaphysical but soteriological, as Rudolf Schnackenburg wrote: "It is only as the Son who has always belonged to God and who 'remains in the house' that Jesus can lead us to true freedom (v. 36) and give the life that overcomes death (v. 51)."[10]

The final two references to preexistence occur in Jesus' prayer in John 17. Preexistence here reaches its furthest point; it is existence "before the world existed" (v. 5), "before the foundation of the world" (v. 24). The beginning of the Christ-event is now pushed back before John, before Abraham, and even before the creation of the world. Indeed, this is where the prologue begins, and the narrative only now catches up.

Preexistence is here connected with glory, the glory which is manifested in the hour of Jesus' death, resurrection, and ascension. The Gospel transforms the cross from humiliation (as in the synoptics, Acts, and Paul) to glorification. Here preexistence assists in that process of transformation. The glory which shines in the hour is the luminous glory of preexistence. The cross is glory because it is the

---

[10]Rudolf Schnackenburg, The Gospel According to St. John, trans. Cecily Hastings, et al. (New York: Crossroad, 1982), II, 223.

preexistent Word who is on the cross. Preexistence and the hour are brought together under the rubric of glory.

Chapter 17 is typically divided into three sections: Jesus prays for himself (vv. 1-5), for his disciples (vv. 6-19), and for those who will believe through the disciples' preaching (vv. 20-26).[11] In this first section, Jesus prays for his own glorification in the "hour." He prays in verse 5, "And now Father, glorify me in your own presence with the glory that I had in your presence before the world existed."[12] Jesus prays that God might grant him the same glory which he had in preexistence.[13] He prays that the eternal glory of the Word might be manifested in the hour of his death and resurrection.

Before creation Jesus enjoyed an intimate relationship with the Father: he was with the Father before the world was made (v. 5); God loved him before the foundation of the world (v. 24). Existence before creation is existence with God. Again the Gospel narrative comes back full circle to the prologue: the παρὰ σοί of 17:5 corresponds to the πρὸς τὸν θεόν of 1:1-2; both express preexistent accompaniment. The preexistence of Jesus relates to both the temporal and the eternal; he was before creation and he was with God. Jesus is then placed on the side of the eternal.

In the third section (vv. 20-26), Jesus prays that those who believe through the disciples' word may be one. This oneness is oneness in preexistent glory. Jesus prays that these believers might "see my glory, which you have given me be-

---

[11]Cf. Raymond E. Brown, The Gospel According to John, XIII-XXI, AB 29A (Garden City, NY: Doubleday and Co., 1970), p. 759. For a careful survey of the variety of divisions proposed for John 17, cf. J. Becker, "Aufbau, Schichtung und theologiegeschichtliche Stellung des Gebetes in Johannes 17," ZNW, 60 (1969), 56-61.

[12]J. M. Ballard, "The Translation of John xvii.5," ExpTim, 47 (1935-36), 284, translated, "with that glory which I had before the world existed beside you." This is doubtful, for the focus is on the relationship of the Son to the Father, not the world to the Father.

[13]A number of commentators have contrasted this perspective with that of Phil. 2:6-11 in which God exalted Jesus after his death to a place above his previous status. Cf. Bultmann, Gospel, p. 407 n. 1; Brown, Gospel, XIII-XXI, p. 752; Schnackenburg, Gospel, II, 174. Cf. also Ernst Käsemann, The Testament of Jesus, trans. Gerhard Krodel (Philadelphia: Fortress Press, 1968), p. 10. Cf. James D. G. Dunn, Christology in the Making: A New Testament Inquiry into the Origins of the Doctrine of the Incarnation (Philadelphia: Westminster Press, 1980), pp. 114-123, for his discussion of Phil. 2:6-11. Interpreting it according to Adam Christology, he challenged the consensus that Paul here teaches the preexistence of Christ. In other passages, such as Col. 1:15-20 and 1 Cor. 8:6, Dunn continued, Paul used the Wisdom terminology to speak of an ideal preexistence (cf. pp. 176-196). Real preexistence is not present until the Gospel, Dunn concluded (p. 249).

cause you loved me before the foundation of the world" (v. 24). The prologue confesses that in Jesus' earthly life the community beheld his glory (1:14); Jesus now prays that they might behold his glory in the hour. This beholding is possible only by being where Jesus is. Indeed, this is the purpose of the hour, of Jesus' going to the Father, that the disciples may be where he is (14:3; cf. also 12:26). Preexistence and glory are here joined with love. The Father's love for the Son is the basis of the Son's preexistent glory.

Preexistence, then, functions in two important ways in the Gospel. First, it substantiates Jesus' superiority to John (1:30), to Abraham (8:58), and to the world (17:5, 24). Thus, preexistence is existence with God (17:5); Jesus is set on the divine side of reality. Second, preexistence substantiates the lofty claims made about Jesus. The preexistent one is the Lamb of God and the Son of God (1:29-34); he offers freedom and life and enjoys intimacy with God (8:31-59); his death is not humiliation but glory (chap. 17).

Wisdom too is preexistent, as seen in the survey of the pictures of Wisdom in the previous chapter.[14] The interest here, however, will be on the function of preexistence in the Wisdom passages, for preexistence functions in much the same way as it does in the Gospel; it substantiates Wisdom's superiority over the created order and substantiates lofty claims about her.

First, Wisdom is superior to all created things because she existed before them. This idea receives signal expression in Proverbs 8:22-31 in which Wisdom says that she was brought forth before ($\pi\rho\acute{o}$, LXX) the beginning of the earth, before the depths and the mountains. The repetition drives the point home: Because Wisdom was before all things, she is greater than all things; because she existed prior to any created thing, she is superior to any created thing (cf. also Job 28:24-27). So also Jesus existed before ($\pi\rho\widehat{\omega}\tau\circ\varsigma$) John (John 1:30), before ($\pi\rho\acute{\iota}\nu$) Abraham (8:58), indeed, before ($\pi\rho\acute{o}$) creation (17:5, 24); therefore, he is superior to all these. The net effect of these statements in the Gospel and in the Wisdom material is that both Jesus and Wisdom area placed on the divine side of reality. In both cases a temporal metaphor is used to make a theological statement. Just as Wisdom was beside ($\pi\alpha\rho\acute{\alpha}$) God (Prov. 8:30 LXX) and with ($\mu\epsilon\tau\acute{\alpha}$) God at creation (Wis. 9:9), so also Jesus was with ($\pi\alpha\rho\acute{\alpha}$) God before the world was made

---

[14]Cf. above, pp. 10-21.

(John 17:5). Wisdom had a warm, intimate relationship with God in creation; she was "daily his delight, rejoicing before him always" (Prov. 8:30b). So also in giving glory the Father loved Jesus before the foundation of the world (John 17:24). Jesus and Wisdom are not of this world; they are of God.

Second, preexistence in the Wisdom material substantiates the lofty claims which are made for Wisdom. Job 28 maintains that Wisdom is more valuable than gold, silver, or precious stones (vv. 15-19), and this statement is grounded in the concept of preexistence (vv. 25-27). In Proverbs 8 Wisdom offers knowledge, understanding, and riches (vv. 6, 21). She follows up this offer with an elaborate claim to preexistence (vv. 22-31). In Wisdom of Solomon 9 the king prays that God will send Wisdom to him in order that he might possess understanding and right judgment. Wisdom can grant these things because she was present when God made the world. Preexistence guarantees the worth of Wisdom and her gifts. In the same way, freedom from sin is available through Jesus because he is preexistent (John 1:29-30; 8:31-32, 58). Furthermore, we know that he came from God and knows God because he was preexistent with God (8:42, 55, 58).

Preexistence, then, is characteristic of both Jesus and Wisdom. More than that, preexistence functions in the same way in both the Gospel and the Wisdom material. It preserves both Jesus' and Wisdom's superiority over all created things, thereby placing them on the side of God. Furthermore, it substantiates the claims made for them. These parallels lead one to the conclusion that the Gospel was influenced by wisdom in its portrait of the preexistent Jesus. Indeed, scholars have previously linked preexistence in the Wisdom material and preexistence in the New Testament. Eduard Schweizer wrote in an article on preexistence in Paul, "The idea (Vorstellung) of the preexistence of Jesus came to Paul through Wisdom speculation."[15] James D. G. Dunn nuanced Schweizer's proposal; he maintained that Paul's use of wisdom terminology paved the way for a full-blown conception of preexistence found only in the Gospel.[16] However Paul is judged, it is beyond dispute that the evangelist paints a picture of the preexistent Christ. The primary influence for this portrait was preexistent Wisdom. In order to highlight the ulti-

---

[15]Eduard Schweizer, "Zur Herkunft der Praexistenzvorstellung bei Paulus," in Neotestamentica: Deutsche und Englische Aufsätze 1951-1963 (Zürich/Stuttgart: Zwingli-Verlag, 1963), p. 109.

[16]Dunn, Christology, pp. 194-195, 211-212.

macy of Jesus, the evangelist borrowed the bright hue of preexistence from the wisdom palette. When this color is applied to the portrait of Jesus, however, it takes on a different shade. The preexistence of Wisdom is preexistence of a personification. In other words, it is further elaboration of the basic metaphor of Wisdom. The preexistence of Jesus, however, is preexistence of a person. It is a description in metaphorical language of the significance of that person. To put it more theologically, discussion of the preexistence of Jesus is an attempt to give eternal significance to an historical event. The Gospel proclaims that in this man the transcendent encounters the mundane, the eternal enters the historical, the divine meets the human. In this way, the preexistence of Jesus goes beyond that of Wisdom, for unlike her, he has become flesh and lived among us.

Descent-Ascent

The true light, which enlightens everyone, was coming into the world (John 1:9)

From his preexistent position with God, Jesus descended into the world, and he ascended out of the world to return to preexistent glory. A statement which tracks Jesus' trajectory in the Gospel is found in 16:28: "I came from the Father and have come into the world; again, I am leaving the world and am going to the Father" (cf. also 13:3). A focal concern of the Gospel is Jesus' origin and destiny; he has come from God and is going to God. Godfrey Nicholson called this the Descent-Ascent Schema (DAS) and contended that it underlies the literary structure, the understanding of Christology, and the understanding of Christian belief in the Gospel.[17] He argued that the question of Johannine Christology is: Where is Jesus from and where is he going?[18] R. Alan Culpepper wrote of the "stereotypic perspective" of the Gospel narrator: "The narrator views Jesus and his ministry from the twin perspectives of his 'whence and his 'whither,' his origin as the preexistent logos and his destiny as the exalted Son of God."[19] Similarly, Wayne Meeks maintained that this DAS is "the cypher for Jesus' unique self-knowledge as well as for his foreignness to the men of this world."[20]

---

[17]Godfrey C. Nicholson, Death as Departure: The Johannine Descent-Ascent Schema, SBLDS 63 (Chico, CA: Scholars Press, 1963), p. 21.

[18]Ibid., p. 107.

[19]Culpepper, Anatomy, p. 33; cf. also pp. 37-38.

[20]Wayne Meeks, "Man from Heaven in Johannine Sectarianism," JBL, 91 (1972), 60.

For a number of years it has been argued that this DAS is rooted in the gnostic redeemer myth.[21] Recent scholarship, however, has grown dissatisfied with this hypothesis and has turned toward Jewish motifs. Charles Talbert, for example, has identified at least two streams of Jewish tradition in which the DAS appears: the wisdom tradition and Jewish angelology.[22] This section will give attention to the former stream. It will show that the DAS is best interpreted against the background of the Wisdom material. In order to do so, the presupposition of the DAS, the Johannine spatial dualism, will be explored. Then the two halves of the DAS, the sending by the Father and the ascent to the Father, will be examined. Finally, attention will be given to the descending-ascending Son of Man. All along the way, the wisdom background will be noted.

Presupposition: Spatial Dualism

The raw material out of which the Gospel builds his DAS is the much-discussed Johannine dualism.[23] In the Gospel there is both a soteriological dualism and a spatial dualism.[24] The spatial dualism slices reality into two spheres: the world above and the world below. The primary world is the world above. It is where God is; it is the source of light, life, spirit, and truth, which are communicated through Jesus to the world below. As James Charlesworth pointed out, the world below is the object of action from above.[25] "This world" (ὁ κόσμος οὗτος, 8:23; 9:39; 11:9; 12:25, 31; 13:1; 16:11; 18:36) is the world below (cf. 8:23), contrasted with the world above.[26]

---

[21]Cf. above, p. 1 n. 2, p. 30 n. 93.

[22]Charles H. Talbert, What is a Gospel? The Genre of the Canonical Gospels (Philadelphia: Fortress Press, 1977), pp. 56-57.

[23]For discussions of the Johannine dualism, cf. J. Becker, "Beobachtungen zum Dualismus im Johannesevangelium," ZNW 65 (1974), 71-87; Rudolf Bultmann, Theology of the New Testament, trans. K. Grobel (New York: Charles Scribner's Sons, 1955), II, 15-32; James H. Charlesworth, "A Critical Comparison of the Dualism in 1QS 3:13-4:26 and the 'Dualism' Contained in the Gospel of John," in John and Qumran (London: Geoffrey Chapman, 1972), pp. 89-96; Robert Kysar, John the Maverick Gospel (Atlanta: John Knox Press, 1976), pp. 47-64.

[24]The term spatial dualism is used instead of cosmic dualism because it is more exact. Cf. John G. Gammie, "Spatial and Ethical Dualism in Jewish Wisdom and Apocalyptic Literature," JBL, 93 (1974), 357, 360.

[25]Charlesworth, "Dualism," pp. 90-91.

[26]Cf. C. K. Barrett, The Gospel According to St. John: An Introduction with Commentary and Notes on the Greek Text, 2d ed. (Philadelphia: Westminster Press, 1978), p. 161.

58

Jesus has come into this world from above. He is the one from above; he is not of this world (3:31; 8:23; 17:14, 16). This note is sounded loudly in John 6, in which Jesus declares that he is the living bread that has come down from heaven (καταβαίνω, vv. 33, 38, 41, 42, 50, 51). Jesus' origin from above functions in much the same way as his preexistence; it locates Jesus in the divine sphere. He is not only "before" all things but "above" all things. He and the salvation that he brings do not have their origin in the human sphere; they are from God.

Though not as pronounced as in the Gospel, the Wisdom material contains a spatial dualism. This matter has been given significant attention by John Gammie.[27] He showed how a spatial dualism had influenced each book in the wisdom literature.[28] He continued that this dualism is "recapitulated and summarized" in the Wisdom passages.[29] In Job 28 Wisdom is not found in the land of the living, not in the deep, not in the sea (28:13-14, 23-34); she is, by implication, in heaven. The situation is the same in Sirach 1, where God sits on his throne, and pours out Wisdom on all his works (vv. 8, 9). Sirach 24 is more explicit: Wisdom is in the assembly of the Most High and says, "I dwelt in the highest heavens, and my throne was in a pillar of cloud" (vv. 2, 4). In Wisdom of Solomon 9:1-8 Solomon prays for God to send Wisdom from heaven: "Send her forth from the holy heavens, and from the throne of your glory send her" (v. 10). "Who has learned your counsel, unless you have given Wisdom and sent your holy spirit from on high?" (v. 17) Wisdom's home is in heaven. In this way Wisdom is placed on the divine side of reality; she too is "above" all things. Therefore, she and her benefits are worthy to be acquired.

Like the Gospel, the Wisdom passages contains a spatial dualism between the world above (heaven) and the world below (earth). Like Jesus, Wisdom is from the world above. Both the Gospel and the Wisdom material share this dualistic perspective. A spatial metaphor is combined with a temporal metaphor to make a theological statement: Jesus-Wisdom does not originate in this time-space continuum. In other words, "before" and "above" means "beyond." The Gospel and the Wisdom material use temporal and spatial language to point to another dimension, the dimension of the divine.

---

[27]Gammie, "Dualism," pp. 362-366.
[28]Ibid., pp. 363-364.
[29]Ibid., p. 365.

The Father Sent the Son

Jesus has not come down from above on his own accord; he has been sent by the Father. Jesus is known repeatedly as the one whom God has sent (John 3:34; 5:38; 6:29; 10:36; 17:3, 21). God, who is otherwise a shadowy figure in the Gospel, is known primarily as the one who sent Jesus (5:23, 30, 36, 37; 6:38, 39, 44, 57; 7:16, 29, 33; 8:16, 18, 26, 29; 12:44).[30] Loader maintained that on the lips of Jesus "he who sent me" becomes almost a formal designation of God and is the ground of Jesus' authority.[31] The fact that Jesus has been sent from the Father validates his message. As the one who has been sent, he uttered the words of God (3:34). Jesus, the one sent by God, is part of the divine movement toward humanity.

The Gospel uses two different terms for the sending of Jesus by God, πέμπω and ἀποστέλλω. Karl Rengstorf maintained that there is a distinction between these two words; ἀποστέλλω is used to ground Jesus' authority in that of God, while the formula ὁ πέμψας με affirms the participation of God in his work.[32] This distinction is artificial, for the two verbs seemed to be used without any apparent distinction of meaning.[33]

The sending of Jesus is described in two brief statements in 3:16-17:

For God so loved the world that he gave his only Son, so that (ἵνα) everyone who believes in him may not perish but may have eternal life. Indeed, God did not send (ἀπέστειλεν) the Son into the world to condemn the world, but in order that (ἵνα) the world might be saved through him.[34]

---

[30]Cf. Culpepper, Anatomy, p. 113: "[God's] predominant characteristic is that he sent Jesus."

[31]Loader, "Central Structure," p. 190. Cf. also Juan Peter Miranda, Der Vater, der mich gesandt hat: Religionsgeschichtliche Untersuchungen zu den johanneischen Sendungsformeln (Frankfurt: Herbert Lang, 1972).

[32]Karl Rengstorf, "ἀποστέλλω (πέμπω)," TDNT, ed. Gerhard Kittel and G. W. Bromiley (Grand Rapids: Wm. B. Eerdmans, 1964), I, 405.

[33]Cf. the discussion in David A. Fennema, "Jesus and God According to John: An Analysis of the Fourth Gospel's Father/Son Christology" (Ph.D. dissertation, Duke University, 1979), pp. 2-5. Cf. also Brown, Gospel, I-XII, p. 134. Cf. also Josef Kuhl, Die Sendung Jesu und der Kirche nach dem Johannes-Evangelium, SIMSVD 11 (St. Augustin: Steyler Verlag, 1967), p. 54.

[34]Cf. 1 John 4:9: "In this the love of God was made manifest among us, that God sent (ἀπέσταλκεν) his only Son into the world, so that (ἵνα) we might live through him." Cf. also Gal. 4:4-5; Rom. 8:3-4.

60

The purpose of the sending is for meaningful relationship with God, referred to as eternal life and salvation. The sending of the Son is salvifically oriented; these verses contain not only christological statements but soteriological ones as well. Christology and soteriology are intertwined.

The end of the sending of the Son is salvation; its origin is love, according to verse 16; the Father's love results in sending his Son. C. K. Barrett wrote: "The mission of the Son was the consequence of the Father's love; hence also the revelation of it."[35] Verse 16 terms the sending a giving (ἔδωκεν).[36] The transition is here being made from the death of Jesus as a "lifting up" (vv. 14-15) to his sending (v. 17). The focus shifts from the crucifixion to the incarnation. The Christ-event takes in both, resulting in eternal life for the believer.

Scholars have looked for the background of the sending motif in two traditions from the Hebrew scripture: the prophetic tradition and the wisdom tradition. C. H. Dodd was probably the most famous proponent of the former position. He wrote in his commentary, "John has deliberately moulded the idea of the Son of God in the first instance upon the prophetic model."[37] Yet the prophetic background is not sufficient to explain the whole of the Johannine sending motif, for it is not a sending from ordinary existence to a particular task but a sending from pre-existence into the world, from above to below. Furthermore, the one who is sent does not say, "Thus saith the Lord," like the prophets, but "I am." While acknowledging the influence of the prophetic tradition, André Feuillet noted the great distance between the prophets and Jesus. He contended that the mission of the Son

---

[35]Barrett, Gospel, p. 215.

[36]Cf. 6:32: "My Father gives (δίδωσιν) you the true bread from heaven." Schnackenburg, Gospel, I, 399, noted, "Jesus is the gift of God to humankind."

[37]C. H. Dodd, The Interpretation of the Fourth Gospel (Cambridge: Cambridge University Press, 1953), p. 255. Cf. also Miranda, Der Vater, pp. 308-388; and his more recent Die Sendung Jesu im vierten Evangelium: Religions und theologieschichtliche Untersuchungen zu den Sendungsformeln (Stuttgart: Verlag Katolisches Bibelwerk, 1977), pp. 47-51; J. Buhner, Der Gesandte und sein Weg im 4. Evangelium, WUNT II 2 (Tübingen: J. C. B. Mohr, 1977); F. M. Braun, Jean le Théologien: Les grandes traditions d'Israel et l'accord des Escritures selon Le Quatrième Evangile (Paris: J. Gibalda, 1964), pp. 49-114; Fennema, "Jesus," pp. 6-8, 31-32. Cf. further Peder Borgen, "God's Agent in the Fourth Gospel," in RAERG, ed. Jacob Neusner (Leiden: E. J. Brill, 1968), 137-147, who noted the similarities between the halakhic principles of agency and ideas in the Gospel.

is roughly of the same type as that of Wisdom.[38] Similarly, Schweizer maintained that the New Testament sending formulae, John 3:16-17, Romans 8:3, Galatians 4:4, and 1 John 4:9, originate in Wisdom speculation.[39] It will here be argued that not only is John 3:16-17 influenced by the wisdom tradition but that the whole Johannine sending motif has been significantly influenced by it.[40]

The sending of Wisdom by God is best stated in Solomon's prayer for Wisdom (Wis. 9:1-18). As a prelude to this prayer, Solomon says, "I perceived that I would not possess Wisdom unless God gave (δῷ) her to me" (8:21). Then he prays, "Give (δός) me the Wisdom that sits by your throne" (9:4). Here the sending, as in John 3:16 and 6:32, is expressed in terms of giving. Like Jesus, Wisdom is God's gift (Wis. 8:21). Here, however, she is not a gift to the world or to the community but to the individual. The giving is a transfer of position from heaven to earth; the Wisdom that sits by God's throne comes to be with Solomon. It is similar to the Father's giving of the Son as described in John 3:16.

God's sending of Wisdom is also described in verse 10 of Solomon's prayer: "Send her forth (ἐξαπόστειλον) from the holy heavens, and from the throne of your glory send (πέμψον) her, that (ἵνα) she may be with me and toil, and that I may learn what is pleasing to you." It is interesting to note that the same verbs, πέμπω and ἀποστέλλω, which are used of the Father's sending of Jesus, are also used here to speak of God's sending of Wisdom. As in the Gospel, the two verbs are interchangeable. The Gospel and the Wisdom material use the same vocabulary in their description of the sending motif. The same dualistic world-view also underlies the sending motif. Wisdom is sent from the holy heavens, from the throne of God's glory. In the same way, Jesus is sent from the Father; he has come down from above.

The parallels between this verse and John 3:17 are striking. Just as Solomon asks God to send Wisdom forth (ἐξαπόστειλον), the Gospel states that

---

[38]André Feuillet, "Redemptive Incarnation in the Johannine Writings," in Introduction to the New Testament, ed. André Robert and André Feuillet and trans. Patrick Skehan, et al. (New York: Desclee Co., 1965), p. 874.

[39]Eduard Schweizer, "Zum religionsgeschichtlichen Hintergrund der 'Sendungsformel' Gal 4.4f., Rom 8.3f., Jn 3.16f., I Jn 4.9," in Beiträge zur Theologie des Neuen Testaments (Zürich: Zwingli-Verlag, 1970), pp. 83-95.

[40]This does not, of course, deny the influence of the prophetic tradition. In addition to Feuillet, "Redemptive Incarnation," p. 874, F.-M. Braun, Jean, pp. 115-150, also argued that prophetic and wisdom themes are interwoven in the sending motif.

God sent (ἀπέστειλεν) his Son. The purpose of that sending is expressed in both verses by an ἵνα clause: Wisdom is sent so that she may be with Solomon and teach him what is pleasing to God; Jesus is sent in order that the world might be saved through him. The purpose of the sending is so that humanity might enjoy intimate communion with God. Wisdom is a spirit that loves humanity (Wis. 1:6); she desires that persons experience full and meaningful life coram Deo. Similarly, God loves the world and has therefore sent the Son in order that the world might be saved (John 3:16-17). The basis of the sending is love.

The final verse of Solomon's prayer (Wis. 9:17) sums up much of the prayer: "Who has learned your counsel, unless you have given (ἔδωκας) Wisdom and sent (ἔπεμψας) your holy Spirit from on high?" Two verbs used previously for the sending (δίδωμι, v. 4; ἀποστέλλω, v. 10) are here placed in parallel; the giving and the sending are equivalent concepts in Wisdom of Solomon, as they are in the Gospel (cf. John 3:16-17).

The dualistic perspective is present here: Wisdom is sent from on high (cf. Wis. 9:4, 10). Furthermore, the purpose of the sending is revelation, that one might learn God's counsel (cf. v. 10). Just as Word and Wisdom are placed in parallel in verse 2, Wisdom and Spirit are placed in parallel here. Furthermore, Wisdom is elsewhere in the book characterized as a spirit (1:6; 7:7, 22b).[41] The Gospel does not identify Jesus and the Spirit-Paraclete, but the two are closely related; both have been sent from the Father. The Father will give the Spirit-Paraclete (John 16:16), just as he gave Jesus (3:16). He will send the Spirit-Paraclete (πέμπει, 14:26), just as he sent (ἀπέστειλεν, 3:17) the Son. The sending of the Spirit, as well as the sending of the Son, seems to be modeled on the sending of Wisdom.[42]

God's giving of Wisdom is also a major theme in Sirach 24 and Baruch 3:9-4:4. The themes are much the same as in Wisdom of Solomon: the sending of Wisdom by God, the preexistence of Wisdom with God, and a dualism between heaven and earth. Sirach 24:8-12 tells of Wisdom being given to Israel. She "dwelt in the highest heavens" (v. 4), but then God commanded her to make her

---

[41]Cf. above, pp. 16-17.

[42]Cf. Brown, Gospel, XIII-XXI, p. 1139, who listed Wisdom as a background for the Spirit-Paraclete. He also discussed the resemblance of the Spirit of Jesus under four headings. He first showed how the coming-giving-sending of the Paraclete resembles that of Jesus (p. 1140).

dwelling in Israel (vv. 8-11). Wisdom is depicted as an independent moral agent who obeys God's command to leave her home in heaven and go to the land which God has prepared for her. The verbs πέμπω, ἀποστέλλω, and δίδωμι do not appear in Sirach, but in Baruch it says that God gave (ἔδωκεν) Wisdom to Israel (Bar.3:36, 37 LXX).

The sending of Wisdom by God into the world in order to dwell with Israel or the individual was the model by which the Gospel expresses the sending of Jesus by God into the world. Indeed, the Gospel even takes up some of the terminology from the Wisdom passages. Thus the Christ-event is grounded in eternity. What was significant about this Jesus of Nazareth? He was sent by God from pre-existence into the world. His words are of God; his person partakes of divinity. In order to communicate the divine origin of Christ, the evangelist chose a pattern which had previously communicated the divine origin of another salvific figure, the sending of Wisdom. So Jesus is Wisdom who has "appeared upon earth and lived with humankind" (Bar. 3:37).

Ascent

Along with the descent from the Father, there is a corresponding ascent to the Father. Jesus says, "I am going to the one who sent me" (John 7:33). Just as Jesus has been sent by the Father, so he also goes to the Father. This theme is particularly prominent in the farewell discourse (cf. 14:12, 28; 16:5, 9, 16). Jesus' impending return to the Father casts its shadow over his final words to the disciples. It is the basis for the "greater works" which the disciples will do (14:12); it opens the way for the Paraclete to come (16:7); it gives the disciples power to ask anything in Jesus' name (14:12-14). Jesus is on his way to the Father (cf. 17:11).

The ascent is referred to not only as a "going to the Father" or a going away" but also as a "lifting up" (3:14; 8:28; 12:32) and "glorification" (12:23; 13:31; 17:1, 5). The Gospel, however, does not place this lifting up or glorification at the ascension, as Luke does (Luke 24:51; Acts 1:9), but at the cross. When Jesus in John 12:32 says that he will be lifted up, that saying is explained as an indication of "the kind of death he was to die" (12:33). Jesus ascends by way of the cross; he goes to the Father by dying. Nicholson argued that the death of Jesus is reinterpreted under the rubric of the DAS: "The crucifixion receives its 'meaning' by being understood as a part of a larger schema: the crucifixion was the beginning of the ascent to the Father, the means by which the Son of Man left the world κάτω to return to the world ἄνω."[43]

In the Wisdom material the emphasis is on the descent of Wisdom rather than on her ascent. Although a few passages depict her withdrawal (cf. Prov. 1:28; Sir. 4:19), the only description of Wisdom's ascent to heaven appears in 1 Enoch 42:1-2.[44] While the descent of Wisdom is firmly established in the Wisdom material, it is matched with a corresponding ascent only in 1 Enoch 42. Although it is possible that the ascent of Wisdom stands behind the ascent of the Son, it is better to look for another motif which combined with the descent of Wisdom to create the DAS.[45]

The Son of Man

The Son of Man sayings have been an area of intense interest for New Testament scholars,[46] and their occurrence in the Gospel has not been overlooked.[47] Aside from the Son, the Son of Man is the Gospel's favorite title for Jesus.[48] As

---

[43]Nicholson, Death, p. 143.

[44]Cf. above, p. 20. Talbert, Gospel, p. 56, however, considered 2 Esdr. 5:10 as a reference to the ascent of Wisdom

[45]Catherine Cory, in an unpublished paper, "Docetism and the 'Glorification' of the Johannine Jesus," read at the SBL annual meeting, Kansas City, MO, November 23, 1991, suggested that the motif of Jesus' being lifted up has been influenced by the picture of the vindication of the suffering righteous person in Wis. If so, then, perhaps both elements of the DAS were indebted to the wisdom tradition: the descent from the sending of Wisdom and the ascent through the vindication of the suffering righteous one. Nevertheless, the suffering righteous one, though exalted after death, does not actually ascend.

[46]The literature is vast. Cf. Dunn, Christology, p. 291 nn. 2-3, for a number of recent works. More recently, cf. Barnabas Lindars, Jesus Son of Man (Grand Rapids: Erdmans, 1983); Douglas R. A. Hare, The Son of Man Tradition (Minneapolis: Fortress Press, 1990).

[47]For a full survey of work on the Son of man in John up to 1969, cf. E. Ruckstuhl, "Die johanneische Menschensonforschung 1957-1969," in Theologische Berichte, ed. J. Pfammatter and F. Furger (Zürich: Zwingli-Verlag, 1972), I, 171-284. More recently, cf. Robert Maddox, "The Function of the Son of Man in the Gospel of John," in RHLLM, ed. R. J. Banks (Exeter: Paternoster Press, 1974), pp. 186-204; Joseph Coppens, "Le Fils de l'homme dans l'evangile johannique," ETL 52 (1976), 28-81; Margaret Pamment, "The Son of Man in the Fourth Gospel," JTS, 36 (1985), 56-66; Lindars, Jesus, pp. 145-157; Hare, Son of Man, pp. 79-111; and esp. F. J. Moloney, The Johannine Son of Man, 2d ed., BSR 14 (Rome: Libraria Ateneo Salesiano, 1979). The most current studies include Mary Margaret Pazdan, The Son of Man: A Metaphor for Jesus in the Fourth Gospel, Zacchaeus Studies: New Testament (Collegeville, MN: Liturgical Press, 1991); Delbert Burkett, The Son of Man in the Gospel of John, JSNTS 56 (Sheffield: JSOT Press, 1991).

[48]Kysar, Maverick, p. 35, contended that the Son is the evangelist's abbreviation for the Son of Man. This is unlikely, for the pairing of the Father and the Son in the Gospel suggests that the Son is an abbreviation for the Son of God.

in the synoptics, it is placed on the lips of Jesus. The Gospel's special contribution, however, is that it depicts a descending-ascending Son of Man. "No one has ascended into heaven except the one who descended from heaven, the Son of Man" (John 3:13; cf. also 1:51; 6:62).[49] The emphasis, however, falls on the ascent.[50] It is in the hour of his ascent that the Son of Man will be lifted up (3:14; 8:28; 12:34c) and glorified (12:23; 13:31-32). This ascent-lifting-up-glorification takes place through the cross and resurrection.

David Fennema argued that the Johannine ascent motif has been adapted from the early Christian tradition of Jesus' post-resurrection ascent to heaven. This tradition was often expressed, he continued, in terms of Son of Man imagery borrowed from the apocalyptic tradition (Dan. 7:14; 1 Enoch 37-71).[51] The ascent of the Son of Man, in which he is glorified and lifted up, is pushed back from the post-resurrection ascension to the cross. Thus, the cross, resurrection, and ascension are collapsed into one event, the hour of Jesus' glorious ascent to the Father.

Furthermore, the Gospel takes the ascent, influenced by the apocalyptic tradition, and combines it with the descent, influenced by the wisdom tradition.[52] Thus is formed the DAS, in which preexistent Wisdom and the eschatological Son

---

[49]Moloney, Son of Man, pp. 226-230, however, contended that the Johannine Son of Man is never involved with a DAS but is intimately linked to the earthly task of the man Jesus of Nazareth. While he admitted that 3:13 does speak of a descent, he refused to acknowledge a corresponding ascent either here or in the lifting up sayings. He translated 3:13, "No one has ascended into heaven, but one has descended from heaven, the Son of Man" (p. 55). Furthermore, he understood the lifting up sayings (3:14; 8:28; 12:32, 34) as references to the cross and not to the ascent. On the other hand, John W. Pryor, "The Johannine Son of Man and the Descent-Ascent Motif," JETS 34 (1991), 341-351, argued that while the Son of Man does ascend in glory, he does not descend.

[50]Loader, "Central Structure," pp. 199-200, noted that the Son of man cluster is not integrated within the central structure of Johannine Christology. In the Son of man cluster, the descent is a presupposition of the all-significant ascent. In the central structure, however, the coming is the essential presupposition of the earthly work of revelation, while the going is but a return to the Father. Cf. also his Christology, pp. 208-211, in which he discusses further the relationship between the "revealer envoy model" and the Son of Man cluster. In summing up that discussion he wrote, "The author has, therefore, employed the Son of Man cluster of ideas in order to point readers to the reality that the life then is even more fully present now in the post Easter mission and community of faith which lives from the benefits which flow from the Son's return to the Father, as the exalted, glorified, ascended Son of Man" (p. 211).

[51]Fennema, "Jesus," pp. 99-106.

[52]Cf. Fennema, "Jesus," pp. 107-111; also Barnabas Lindars, The Gospel of John, NCB (Grand Rapids: Wm. B. Eerdmans, 1981), pp. 41-42; F.-M. Braun, "Messie, Logos, et Fils de l'homme," in La Venue du Messie, ed. E. Massaux, et al. (Paris: Desclee de Brouwer, 1962), 133-147; Rudolf Schnackenburg, "Der Menschensohn im Johannesevangelium," NTS 11 (1965), 123-137; Hamerton-Kelly, Pre-existence, p. 241.

of Man are brought together. The beginning and the end are met in Jesus; he is the Alpha and the Omega (Rev. 21:6). In chapter 1 it was noted that the Wisdom and Son of Man traditions merge in 1 Enoch; Wisdom becomes a possession of the Son of Man; she gives over to him her preexistence.[53] The combination in the Gospel, however, is stronger. Wisdom gives to Jesus not only her preexistence but also her descent from above. The Son of Man gives to Jesus his exalted status so as to give life and judgment. He also gives him his title, a title deeply embedded in the Jesus tradition. Jesus is the descending-ascending Wisdom-Son of Man.[54]

It was noted above that the sending motif is influenced both by the prophetic and wisdom tradition.[55] The DAS, then, takes up themes from three figures from the Hebrew scriptures, the prophet, Wisdom, and the Son of Man. The Gospel's Christology is built from the raw material of Jewish faith. As a prophet, Jesus is sent by God to complete a mission. As Wisdom, he is the preexistent one who has come down from heaven. As the Son of Man, he is the glorified one who gives life and exercises judgment. All of these contribute to the DAS. Of primary interest, however, is Wisdom: she is sent from God; she descends from heaven. As the one who is sent from the Father, who has come down from above, Jesus is Wisdom incarnate.

Revelation-Hiddenness

No one has even seen God. It is God the only Son, who is close to the Father's heart, who has made him known (John 1:18).

This sending by the Father, this descent from above, is for the purpose of revelation. Jesus appears in the Gospel primarily as revealer. He is the exegete of God; he has been sent in order to reveal the Father. A number of scholars have highlighted the motif of revelation in the Gospel. Loader noted that this motif is central to Johannine Christology.[56] Ernst Käsemann wrote, "The revelation of the

---

[53]Cf. above, pp. 20-21.

[54]Building upon Loader's distinction between the central structure of Johannine Christology and the Son of man cluster (cf. above, p. 65 n. 50), it might be said that Wisdom primarily influenced the central structure while the apocalyptic Son of man primarily influenced the Son of man cluster.

[55]Cf. above, pp. 60-61. Significantly, J. Becker, Das Evangelium des Johannes (Gutersloh: Mohn, 1979/1981), p. 55, noted that in the Gospel the sending stream, which includes prophets, envoys, and angels, is combined with the wisdom stream.

[56]Loader, "Central Structure," p. 190.

Logos is the meaning and the criterion of the incarnation."[57] Terence Forestell demonstrated that even Jesus' death on the cross is portrayed in the Gospel as revelation.[58] The strand which runs through Rudolf Bultmann's work on the Gospel is that Jesus is the revealer.[59]

This section will investigate the Johannine concept of revelation and its corresponding opposite, hiddenness. It will be demonstrated that striking similarities exist between the revelation of God in Jesus and that in Wisdom. Indeed, the Gospel was dependent on the wisdom tradition in presenting Jesus as revealer of God. In order to substantiate this assertion, this chapter will first consider the presupposition of revelation, the intimacy between the Father and the Son, as defined as will, knowledge, and love. The concept of revelation will then be plumbed. Attention will be drawn to the discourse of revelation: the "I am" sayings and the images. Finally, the concept of hiddenness will be explored.

Presupposition: Intimacy

That Jesus reveals God presupposes that Jesus enjoys a unique relationship with God. Jesus says, "I am in the Father, and the Father is in me" (10:38; cf. also 14:10, 11). Marinus de Jonge wrote, "Jesus' kingship and his prophetic mission are both redefined in terms of the unique relationship between Father and Son, as portrayed in the Fourth Gospel."[60] Mark Appold went further; he maintained that all the titles bestowed upon Jesus in the Gospel are expressions of the unity between Father and Son.[61]

---

[57]Käsemann, Testament, p. 43.

[58]J. Terence Forestell, The Word of the Cross: Salvation as Revelation in the Fourth Gospel, AnBib 57 (Rome: Biblical Institute Press, 1974), pp. 74-82.

[59]Cf. Bultmann, Gospel, in which the idea of revelation is discussed 58 times! Cf. also his Theology, II, 46-69.

[60]Marinus de Jonge, "Jesus as Prophet and King in the Fourth Gospel," in Jesus: Stranger from Heaven and Son of God, ed. and trans. John E. Steeley, SBLSBS 11 (Missoula, Mont.: Scholars Press, 1977), p. 52. He was responding to Meeks, Prophet-King, p. 1. However, de Jonge found himself in substantial agreement with Meeks' later article, "Man from Heaven," pp. 44-72.

[61]Mark J. Appold, The Oneness Motif in the Fourth Gospel: Motif Analysis and Exegetical Probe into the Theology of John, WUNT 2, 1 (Tübingen: Mohr-Siebeck, 1976), pp. 48-85. His treatment concerning Son of God is indicative of his treatment of all titles: "The title appears as an integral expression of a theology which has as its root the proclamation that Jesus and God are one" (p. 58).

This intimacy manifests itself in three ways: will, knowledge, and love. Jesus does what the Father does, he knows the Father, and he loves the Father. Each of these categories will be discussed in order to discern the contours of Jesus' relationship with the Father.

Will. The oneness of Jesus and the Father is not primarily a oneness of essence but of operation. They are one in revelatory and salvific purposes. The priority, however, is always with God. Jesus says, "The Father is greater than I" (14:28). Jesus, then, is dependent upon the Father. J. Ernest Davey contended in his study of Johannine Christology that dependence is "the ruling element in John's portrait of Christ."[62] Similarly, J. A. T. Robinson wrote that the Gospel presents Jesus as "a man whose life was lived in absolutely intimate dependence (stressing all three words) upon God as Father."[63]

The dependence of Jesus upon the Father is a river that flows throughout the Gospel, but it runs deepest in 5:19-30. Here Jesus debates with the Jews, prompted by his healing of the lame man on the sabbath (5:1-9). The discourse is framed by two statements about Jesus' dependence upon God: "The Son can do nothing on his own, but only what he sees the Father doing; for whatever the Father does, that the Son does likewise" (v. 19). "I can do nothing on my own" (v. 30a). Brown wrote, "[Jesus] is not a rebellious son setting himself up as a rival to the Father, he is completely dependent on the Father and claims nothing on his own."[64] Jesus' works are not his (cf. also 9:4); indeed, his words are not his, either (3:34; 8:26; 12:29). All that Jesus has has come from God.

The body of the discourse concerns the "greater works" (5:20) which the Father shows the Son: giving life and passing judgment. Unlike apocalypticism, the Gospel gives priority to giving life rather than judgment:[65] "Just as (ὥσπερ) the Father raises the dead and gives them life, so (οὕτως) also the Son gives life to whomever he wishes" (5:21). Barrett noted that the expression ὥσπερ . . . οὕτως

---

[62]J. Ernest Davey, The Jesus of St. John: Historical and Christological Studies in the Fourth Gospel (London: Lutterworth, 1958), p. 77. He organized his book around this concept, discussing Jesus' dependence for power, knowledge, authority, and love.

[63]J. A. T. Robinson, "The Use of the Fourth Gospel for Christology Today" in CSNT, ed. B. Lindars and S. Smalley (Cambridge: Cambridge University Press, 1973), p. 68. Cf. also C. K. Barrett, "'The Father is Greater than I,' John 14:28: Subordinationist Christology in the New Testament," in Essays in John (Philadelphia: Westminster Press, 1982), pp. 19-36.

[64]Brown, Gospel, I-XII, p. 218.

[65]Cf. Schnackenburg, Gospel, II, 105.

(cf. also v. 26) is the keynote of this passage, for it denotes the exact parallelism between the actions of the Father and the Son.[66] Also unlike apocalypticism, the Gospel pictures this giving of life in the present. Jesus says, "The hour is coming, and is now here" (v. 25). Such is the realized eschatology of the Gospel; eternal life is granted, not at the end of time, but in the midst of time, in the ministry of Jesus, for it has been granted the Son by the Father (v. 26). It is reminiscent of the prologue: "What which came to be in him was life" (1:3b-4a). The life-giving function of the Son is spoken of in apocalyptic language (5: 28-29),[67] yet it is transported into the present. Indeed, these words are fulfilled in the raising of Lazarus, who hears Jesus' voice and comes out of the tomb (11:43-44).

The flipside of Jesus' life-giving power is his authority to pass judgment. Parallel to verse 21, which speaks about the Son's life-giving power, stands verse 22, which speaks about his authority to judge: "The Father judges no one but has given all judgment to the Son." Judgment is an important concept in the Gospel. The coming of Jesus brings judgment as well as life. "And this is the judgment, that the light has come into the world, and people loved darkness rather than light because their deeds were evil" (3:19). Judgment is given to the Son because it is one's response to him which determines whether one receives life or falls under judgment. Jesus says, "Anyone who hears my word and believes him who sent me has eternal life, and does not come under judgment, but has passed from death to life" (5:24). Again, this judgment happens not at the end of time but in the present.

The discourse ends by returning to the theme of dependence. Jesus' judgment is just because he seeks the will of the one who sent him (v. 30). The oneness of the Father and the Son is primarily a oneness of will and therefore a oneness of essence; his purposes are so attuned to God's that he becomes one with God.[68] It is in this sense that Jesus says, "I and the Father are one" (10:30; cf. also 17:11, 22). The unity of the Father and the Son is a unity of operation in which the Son enacts the Father's will of giving life and judgment.

---

[66]Barrett, Gospel, p. 260.

[67]Cf. Matt. 25:46; Acts 24:15; 2 Cor. 5:10; 1 Thess, 4:16, in which this language is used of the final judgment.

[68]Cf. Oscar Cullmann, The Christology of the New Testament, rev. ed., trans. Shirley Guthrie and Charles A. M. Hall (Philadelphia: Westminster Press, 1963), p. 300.

In the same way Wisdom is pictured as being one with God; she enacts God's will of giving life and judgment. In Proverbs 1:20-33 she pronounces judgment on those who have rejected her. Just as all judgment has been handed over to the Son (John 5:22), so also judgment here has been handed over to Wisdom. She will not answer when trouble strikes those who have rejected her; rather, she will laugh at them (Prov. 8:24-28). Judgment has been handed over to Wisdom, and so has giving life. Paired with Wisdom's pronouncement of judgment in Proverbs 1 is her invitation to life in Proverbs 8. "Whoever finds me finds life and obtains favor from the Lord" (v. 35). Life here is defined in terms of knowledge (v. 10), right judgment (vv. 15-16), and wealth (v. 18). Like Jesus, Wisdom has been given authority to give life and execute judgment.

Similarly, Wisdom of Solomon depicts Wisdom as an associate in God's works (Wis. 8:4). These works include creation, for Wisdom is the fashioner of all things (7:22a; 8:6). They also include redemption, both as friendship with God (7:14, 27) and as physical salvation (chap. 10). God accomplishes his purposes with humanity through Wisdom. As the outreaching love of God, she brings forth creation and facilitates reconciliation. Wisdom is God in action, God turned toward the world enacting God's will among humanity.

The Gospel draws upon this picture in depicting the action of God in Christ. The Wisdom material depicts oneness between God and Wisdom. The Gospel takes it over in the form of the oneness of the Father and the Son in order to authorize Jesus' ministry. This man Jesus was so attuned to God's purposes that he was one with God, just as Wisdom was one with God. This theme of "one will" was heightened because of Jesus' personhood over against Wisdom's personification. This person was of God. The Gospel, unlike the Wisdom passages, deals with the history of this man Jesus. His history is viewed, however, through the lens of Wisdom.

Knowledge. The intimacy of the Father and the Son is not only one of will but also one of knowledge. Only the Son has perfect knowledge of the Father and thus is able to reveal him. This knowledge is not merely information about the Father but relationship with the Father based on being close to his heart (John 1:18).

In order to speak about this intimate knowledge which the Son has of the Father, the Gospel uses two different verbs for knowing, γίνωσκω and οἶδα.

Ignace de la Potterie made a distinction between the two,[69] but such a distinction is unlikely.[70] Jesus says that he knows (οἶδα or γίνωσκω) the Father in 7:29, 8:55, 10:15, and 17:25.[71] Furthermore, Jesus says that he has seen the Father in 6:46. A brief glance will be taken at each of these.

The first saying, 7:29, occurs in a passage united by the theme of knowledge (7:25-31). After hearing Jesus teach in the temple, the people in Jerusalem wonder if the authorities know that Jesus is the Christ (v. 26). The crowd claims to know where Jesus is from, but they claim that no one will know where the Christ comes from (v. 27). Jesus challenges their knowledge both of him and of the one who sent him (v. 28). The climax of the passage is verse 29, in which Jesus says, "I know him, because I am from him, and he sent me." Because the people do not know where Jesus comes from, they do not know God. But Jesus knows him, and this knowledge is based on Jesus' having been sent from God. His intimacy with the Father is grounded in his descent from the Father. Sending by God and knowledge of God are brought together in order to authorize Jesus' mission. As Bultmann wrote, knowledge of God is knowledge of his commission.[72]

Jesus again asserts his knowledge of the Father in controversy with the Jews in 8:55. This saying occurs in the context of the discussion over whether Jesus is greater than Abraham (8:31-59). Jesus grounds his superiority to Abraham in his intimate knowledge of the Father. Again he contrasts his knowledge of the Father with the Jews' lack of knowledge: "You do not know him. But I know him" (v. 55a). Such knowledge is bound up with keeping the Father's word: "If I would say that I do not know him, I would be a liar like you. But I do know him and I keep his word" (v. 55b). Jesus' intimacy with the Father is integrally related to keeping his commandments (cf. 15:10). As Barrett observed, "Obedience is a characteristic of Johannine 'gnosis.'"[73]

---

[69]Ignace de la Potterie, "οἶδα et γίνωσκω," les deux modes de la connaissance dans le quatrième évangile," Bib, 40 (1959), 709-725. He contended that οἶδα refers to the progressive acquisition of knowledge while γίνωσκω refers to absolute knowledge not acquired.

[70]Cf. Brown, Gospel, I-XII, p. 514; James Gaffney, "Believing and Knowing in the Fourth Gospel," TS, 26 (1965), 228.

[71]The synoptic parallel is the so-called Johannine logion: "No one knows the Father except the Son and anyone to whom the Son chooses to reveal him" (Matt. 11:27; Luke 10:22).

[72]Bultmann, Gospel, pp. 298, 301.

[73]Barrett, Gospel, p. 351.

The Good Shepherd discourse provides the context for 10:15. The setting is again one of controversy, for this discourse is directed toward the Pharisees who have just cast the healed blind man out of the synagogue (9:40). The dispute, however, is not as sharp as in 7:25-31 or 8:31-59; Jesus makes no reference to their lack of knowledge of the Father. Here, however, the mutual knowledge between Jesus and the Father is compared with the mutual knowledge between Jesus and the disciples. Jesus says, "I am the good shepherd" (10:11, 14). This is true first because he "lays down his life for the sheep" (v. 11). Jesus adds a second reason: "I know my own and my own know me, just as (καθώς) the Father knows me and I know the Father" (v. 14). A mutuality of knowledge is set up: The Father knows the Son who knows the flock; the flock knows the Son who knows the Father.[74] The knowledge between the Father and the Son is a model for the knowledge between the good shepherd and his flock.

Jesus' prayer for the disciples in John 17 contains the only reference to Jesus' knowledge of the Father which is not couched in controversy: "Righteous Father, the world does not know you but I know you; and these know that you have sent me" (v. 25). Nevertheless, a contrast is still set up between knowledge and lack of knowledge. The reference, however, is to the world, rather than to the Jews.[75] A reference is also made to the disciples' knowledge, that is, faith, the knowledge that he sent Jesus (cf. also vv. 3, 8).

This reference to Jesus' knowledge of the Father sums up the intimacy of the Father and the Son expressed in the prayer. Jesus had glory with the Father before creation (vv. 5, 24). Jesus was sent from preexistence into the world by the Father (vv. 8, 18, 21, 25). The Father gave Jesus disciples from out of the world (vv. 6, 9). The Father and the Son are one, dwelling within one another (vv. 11, 21-23). All these statements give content to Jesus' statement that he knows the Father.

Seeing is related to knowledge; Jesus has seen the Father. Aside from passages where this is implied (1:18; 5:37; 14:9), this explicit statement appears only in 6:46, in the context of the Bread of Life discourse (6:25-59). This saying is also forged in controversy, for Jesus is here responding to the Jews' complaints (vv.

---

[74]It is interesting to note that nothing is said of the knowledge between the Father and the flock.

[75]These two terms often coincide in the Gospel; cf. below, p. 103.

41-42). He argues that all who have heard and learned from the Father (through scripture) come to him. Yet, no one has actually seen God save one: "Not that anyone has seen the Father except the one who is from God; he has seen the Father" (v. 46). The theme of this pericope is that Jesus is the living bread which came down from heaven (vv. 33, 41, 50, 51, 58). An accompanying theme is that the Father sent Jesus (vv. 38, 39, 44, 57). Both these authenticate Jesus' message; the source of his words and his being is in God. Also supporting this statement is Jesus' claim to have seen the Father; he alone has that intimate knowledge of God. Yet this is not a major component of the argument. Jesus returns quickly to his major theme: "I am the bread of life" (v. 48). Seeing God, then, is not the primary way in which Jesus expresses his intimacy with the Father; he speaks more often of his knowledge of the Father.

Jesus not only knows the Father, but he knows all things (16:30). In the Gospel the reader meets an omniscient Jesus. Primarily he knows what is in humanity (2:25); thus, he knows who would not believe and who would betray him (6:64). He knows that the Jews do not have God's love within them (5:42). He knows that the people who saw the multiplication of the loaves want to make him king (6:15). Jesus alone has omniscient knowledge concerning his disciples. He sees Nathanael under the fig tree (1:48). He knows that his disciples are grumbling (6:61) and questioning (16:19). He knows how Peter will die (21:18-19). Jesus' omniscient knowledge serves as a stimulus to faith for the Samaritan woman and the Samaritans of the city. Because Jesus told her about her past (4:18), the woman first confesses Jesus as a prophet (4:19), then as the Christ (4:29). The Samaritans believe in Jesus because of the woman's testimony to Jesus' omniscience (4:39), leading them to encounter with Jesus and confession that he is the Savior of the world (4:40-42).

Jesus also knows his own past and future. He knows exactly what he is going to do concerning the hungry multitude (6:6). As the soldiers approach to arrest him, Jesus knows what is going to happen to him (18:4). Most of all, he knows that he has come from God and is going to God (13:3). He knows his origin and destiny, his whence and his whither.[76]

---

[76]Cf. Culpepper, Anatomy, pp. 36-38, for a discussion of Jesus' omniscience as evidenced in the farewell discourse. He showed how Jesus' point of view corresponds to that of the narrator.

Jesus' omniscience, as well as his knowledge of the Father, indicates he is "not of this world"; he is from above. He knows God; he knows all things. He does not originate from the human plane but comes from beyond.

This emphasis on knowledge is also a characteristic of the wisdom literature, as John Painter noted.[77] In the Wisdom material, knowledge often appears parallel to Wisdom. In her speech in Proverbs 1:20-33, Wisdom equates the people's refusal to listen to her with their hatred of knowledge (vv. 22, 29). Furthermore, Wisdom often appears parallel to knowledge and understanding: "For the Lord gives wisdom, from his mouth come knowledge and understanding" (Prov. 2:6; cf. also 2:10; 3:19, 20). In Wisdom's speech in Proverbs 8, she offers knowledge as one of her gifts (vv. 9, 12). Furthermore, Sirach says that God saw and apportioned Wisdom, and she rained down knowledge and discerning comprehension (1:19). Furthermore, the Law fills people with wisdom, understanding, and instruction (24:25-27). According to Baruch, Israel has forsaken the fountain of Wisdom and has not learned the way to knowledge (3:12, 20; cf. 3:27, 36).

The relationship between the Father and the Son stands parallel to God's relationship with Wisdom. It is never said that God knows Wisdom or vice-versa.[78] Nevertheless, the close association between God and Wisdom implies mutual knowledge. For example, in Job 28 God is the only one said to know Wisdom's location: "God understands the way to [Wisdom] and he knows its place. . . . he saw it and declared it; he established it, and searched it out" (vv. 23, 27). In the same way Wisdom knows God's works and understands what is pleasing and right to him (Wis. 9:9). Furthermore, she is "an initiate in the knowledge of God, and an associate in his works" (8:4). This knowledge is based on Wisdom's preexistent presence with God (9:9). The relationship between God and Wisdom, like that between the Father and the Son, is an intimate relationship of mutual knowledge.

Wisdom not only knows God; she knows and understands all things (9:11). Her knowledge is defined in Wisdom of Solomon 8:8: "She knows the things of old, and infers the things to come; she understands turns of speech and

---

[77]John Painter, John: Witness and Theologian (London: SPCK, 1975), p. 86.

[78]Fennema, "Jesus," pp. 175-176, suggested a number of reasons for this, e. g. God's knowledge of his own attributes may be too obvious to require an explicit statement; to say that God "knows" Wisdom would carry sexual connotations.

the solutions of riddles; she has foreknowledge of signs and wonders and of the outcome of seasons and times." Her knowledge is more specifically defined as knowledge of "the structure of the world and the activity of the elements" (Wis. 7:17-22). The Wisdom material presents an omniscient Wisdom, just as the Gospel presents an omniscient Jesus.

The Gospel's picture of a Jesus who knows the Father intimately and all things omnisciently parallels the Wisdom material's picture of Wisdom. She too knows God and all things. In order to express the intimate yet eternal relationship of the Father and the Son, the Gospel appropriates the wisdom theme of knowledge between God and Wisdom. In order to demonstrate that Jesus was from the eternal rather than the temporal plane and that he has the capacity to reveal the Father, the Gospel appropriates the theme of Wisdom's omniscience. As Wisdom incarnate, Jesus knows the Father, and he knows all things.

Love. The relationship between the Father and the Son is expressed in terms of will, knowledge, and love, "but the greatest of these is love" (1 Cor. 13:13b). Above all, love describes the intimate communion of the Father and the Son . Primarily it is the Father's love for the Son which is in view; only once is it said that the Son loves the Father. The initiative lies with the Father; it is his love for the Son and for the world which sets the drama of redemption in motion.

The usual word for the Father's love of the Son and the Son's love of the Father is $\dot{\alpha}\gamma\alpha\pi\dot{\alpha}\omega$. Ceslaus Spicq wrote that this kind of love was an outgoing, effect-producing, gift-giving love.[79] God's love for the world resulted in sending his Son (3:16); his love for his Son resulted in giving him all things (3:35). In one passage, however, $\phi\iota\lambda\dot{\epsilon}\omega$ is used for the Father's love of the Son (5:20). A number of commentators have seen a difference in meaning. B. F. Westcott maintained that $\phi\iota\lambda\dot{\epsilon}\omega$ "marks personal affection based upon a special relation," while $\dot{\alpha}\gamma\alpha\pi\dot{\alpha}\omega$ refers to "the general feeling of regard, esteem, consideration which comes from reflection and knowledge."[80] This distinction is artificial. As Brown and others have shown, these verbs are used interchangeably in the Gospel for God's love for

---

[79]Ceslaus Spicq, "Notes d'exégèse johannique. La charité est amour manifeste," RB, 65 (1958), 358-370; Agápē in the New Testament, trans. M. A. McNamara and M. H. Richter (St. Louis and London: B. Herder Book Co., 1966), III, 14-85.

[80]B. F. Westcott, The Gospel According to St. John (London: John Murray, 1892), p. 85. Cf. also Spicq, Agápē, III, 86-87; R. C. Trench, Synonyms of the New Testament, 8th ed. (London: Macmillan and Co., 1980), p. 42.

the disciples and their love for Jesus (14:23; 16:27), for Jesus' love for Lazarus (11:3, 5), and for Jesus' love for the special disciple (13:23; 20:2).[81] Consequently, no distinction exists between ἀγαπάω and φιλέω in characterizing the Father's love for the Son.

The Gospel contains five passages in which it is said that the Father loves the Son (3:35; 5:20; 10:17; 15:9; 17:23, 24, 26). These passages will be surveyed in order to determine the shape of the Father's love for the Son.

In the summary of Johannine Christology (3:31-36), the Gospel states, "The Father loves the Son and has given all things into his hand" (v. 35). The Father's giving all things to the Son is a frequent theme in the Gospel.[82] It is again stated in the summary statement in 13:3: "Jesus, knowing that the Father had given all things into his hands, and that he had come from God and was going to God. . ." The "all things" given to the Son include power to give life and to judge (5:21-27), power over all flesh (17:2), followers (6:37; 17:6), what to say (12:49; 17:8), the divine name (17:11,12), and glory (17:22). According to 3:35, the basis for this giving is the Father's love for the Son. His love is also related to his sending of Jesus, as the previous verse attests. The Father's love for the Son is a giving love.

The second reference to the Father's love for the Son occurs in the context of Jesus' discourse about his dependence on the Father (5:19-30). Love and will are interrelated. "For the Father loves the Son and shows him all that he himself is doing" (5:20). Because of the love which the Father has for the Son, the Father reveals his words to the Son, so that the Son might reveal these works in the world. The Father's love is a showing love.

In 3:35 and 5:20 the Father's love for the Son is part of the eternal relationship between the two, resulting in the Son's authority and mission. In 10:17, however, the Father's love is a response to an action of the Son. "For this reason the Father loves me, because I lay down my life, that I may take it up again" (10:17). Jesus brings forth "laying down his life" as evidence that he is the good shepherd

---

[81]Brown, Gospel, I-XII, pp. 498-499; J. H. Bernard, A Critical and Exegetical Commentary on the Gospel According to St. John, ICC, ed. A. H. McNeile (Edinburgh: T. & T. Clark, 1928), pp. 702-704. For more on this debate concerning ἀγαπάω and φιλέω, cf. André Feuillet, Le mystère de l'amour divin dans le johannique, EBib (Paris: J. Gibalda, 1972), pp. 5-13.

[82]Loader, "Central Structure," pp. 190-191, listed it as one of the motifs in the central structure of Johannine Christology.

(10:15); here it is the reason why the Father loves him. This does not mean that the Father's love is dependent upon the Son's laying down his life, for this love is "from the foundation of the world" (17:24). Barrett wrote, "The love of the Father for the Son is a love that is eternally linked with and mutually dependent upon the Son's complete alignment with the Father's will and his obedience unto death."[83] The Father's love evokes obedience from the Son which in turn evokes further love from the Father. Jesus has also said that the Father knows him (10:15), and now he adds that the Father loves him. An intimacy of knowledge and love is built up between the Father, the Son, and the flock.

A community of love between Father, Son, and believers is again mentioned in 15:9. The context is Jesus' allegory of the vine, in which the key word is abide, occurring ten times in 15:1-11. Jesus says, "As the Father has loved me, so have I loved you; abide in my love."[84] The love between the Father and the Son models the love between the Son and the community.[85] Abiding in Jesus' love is defined as keeping his commandments, that is, his commandment to love one another (v. 10a; cf. 13:34). In the same way, Jesus has kept the Father's commandments and abides in his love (v. 10b). Love is again bound up with obedience.

The final reference to the Father's love for the Son occurs in Jesus' prayer for the disciples (17:1-26). Here Jesus compares the Father's love for the disciples with the Father's love for him.

> I in them and you in me, that they may become perfectly one, so that the world may know that you have sent me and have loved them even as you have loved me . . . I made known your name to them, and I will make it known, so that the love with which you have loved me may be in them, and I in them (vv. 23, 26).

The Father's love for the Son continues in the community. The Father loves the disciples with the same love with which he loved the Son. The Father's love for the Son is inclusive; it opens up to embrace all who believe.

Sandwiched between these two references to the Father's love for the disciples is a reference to the preexistent love which the Father had for the Son. Jesus

---

[83]Barrett, Gospel, p. 377.

[84]The aorist here as in 17:23, 24, 26 contrasts with the present in the passages previously discussed. The farewell discourse is spoken from the perspective of the hour; Jesus' life is presented as having been complete.

[85]An important principle of Johannine ecclesiology is that the Father-Son relationship corresponds to the Son-disciples relationship. Cf. below, p. 105, 110.

prays that the disciples might "see my glory, which you have given me because you loved me before the foundation of the world" (v. 24). The Father has loved the Son from all eternity. Before creation this love manifested itself in glory. In the sending of the Son it manifested itself in equipping him for mission. In the hour of the Son's death and resurrection it manifested itself in love for the community. The Father loves the Son with an eternal love which continually goes out from himself.

Only once does Jesus refer to his own love for the Father (14:31). Jesus explains what he means by saying, "I am going to the Father" (14:28): it is the hour in which he does battle with the ruler of this world, Satan (cf. also 12:31; 16:11). He enters this conflict upon command from the Father. "But I do as the Father has commanded me, so that the world may know that I love the Father" (14:31). Again, obeying the commandments is coupled with love. Jesus demonstrates his love for the Father by doing what the Father commands him to do. Indeed, Jesus always does what is pleasing to the Father (8:29). The paramount way, though, that Jesus demonstrates his obedience in love is by going to the Father (14:28).

In the love relationship between the Father and the Son, the initiative lies with the Father. He loves the Son by showing him his mission to the world and by giving him authority to complete that mission. The Son loves the Father by completing the mission given to him by the Father. The Father in turn loves the Son because he has completed that mission. As the ocean tide flows back and forth, so love flows back and forth between the Father and the Son. This love, however, does not consist of warm feelings toward one another or a kind of contemplative mysticism; rather, it is a love which is clustered around doing the Father's will. Love, will, and knowledge are intertwined.

In only one passage is it said that God loves Wisdom, but this passage is significant. "She glorifies her noble birth by living with God, and the Lord of all loves (ἠγάπησεν) her. For she is an initiate in the knowledge of God, and an associate in his works" (Wis. 8:3-4). The same verb, ἀγαπάω, used in most of the Gospel passages is used here. God's love for Wisdom is tied in with her living with God; both ideas press home the intimacy between God and Wisdom. Likewise, one way in which the Father expresses his love for the Son is by always being with him (John 8:29). As in the Gospel, God's love is tied in with doing God's will. God loves Wisdom because she participates with God in his works.

These works include creation and redemption. So also the love between the Father and the Son manifests itself in terms of the Father showing the Son his works such as life and judgment (5:19-30) and the Son carrying out these works.

Love and knowledge are closely related here: God loves her, "for she is an initiate in the knowledge of God" (Wis. 8:4). Love and knowledge are also brought together in the Gospel (cf. John 10:14-15, 17). Jesus, like Wisdom, is "an initiate in the knowledge of God" because the loving Father shows him what he is doing (John 5:20).

John 17:24 speaks of the Father's love for the Son "before the foundation of the world." Preexistent intimacy is also found in Proverbs 8:30-31. At creation, Wisdom was beside (παρά, LXX) God and "was daily his delight, rejoicing before him always, rejoicing in his inhabited world and delighting in the human race." The Gospel's vocabulary of love is absent here, but the same essential meaning is present: the intimate relationship between God and his agent from all eternity.

God loves Wisdom because she knows God intimately, she participates with God in the divine works, and she has been with God from the beginning of time. The Father loves the Son in much the same way. Nevertheless, God's love for Wisdom is a far less frequent theme in the Wisdom material than is the Father's love for the Son in the Gospel. Furthermore, Wisdom is never said to love God.[86] A fuller development of the love between God and his agent awaited the incarnation; love is fully expressed only between persons. It is not immediately clear what it means to speak of God's love for a personification of divine action in the world; however, to speak of God's love for Jesus, the Father's love for the Son, means that God has poured Godself into Jesus, that God accomplishes the divine purposes through him, that God is for this man.[87] The Gospel uses this theme of the Father's love for the Son to authorize Jesus' mission: he has intimacy with God as Father with Son. The Gospel then takes a note from the wisdom score--God's love for a divine agent--and expands it into a major theme.

The intimacy between the Father and the Son is an intimacy of will, knowledge, and love. The Father and the Son are one in operation; the Son knows the

---

[86]The reasons for this are similar to those concerning knowledge; cf. above, p. 74 n. 78.
[87]Cf. Bultmann, Gospel, pp. 521-522, for his discussion of love as "being for."

Father intimately; the Father loves the Son, and the Son loves the Father.[88] Such a close relationship is presaged by the close relationship of God and his agent Wisdom. The intimacy between God and Wisdom is an intimacy of will, knowledge, and love. The Gospel found in the wisdom cluster ideas to express the eternal relationship of the Father and the Son.

Revelation

Out of the intimacy which the Son has with the Father, the Son reveals the Father on earth. Barrett wrote that the Johannine Christology is a Christology of mediation.[89] Jesus mediates to those who believe the kind of intimacy which he has with the Father.

It is best to look first at the vocabulary of revelation.[90] The Gospel frequently uses the verb φανερόω, "reveal": Through his signs Jesus reveals his glory (John 2:11); in him the works of God are revealed (9:3); he reveals the Father's name to the disciples (17:6). Also frequently appearing is μαρτυρέω, "bear witness": Jesus bears witness to heavenly things which he has heard and seen (3:11-12, 32); he bears witness to himself (8:18); he bears witness to the truth (18:37). The Gospel also uses δεικνύω, "show": Jesus shows many good works from the Father (10:22); he shows the Father to his disciples (14:8-9). Occasionally γνωρίζω, "make known," appears: Jesus makes known to the disciples all that he has heard from the Father (15:15); he makes known his Father's name (17:26). Even the verb λαλέω, "speak" is taken up in the service of revelation: Jesus speaks the words of God (3:34); he speaks to the world what he has heard and seen from the Father (8:26, 28); he speaks as his Father has commanded him (12:49-50).

What, then, does Jesus reveal? Aside from the references in which Jesus reveals himself (2:11; 7:4; 8:18; 21:4, 14), he is depicted as revealing that which belongs to the Father, or more specifically, that which he has heard and seen from the Father (3:11-12, 32; 8:26, 38; 15:15). Such things are variously referred to as glory (2:11), truth (18:37), the Father's name (17:6, 26), good works from the

---

[88]Fennema, "Jesus," pp. 197-220, 215-218, 227-231, wrote concerning knowledge, love, and unity that the Father has priority but the Father and the Son enjoy equality and mutuality.

[89]C. K. Barrett, "Christocentric or Theocentric? Observations on the Theological Method of the Fourth Gospel," Essays, p. 8.

[90]Helpful at this point is Feuillet, "Redemptive Incarnation," p. 879.

Father (9:3; 10:22), and the words of God (3:34). In two instances Jesus is said to reveal the Father (1:18; 14:8-9). Nevertheless, despite this multi-faceted vocabulary, precisely what Jesus reveals remains a bit vague.

Bultmann, in his analysis of the Johannine concept of revelation, wrote, "Jesus as the Revealer of God reveals nothing but that he is the Revealer."[91] He went on to speak of the "bare fact" of the revelation: "John . . . presents only the fact (das Dass) of the Revelation without describing its content (ihr Was)."[92] Bultmann corrected a propositional view of revelation; the revelation which Jesus brings does not consist solely of teaching.[93] Yet he went a bit too far in speaking about Jesus as the revealer without a revelation. Jesus reveals the Father; it is a personal revelation which cannot be captured in propositions. Jesus' person is integrally tied to his revelation, for the person of the Father is revealed in the person of the Son, and met only in personal encounter with the Son.[94] Jesus brings the divine dimension to bear upon human life. The Gospel's varied vocabulary of revelation is an attempt to express the inexpressible, to plumb the mystery of eternity. Forestell wrote, "Revelation is not merely teaching about God or Jesus or the way of salvation, but event, i.e. the event of God's self-manifestation in Jesus Christ, the λόγος σὰρξ γενόμενος."[95]

At this point, the motifs of sending and revelation coincide. The Father has sent the Son to reveal the Father. As divine emissary he is divine revealer. According to de Jonge, "An emissary is not simply someone who is sent, but also an envoy, a plenipotentiary; he speaks and acts in the name of the one who sent him."[96] This is precisely Jesus' function in the Gospel; he is God's authorized representa-

---

[91]Bultmann, Theology, II, 66.

[92]Ibid.; cf. also references throughout his commentary.

[93]Brown, Gospel, I-XII, p. 32, however, in response to Bultmann, pointed out that there is a considerable amount of teaching in the Gospel, such as teaching about the Paraclete and about the commandment to love. It must be emphasized, though, that this teaching always points back to the person of Jesus.

[94]At this point, Bultmann was correct. Cf. his Gospel, pp. 65-66: "The encounter with the Incarnate is the encounter with the Revealer himself; and the latter does not bring a teaching which renders his own presence superfluous; rather as the Incarnate he sets each man before the decisive question whether he will accept or reject him."

[95]Forestell, Word, p. 192. Cf. also Loader, Christology, pp. 139-142, for a discussion of Jesus' revelation as encounter.

[96]de Jonge, "The Son of God and the Children of God," in Jesus, p. 147.

tive here on earth.[97] This perspective is best summarized in 12:44-45: "Whoever believes in me believes not in me but in him who sent me. And whoever sees me sees him who sent me." Brown noted that πιστεύω εἰς refers to the Father twice in the Gospel, to Jesus thirty-one times, and to the name of Jesus four times.[98] The Johannine concept of faith differs from that of the synoptics in that Jesus becomes the object of faith. He says, "Believe in God, believe also in me" (14:1).[99] The farewell discourse gives further definition to believing in Jesus; it means keeping his commandments (14:15; 15:10) and abiding in his love (15:1-10).

Faith in Jesus does not supplant faith in God; on the contrary, faith in Jesus is faith in God, as 12:44 makes clear. Jesus makes God present in such a way that believing in Jesus means believing in God. Twice faith in Jesus is coupled with faith in God (14:1; 17:3). Coming to the Father is possible only through Jesus (14:6b). Knowledge of him is knowledge of the Father (8:19; 14:7). A parallel to 12:44 is found in the farewell discourse: "He who receives any one whom I send receives me; and he who receives me receives him who sent me" (13:20). The thought is carried over from 12:44: The response one makes to Jesus, God's authorized agent, is the response one makes to God.

This same thought is repeated in verse 45. Here seeing is believing, for θεωρῶν-θεωρεῖ stands parallel to πιστεύων-πιστεύει. Jesus grants not only faith in God but a vision of God. This idea is repeated in the farewell discourse. In response to Philip's request for Jesus to show them the Father, he says, "Whoever has seen me has seen the Father" (14:9). This is possible only because Jesus himself has seen the Father (1:18; 6:46). Jesus makes God fully present so that humanity might relate meaningfully to the divine.

Jesus' role as Son of Man is tied in with his function as revealer of God. Moloney noted that the title is not simply a title of honor but is linked with the theme of revelation.[100] The Son of Man descends and ascends for the purpose of

---

[97]Loader, Christology, p. 155, wrote, "The central structure of the author's christology depends upon the pattern of the revealer envoy."

[98]Brown, Gospel, I-XII, p. 512.

[99]It makes little difference whether the first πιστεύετε is translated as an indicative or an imperative; the sense is the same: faith in God is matched by faith in Jesus. Cf. Schnackenburg, Gospel, III, 58-59.

[100]Moloney, Son of Man, p. 40. Following Moloney, Lindars, Jesus, p. 155, wrote, "The Son of Man in John is the agent of the revelation which is disclosed in the cross."

revelation. This role as revealer is highlighted in the first Son of Man saying. Jesus says to Nathanael and the other disciples, "Very truly, I tell you, you will see heaven opened and the angels of God ascending and descending upon the Son of Man" (1:51). In the background stands Genesis 28:12 in which Jacob dreamed of the ladder extending from earth to heaven upon which the angels of God were ascending and descending."[101] The Son of Man, then, becomes the new ladder from earth to heaven; he is the place where God and humanity meet. In Barrett's words, "Jesus as the Son of Man becomes the means by which men have communion with God."[102]

The lifting up sayings also demonstrate that the Son of Man is the revelation of God. Particularly significant is John 8:28: "When you have lifted up the Son of Man, then you will know that I am he ($\dot{\epsilon}\gamma\omega$ $\epsilon\dot{\iota}\mu\dot{\iota}$), and that I do nothing on my own, but I speak these things as the Father has instructed me." When Jesus is lifted up on the cross, then his accusers will know that he is the revelation of the Father. The cross, then, becomes revelation as well as judgment (12:31). Through it, Jesus will draw all people to himself (12:32). The Son of Man becomes, to use Moloney's words, a "locus revelationis."[103]

Wisdom, too, is the "locus revelationis"; she makes God present for humanity. The vocabulary, however, is different from that of the Gospel. The Wisdom passages use $\dot{\alpha}\pi o\kappa\alpha\lambda\dot{\upsilon}\pi\tau\omega$, "reveal": Wisdom reveals her secrets (Sir. 4:19). They also use $\pi\rho o\gamma\nu\omega\rho\dot{\iota}\zeta\omega$, "make known": she makes herself known (Wis. 6:13). Also appearing is $\delta\iota\delta\dot{\alpha}\sigma\kappa\omega$, "teach": Wisdom teaches both secret and manifest things (Wis. 7:21). Not as much emphasis, however, is placed on verbs as in the Gospel. Often Wisdom appears parallel to knowledge, understanding, and insight (cf. Prov. 2:6, 10-11). All these are included in the revelation which Wisdom brings. Furthermore, her revelation is sometimes stated passively. Coming to Wisdom or Wisdom coming results in knowledge, right judgment, and friendship with God (cf. Wis. 7-9). Though the Wisdom material speaks in a different language than the Gospel, there can be no mistake that Wisdom is revelation.

---

[101]Exegetes since Augustine have made this connection; however, Wilhelm Michaelis, "Joh 1,41, Gen 28,12 und das Menschensohn-Problem," TLZ, 85 (1960), 561-578, called it into question. Others have pointed to rabbinic commentary on Gen. 28:12-13 as background to the saying. Cf. Moloney, Son of Man, pp. 26-30.

[102]Barrett, "Christocentric or Theocentric," p. 11.

[103]Moloney, Son of Man, p. 85.

What does Wisdom reveal? Her revelation is variously referred to as knowledge of what exists (Wis. 7:17), the secret and manifest things (Wis. 7:22), her secrets (Sir. 4:19), knowledge, understanding, and insight (Wis. 6:13). Like Jesus, she reveals the divine dimension. This idea is best expressed in Wisdom of Solomon 7:25-26:

> For she is a breath of the power of God, and a pure emanation of the glory of the Almighty . . . For she is a reflection of eternal light, a spotless mirror of the working of God, and an image of his goodness.

Wisdom is God's breath, emanation, reflection, mirror, and image. Though this language is not used in the Gospel,[104] the same ideas are present: Jesus is a reflection of God, for he says, "Whoever has seen me has seen the Father" (John 14:9), and "Whoever sees me sees him who sent me" (12:45). He is the spotless mirror of the working of God, for he says, "My Father is still working, and I also am working. . . . The Son can do nothing on his own, but only what he sees the Father doing; for whatever the Father does, the Son does likewise" (5:17, 19). The works of the Son mirror the works of the Father (5:21-22). Jesus is also the image of God.[105] He is the only Son from the Father, full of grace, truth, and glory (1:14). As the only Son, he has made the Father known (1:18). This picture of Wisdom as the revelation of God has influenced the evangelist in his picture of Jesus as the revealer of God.

As revealer of God, Wisdom sets herself up in the place of God. Relationship with her determines one's relationship with God: "Those who serve her minister to the Holy One; the Lord loves those who love her" (Sir. 4:14). These words are similar to Jesus': "Whoever believes in me believes not in me but in him who sent me" (12:44). "Whoever receives me receives him who sent me" (13:20). "Those who love me will be loved by the Father" (14:21; cf. also 14:23; 16:27; 17:23). Also, "God loves nothing so much as the person who lives with Wisdom" (Wis. 7:28). This statement parallels that of Jesus' allegory of the vine (John 15:1-11) in which the theme of abiding coalesces with that of love, both Jesus' love and the Father's love (cf. vv. 9-10). Finally, those who obtain Wisdom "obtain friendship with God" (7:14; cf. also 7:27). Jesus too brings persons into an intimate relationship with God.

---

[104]Cf. below, pp. 89, 114, however, for light and glory, respectively.

[105]Although the term image (εἰκών) does not appear in the Gospel, cf. Col. 1:15.

One's relationship to Wisdom is also spoken of in terms of faith or faithful-ness: "If they remain faithful (ἐμπιστεύσῃ), they will obtain her" (Sir. 4:16). Re-maining faithful to her stands parallel to loving her, seeking her (v. 12), holding her fast (v. 13), serving her (v. 14), and obeying her (v. 15). Sirach also speaks of leaning and relying on her (15:4). While the Wisdom material uses a variety of ex-pressions for trust in Wisdom, the Gospel uses almost exclusively the expression "having faith" or "believing" (πιστεύειν) in Jesus.

As one of the sources for his portrait of Jesus as the revealer of God, the evangelist has turned to previous portraits of Wisdom as the revelation of God. Wisdom makes God present to God's chosen people, the Israelites. She makes God known in such a way that the response one makes to Wisdom is essentially the response one makes to God. Trusting Wisdom means trusting God, and vice-versa. In the same way, Jesus makes God known and challenges persons to respond, not only to God, but to his person.

Yet the revelation which Jesus brings in the Gospel is different from that which Wisdom brings in the biblical and early Jewish literature, for Jesus is a per-son, bearing witness to the personal God. He does not meet people in every thought or in the reading of the Law but in the market, in the streets, in the temple. The image of a wandering revealer confronting people with the Word is now actual-ized in the ministry of Jesus. The Wisdom metaphor is employed to elaborate the significance of this man. According to the Gospel, Wisdom, the revelation of God, has become known in Jesus Christ.

Discourse of Revelation

Jesus reveals the Father in both word and deed, that is, through his dis-courses and through his signs. Indeed, the Gospel makes little distinction between Jesus' words and his works.[106] This section will consider Jesus' discourse under two rubrics, the "I am" sayings and the images which the Gospel uses to portray the revelation of God, such as bread, wine, water, and light. It will be demon-strated that each of these modes of revelation owes much to wisdom influence.

"I am" sayings. A striking difference between the portrayal of Jesus in the synoptics and in the Gospel is the place which Jesus' person has in his own

---

[106]Cf. Bultmann, Theology, II, 60: "The works of Jesus (or seen collectively as a whole: his work) are his words.

proclamation. The hub around which Jesus' message revolves in the synoptics is the kingdom of God. In order to proclaim "the secret of the kingdom," Jesus tells parables (cf. Mark 4:10-12 par.), The parables depict the new situation which results form the advent of the kingdom. In the Gospel, however, Jesus places himself squarely in the center of his own proclamation. In place of the parables of the kingdom stand the "I am" sayings. Jesus directs the believer to himself as the revealer of God.

The "I am" sayings have been a source of much investigation, and only a brief summary can be attempted here.[107] The sayings appear both without a predicate nominative (8:24, 28, 58; 13:19) and with a predicate nominative (6:35, 48, 51; 8:12; 9:5; 10:7, 11; 11:25; 14:6; 15:1, 5).[108] This latter use is the more frequent and the more christologically significant. In proclaiming the revelation which he brings, Jesus sets up a metaphorical relationship between himself and a particular image such as bread, light, or vine. He places himself alongside this image, and the resulting equation shatters the reality of the reader. One is forced to redefine both Jesus and the accompanying image. Faith is defining Jesus as the revelation of God.[109] The "I am," then, is a revelation formula.

---

[107]For more comprehensive treatments cf. Eduard Schweizer, Ego Eimi: Die religionsgeschichtliche Herkunft und theologische Bedeutung der johanneischen Bildreden, zugleich ein Beitrag zur Quellenfrage des vierten Evangeliums, 2d ed. (Göttingen: Vandenhoeck und Ruprecht, 1965); H. Zimmerman, "Das absolute ἐγώ εἰμί als die neutestamentliche Offenbarungsformel," BZ, 4 (1960), 54-69, 266-276; André Feuillet, "Les Ego Eimi christologiques du quatrième Evangile," RSR, 54 (1966), 5-22, 213-240; P. B. Harner, The "I Am" of the Fourth Gospel: A Study in Johannine Usage and Thought, Facet Books (Philadelphia: Fortress Press, 1970). Cf. also material in the following commentaries: Brown, Gospel, I-XII, pp. 533-538; Schnackenburg, Gospel, II, 79-89; Dodd, Interpretation, pp. 93-96, 349-350; Bultmann, Gospel, pp. 225-226 n. 3; Barrett, Gospel, pp. 291-292. Most recently, cf. Jerome H. Neyrey, An Ideology of Revolt: John's Christology in Social-Science Perspective (Philadelphia: Fortress Press, 1988), pp. 213-220

[108]Some commentators add a third category, but no agreement exists as to what belongs in it. Brown, Gospel, I-XII, pp. 533-534, considered 6:20 and 18:5 examples in which the predicate nominative is understood but not expressed; Schnackenburg, Gospel, II, 81, listed 4:26; 8:18, 23, as examples of ἐγώ εἰμί plus a nominalized participle or defining preposition.

[109]Such a treatment of the "I am" sayings is similar to the treatment of the christological titles by Leander Keck, "Jesus in New Testament Christology," AusBR 28 (1980), 12-15. He used the work of Paul Ricoeur on metaphors. Cf. also his "Toward the Renewal of New Testament Christology," NTS 32 (1986), 362-377. For a treatment of the Son of Man as metaphor, cf. Pazdan, Son of Man, pp. 83-84.

Scholars often point to the "I am" in Hebrew scripture.[110] Especially significant is Exodus 3:14, in which the revelation of the divine name occurs at the burning bush,[111] and various passages in Deutero-Isaiah, in which the use of ἐγώ εἰμί is understood as a divine name.[112]

Often overlooked, however, is the Wisdom material. Although Wisdom does not speak in "I am" sayings, her speech pattern is closely related. Like Jesus, the focus of her message is herself. In her speeches in Proverbs 1:20-33 and 8:1-36 she and her words take center stage: "Give heed to my reproof; I will pour out my thoughts to you; I will make my words known to you" (1:23). Here is no humble "Thus saith the Lord." Rather, the message is completely hers; it is her counsel and her reproof (vv. 25, 30). Similarly, in Wisdom's speech in Proverbs 8:1-36 her subject is the words from her mouth (v. 8) and her instruction (v. 10). She says, "I, Wisdom, live with prudence, and I attain knowledge and discretion. . . . I have good advice and sound wisdom, I have insight, I have strength" (vv. 12, 14). In the other speech of Wisdom, Sirach 24, Wisdom praises herself and glories in the midst of her people (v. 1). She traces her travels from heaven and earth (vv. 3-7), to her dwelling in Israel (vv. 8-12), to her growth there (vv. 13-17). Like the speeches in Proverbs 1 and 8, Wisdom again offers an invitation: "Come to me, you who desire me, and eat your fill of my fruits" (v. 19; cf. also vv. 20-22). Wisdom's "I" sayings are followed by a personal invitation to come to her. She states who she is and invites believers to participate in her revelation.

In his study of the Bread of Life discourse Feuillet noted that all three "I am" sayings (6:35, 48-50, 51) are accompanied by an invitation to believe in Jesus. This pattern, he continued, resembles the pattern of Proverbs 8 and 9 and Sirach 24, in which the prayers of Wisdom are followed by an invitation.[113] Indeed, this pattern is true of nearly all of the "I am" sayings with a predicate nominative; they are followed by an invitation to come to Jesus: "I am the light of the world. Who-

---

[110]Cf. Zimmerman, "ἐγώ εἰμί," pp. 62-64, 273-276.

[111]Cf. Karl Zickendraht, "ΕΓΩ ΕΙΜΙ," TSK, 94 (1922), 162-168, who argued that the absolute "I am" sayings were derived from the "I am" of Exod. 3:14. Cf. also the response by Harner, I Am, pp. 15-17.

[112]Cf. Brown, Gospel, I-XII, pp. 536-537. Furthermore, Schnackenburg, Gospel, II, 85, noted that Deutero-Isaiah was a rich source for the images used in the "I am" sayings.

[113]André Feuillet, "The Principle [sic] Biblical Themes in the Discourse on the Bread of Life," in Johannine Studies, trans. Thomas E. Crane (Staten Island, NY: Alba House, 1964), p. 86.

ever follows me will not walk in darkness but will have the light of life" (8:12; cf. also 10:7-9; 11:25; 14:6; 15:1, 5).[114] Jesus confronts humanity with who he is and then invites persons to participate in his identity. While the "I am" sayings have a number of influences, an important one is the influence of Wisdom, who, like Jesus, speaks in discourses of self-praise, inviting the believer to come to her.

Images. Part of the brilliance of the Gospel is that it takes up ordinary images, such as light, bread, and water, and transforms them into bearers of divine revelation. The Gospel has a sacramental view of the world: everything has the potential for pointing to the divine. Because all things came into being through the Word (1:3), all things are a witness to him.[115] This perspective is similar to that of wisdom. Wisdom pervades and penetrates all things and orders all things well (Wis. 7:24; 8:1). She is the divine order of creation, that which is of God which gives meaning to the universe. Creation itself is alive with the spirit of Wisdom, and as a result all created things point back to their Maker. The Gospel stands firmly in the wisdom tradition in the use of ordinary images to express the divine mystery of Christ.

The Gospel not only takes up the attitude from the Wisdom material; it also takes up some of the images, such as light, water, and bread and wine. This section will briefly look at each of these images and their corresponding use in the Wisdom material.

The image of light shines throughout the Gospel. Culpepper called it a "core symbol" in the Gospel.[116] More so than any other symbol it expresses the revelation of God brought in Jesus. Jesus claims that he is the light of the world and that his followers will have the light of life (8:12). Jesus illustrates this saying by healing the man born blind (9:5-7). In a concluding summary of his ministry Jesus says, "I have come as light into the world, that whoever believes in me may not remain in darkness" (12:46). The revelation which Jesus brings--indeed, which Jesus is--is illumination, enlightenment to believers. Jesus enjoins the disciples to

---

[114]The only exceptions to this pattern are 9:5, in which "I am the light of the world" is repeated from 8:12, and 10:11 in which Jesus' being the good shepherd is coupled with his laying down his life for his sheep. An invitation, however, appears in 10:9 in connection with "I am the door."

[115]Cf. Culpepper, Anatomy, pp. 200-202; Stephen S. Smalley, John: Evangelist and Interpreter (Exeter: Paternoster Press, 1978), pp. 208-210.

[116]Culpepper, Anatomy, pp. 190-192.

walk in the light and believe in the light (12:35-36; cf. also 11:9-10). Revelation, however, always brings judgment upon those who do not believe, and the image of light also expresses this idea.

> And this is the judgment, that the light has come into the world, and people loved darkness rather than light, because their deeds were evil. For all who do evil hate the light, and do not come to the light, so that their deeds may not be exposed (3:19-20).

The Father through his Son shines his spotlight upon humanity; some come to the light because they recognize in it the revelation of God, but others flee because it exposes their evil deeds.

Light often accompanies the description of Wisdom. She is depicted as a beacon beckoning persons to come out of their darkness into her light. This image of light was considered in the previous chapter.[117] Wisdom, her instruction, and those who take her instruction are all described in terms of light. The Gospel has taken this image and concentrated it in the figure of Jesus as the revelation of the Father. Just as the moon's light is a reflection of the sun, Wisdom's light is a reflection of eternal light. In the same way, Jesus as the light of the world reflects the light from the Father.

The images of bread, water, and wine form a cluster of symbols which often appear together. Bread becomes most prominent in the Bread of Life discourse (John 6:35-59), in which Jesus asserts that he is the bread which came down from heaven (vv. 50, 51). The Gospel has affixed this discourse to the feeding miracle (6:1-15) and the walking on the water (6:16-21). Because of the feeding miracle the people seek Jesus in Capernaum (6:22-24). Jesus takes the discussion from the bread which perishes to the bread of eternal life (v. 27). Talk about bread brings to mind Moses giving the Israelites bread from heaven. Jesus counters that God, not Moses, gives the true bread from heaven, and Jesus himself is this bread (vv. 31-35). He has come down from heaven to do the Father's will (vv. 38, 41, 42, 50, 51). Finally, as the bread of heaven, believers must eat his flesh and drink his blood (vv. 52-58).[118]

---

[117]Cf. above, p. 38.

[118]For a discussion of whether this discourse is primarily sapiential or sacramental. Cf. Brown, Gospel, I-XII, pp. 272-275; James D. G. Dunn, "John VI--An Eucharistic Discourse?" NTS, 17 (1971), 328-338. A number of scholars, such as Brown, considered vv. 35-50 sapiential

90

Feuillet and Peder Borgen have explored the wisdom background of this passage.[119] Feuillet noted that one of the biblical themes at the base of the discourse is "Wisdom's banquet." He pointed to the feast which Wisdom prepares in Proverbs 9:1-6.[120] She prepares the meat and wine (v. 2); she commissions her maids to make the invitation to the simple "from the highest places in the town (vv. 3-4);[121] Wisdom then makes her own invitation: "Come, eat of my bread and drink of the wine I have mixed" (v. 5).[122]

So also Jesus has prepared his feast and set his table through the feeding miracle, through his "coming down" as the bread from heaven, and through the eucharist. He offers his invitation, first as a general invitation to come to him: "I am the bread of life. Whoever comes to me will never be hungry, and whoever believes in me will never be thirsty" (John 6:35; cf. also vv. 37, 45). Then he makes a specific invitation to eat his flesh and drink his blood: "Very truly, I tell you, unless you eat the flesh of the Son of Man and drink his blood, you have no life in you" (6:53; cf. also vv. 54-56). The eating of Jesus' flesh and drinking of his blood is a direct parallel to the eating of Wisdom's bread and drinking her wine.

Borgen noted that the ideas in the discourse which clearly come from the Jewish wisdom traditions are centered around the words, "to come," "to eat and drink," and "hunger and thirst."[123] He drew particular attention to the resemblance between Sirach 24:19-21 and John 6:35.

Come to me, you who desire me, and eat your fill of my fruits. . . . Those who eat of me will hunger for more, and those who drink of me will thirst for more (Sir. 24:19, 21).

I am the bread of life. Whoever comes to me will never be hungry, and whoever believes in me will never be thirsty (John 6:35).

---

and vv. 51-58 sacramental. As Barrett, Gospel, p. 284, insisted, however, these two interpretations are not inconsistent but complementary.

[119]Cf. Feuillet, "Biblical Themes," pp. 76-118; Peder Borgen, Bread from Heaven: An Exegetical Study of the Concept of Manna in the Gospel of John and the Writings of Philo, NovTSup X (Leiden: E. J. Brill, 1965), pp. 154-158.

[120]Feuillet, "Biblical Themes," pp. 76-118.

[121]Cf. also 1:21 and 8:2 in which Wisdom calls "on the top of the walls" and "on the heights"; Wisdom's message in 1:22 and 8:5 is also to the simple.

[122]Also relevant here is Sir. 15:3, in which Wisdom is said to feed the one who fears the Lord with "the bread of understanding" and give "the water of wisdom to drink."

[123]Borgen, Bread, pp. 154-158.

He noted the parallel invitation of Wisdom (προσέλθετε πρός με) and Jesus (ὁ ἐρχόμενος πρὸς ἐμέ), and their association with eating and drinking.[124] Furthermore, just as Wisdom identifies herself with food and drink, so also does Jesus. Jesus' promise, however, is much more radical for it tells about cessation of hunger and thirst rather than its continuation.[125]

While admitting that the wisdom literature provides background for Wisdom being called food and drink, Borgen found no parallels for the Johannine identification of manna and Wisdom. Such an identification, he continued, is suggested in Exodus Rabbah 25:7 in which Exodus 16:4 concerning the manna is combined with Proverbs 9:5 concerning Wisdom.[126] Richard Dillon, however, contended that the identification hearkens back to the interpretation of the manna miracle in Wisdom of Solomon 16:20-23.[127]

Borgen, however, did not stop there. He maintained that in addition to Wisdom's invitation to eat and drink, features from the theophany at Sinai also appear. "He who shares in the (preparatory) revelation at Sinai accepts the invitation and "comes to" Wisdom/Jesus (John 6:45)."[128] Finally, Borgen added a third influence, the Jewish principle of agency.[129] The Gospel mixes together the colors of Torah, Wisdom, and agency in order to picture the bread which has come down from heaven.

Closely related to the feeding miracle and the Bread of Life discourse is the miracle at Cana (John 2:1-11). Dillon gave significant attention to the wisdom background of the Cana miracle.[130] He noted that this story forms a parallel with John 6, "for in both the notions of reception of the Word by faith and the consummation of this in the Eucharist are developed with the aid of the bread and wine fig-

---

[124]He also pointed to Wisdom's invitation in Prov. 9:5 (LXX ἔλθατε).

[125]F.-M. Braun, "Saint Jean, la Sagesse et l'Historie," in Neotestamentica et Patristica: Freudsgabe für Oscar Cullmann, NovTSupIV, ed. W. C. van Unnik (Leiden: E. J. Brill, 1962), p. 125, however, wrote that the fundamental idea is the same in both passages: Wisdom's produce is so good the person wants to have it always; Jesus' bread satisfies completely.

[126]Borgen, Bread, p. 15.

[127]Richard J. Dillon, "Wisdom Tradition and Sacramental Retrospect in the Cana Account (Jn 2,1-11)," CBQ, 24 (1962), 275.

[128]Borgen, Bread, p. 157. He also noted that this same combination is present in the prologue.

[129]Ibid., pp. 158-164. Cf. also his later "God's Agent," in which he developed this idea in greater detail.

[130]Dillon, "Wisdom Tradition," pp. 268-296.

ures of Wisdom's banquet."[131] Furthermore, a "replacement theme" also runs through both accounts: in John 6 the bread come down from heaven replaces the manna given in the wilderness; in John 2 the wine of Jesus' revelation replaced the water of Jewish tradition.[132]

Related to the images of bread and wine is the image of the vine in John 15:1-11. This image reinforces the message of abiding which sounds throughout the passage. Just as the branches draw their strength from the vine, so also the disciples draw their strength by remaining united with Jesus. They do so by keeping his commandments (v. 10). Though this image is used elsewhere in the Hebrew scripture to symbolize the nation of Israel (cf. Psalm 80:9-20; Isa. 5:1-7; Jer. 2:21) , it appears as a symbol of Wisdom in Sirach 24:17. She says, "Like the vine I bud forth delights, and my blossoms became glorious and abundant fruit" (v. 17). Then follows the invitation to come and eat and drink of her (vv. 19-22). Just as Wisdom compares herself to a vine and offers an invitation to come, so also Jesus identifies himself as the vine and gives the disciples the command to abide. Schnackenburg noted further that buds (branches) and abundant fruit also appear in both discourses.[133] As Brown suggested, the Johannine image of the vine and the branches has been drawn, not only form the image of the Israel as the vine, but also the image of Wisdom as the life-giving vine.[134]

The final image in this cluster is the image of water. Water flows throughout the Gospel, sometimes as a placid stream, other times as a rushing river. Birger Olsson wryly observed that the statement, "There was much water there" (3:23), can be applied to the entire Gospel.[135] As Culpepper noted, the image is less unified and more variable than either light or bread.[136] Nevertheless, like bread and

---

[131]Ibid., p. 294.

[132]Ibid., pp. 287-288. Dillon demonstrated how the rabbis interpreted the bread and wine of Wisdom's banquet as the bread and wine of Torah (cf. above, p. 19). He maintained that John 2 and 6 portray Jesus as true Wisdom offering the bread and wine of his revelation in place of the bread and water of the Torah. Cf. also Brown, Gospel, I-XII, p. 107.

[133]Schnackenburg, Gospel, III, 107.

[134]Brown, Gospel, XIII-XXI, p. 672. Cf. also Feuillet, "Biblical Themes," pp. 87-88.

[135]Birger Olsson, Structure and Meaning in the Fourth Gospel: A Text-Linguistic Analysis of John 2:1-11 and 4:1-42, trans. J. Gray, Con BNT 6 (Lund: C. W. K. Gleerup, 1974), p. 53. Cf. his excursus on "Living Water," pp. 212-218.

[136]Culpepper, Anatomy, p. 193. For the various meanings of water in the Gospel, cf. his concise discussion on pp. 192-195.

wine, water points to the revelation of God which Jesus brings. It meets humanity's basic need for relationship with God.[137]

Water flows to the fore in two pericopes, in the conversation with the Samaritan woman (4:7-15) and in Jesus' words on the last day of the feast (7:37-39). In the first episode, Jesus uses the occasion of a woman coming out to draw water as a setting for his offer of living water. The water has generally been interpreted either as revelation or the Spirit.[138] It is not necessary to choose between these two alternatives.[139] Olsson wrote, "In a Johannine context, a revelation without the Spirit and a Spirit without integration in the revelation of Jesus are unthinkable. . . . The revelation becomes present with the Spirit, and, in a sense, only with the Spirit."[140] In the Gospel the image of water does double duty; it represents both the revelation of God in Jesus and the Spirit which Jesus imparts to believers. In offering the Samaritan woman living water Jesus offers the revelation of God made present in the Spirit, which brings eternal life to those who believe. The one who drinks of this water will never thirst (cf. John 6:35), that is, the believer will never want for fellowship with God, for it is made available in Jesus.

The same promise, as well as the identification of water and the Spirit, is made in 7:37-39:

> Let anyone who is thirsty come to me, and let the one who believes in me drink. As the scripture has said, Out of his heart shall flow rivers of living water. Now this he said about the Spirit which those who believed in him were to receive; for as yet the Spirit had not been given, because Jesus was not yet glorified.[141]

---

[137]Cf. Schnackenburg, Gospel, I, 431: "Jesus' gift of living water . . . is a divine gift brought by Jesus from the heavenly world and given to men to quench fully and for ever their most radical 'thirst for life,' penetrating and permeating man, unfolding its vital powers and continuing to work unfailingly till eternal life."

[138]Maurice F. Wiles, The Spiritual Gospel: The Interpretation of the Fourth Gospel in the Early Church (Cambridge: Cambridge University Press, 1960), pp. 46-47, stated that both these interpretations go back to the second century. For a discussion of each alternative, cf. Brown, Gospel, I-XII, pp. 178-179; Olssen, Structure, pp. 214-215.

[139]So Brown, Gospel, I-XII, p. 179; Olssen, Structure, pp. 217-218; F. J. McCool, "Living Water in John," in The Bible in Current Catholic Thought, ed. J. L. McKenzie, Festschrift for M. Gruenthauer (New York: Herder and Herder, 1962), pp. 226-233.

[140]Olssen, Structure, pp. 217.

[141]The NRSV reading of vv. 37-38b is here adapted.

This passage bristles with exegetical problems, and the reader is referred elsewhere for thorough discussion.[142] Will the rivers of living water flow out of Jesus or the believer? The above translation favors the former: Jesus is the source of living water for the believer. He is the one who gives living water (4:10, 14a) and the Spirit (19:30; 20:22).[143] The two are identified in 7:39, recalling the association of water and spirit in 3:5. This is the only time in the Gospel in which the meaning of a symbol is explained. Furthermore, of the images of revelation water is the only image which is not used in an "I am" saying.[144] It would have been awkward, however, to have identified water as both Jesus and the Spirit. Nevertheless, Jesus possesses the living water and gives it to those who believe. This water is the Spirit, which makes God present in the community.

Not only does water appear in the Wisdom material in conjunction with bread, as noted above,[145] it also stands alone as a symbol of the revelation Wisdom offers. In Sirach 24:30-34 the author compares himself to an irrigation canal leading off from the great river of Wisdom. Perhaps this image was suggested by verse 29 in which Wisdom's thought is said to be more abundant than the sea. The canal, intended only to water his own garden, becomes a river and then a sea (v. 31). Furthermore, Baruch refers to "the fountain of Wisdom," which Israel has rejected (3:12). These images of an ever-expanding river and a fountain are akin to the Johannine images of the spring of water welling up to eternal life (John 4:14) and flowing rivers of living water (7:38). The images are not stagnant but keep on renewing themselves. Such is the revelation of God which is present in Wisdom and in Jesus; through the Spirit it slakes the believer's thirst for eternal life. Again the Gospel takes up an image from the Wisdom material, expands its importance, and concentrates it in Jesus. The revelation which was only glimpsed in Wisdom is now manifest in fullest measure in Jesus.

---

[142]Cf. Brown, Gospel, I-XII, pp. 319-329; Schnackenburg, Gospel, II, 152-157; and now Gary M. Burge, The Anointed Community: The Holy Spirit in the Johannine Tradition (Grand Rapids: Wm. B. Eerdmans, 1987), pp. 88-93.

[143]For further reasons for this reading, cf. Brown, Gospel, I-XII, p. 320; Schnackenburg, Gospel, II, 154; Bultmann, Gospel, p. 303; Dodd, Interpretation, p. 349; Burge, Anointed, pp. 91-93.. Barrett, Gospel, p. 327, and Lindars, Gospel, p. 301, prefer a reference to the believer, as does the NRSV.

[144]Although this is clearly implied in 6:35.

[145]Cf. above, pp. 82-83.

It is interesting to note that this cluster of images, bread, water, and wine, which are taken up from the wisdom tradition, are images which have sacramental overtones. Space does not allow discussion of the question as to what extent the Gospel is sacramental.[146] Suffice it to say that the Wisdom material and the Gospel share a sacramental perspective: all of life can give expression to the divine. This cluster of images symbolizes the revelation brought by Wisdom-Jesus. In the early church, however, these images would have been interpreted as references to baptism and eucharist. The Gospel, then, at a secondary level, gives a deeper interpretation of the sacraments by connecting them to the theme of revelation. The narratives of Jesus' baptism and of the institution of the Lord's Supper are missing, but images suggesting the sacraments pervade the Gospel. The revelation has come in Jesus, and believers participate in that revelation through the water, the bread, and the wine.

Hiddenness

While Jesus brings the revelation of God, there is still a hiddenness about that revelation. The person of Jesus is cloaked in mystery. He and his ways are unfathomable, particularly to unbelievers, but even to the disciples. Such hiddenness is also characteristic of the revelation brought by Wisdom. This section will explore the theme of hiddenness in the Gospel and its background in the Wisdom material.

The object of knowledge which is continually beyond those who encounter Jesus is his "whence-whither." Neither the Jews nor the disciples fully comprehend where he has come from or where he is going. This theme comes to the fore in Jesus' debate with the Jews at the Feast of Tabernacles (7:14-36). An irony appears in verse 27: the people of Jerusalem deny that Jesus is the Christ because they know where Jesus is from and no one is to know where the Christ is from. Jesus questions whether they really know where he is from. Because they know neither him nor his origin, they also do not know the one who sent him (v. 28).

---

[146]The literature on this subject is extensive. Cf. the bibliography in Ernst Haenchen, John 1: A Commentary on the Gospel of John Chapters 1-6, Hermeneia, trans. Robert W. Funk and ed. Robert W. Funk and Ulrich Buse (Philadelphia: Fortress Press, 1984), pp. 287-288. The debate is marked off by Bultmann, Theology, II, 58-59, who observed that the sacraments play no role in the Gospel, and Oscar Cullmann, Early Christian Worship, trans. A. S. Todd and J. B. Torrance (Philadelphia: Westminster Press, 1953), pp. 37-119, who maintained that the sacraments were of central importance to the evangelist.

Jesus then says, "I will be with you a little longer, and then I am going to him who sent me; you will search for me and you will not find me; where I am you cannot come" (vv. 33-34). The Jews do not understand this saying (vv. 35-36). In another bit of irony, they wonder if he is going to the Dispersion to teach the Greeks.[147]

The question again arises in Jesus' debate with the Jews in the treasury (8:12-30). Jesus says frankly to the Pharisees, "You do not know where I come from or where I am going" (8:14). The Jews prove this in verses 21-22, for they think he will kill himself. Jesus explains why they do not understand his destiny by a reference to his origin: "You are from below, I am from above; you are of this world, I am not of this world" (v. 23). The Jews do not understand Jesus' whence-whither because Jesus and the Jews stand on different sides of the Johannine dualism.

In 7:27 the Jews deny Jesus' Messiahship because they know where he is from, but the argument is turned in 9:29. The Pharisees maintain that God has not spoken to Jesus because they do not know where he comes from. While the two passages seem to stand in contradiction, the intent is the same: The Jews deny that Jesus has come from God.

The hiddenness of the "whence-whither" is not only a theme for Jesus but also for his benefits. Nicodemus does not know the whence-whither of the wind (spirit) or of the one who is born of the Spirit (3:8). The steward of the wedding feast at Cana does not know where the extra wine has come from (2:9). The Samaritan woman does not know where Jesus would get living water (4:11). The disciples do not know where he had gotten food (4:32-33). They also do not know where they would get bread to feed the multitude (6:5-7). The answer to all these questions is that spiritual birth, new wine, living water, and bread come from above.

Jesus repeats to the disciples in the farewell discourse his words to the Jews: "Where I am going you cannot come" (13:33; cf. 7:33; 8:21). This saying receives no greater understanding among the disciples than it did among the Jews. Peter asks, "Lord, where are you going?" Jesus answers that Peter will follow later

---

[147]Brown, Gospel, I-XII, p. 318, noted that this suggestion had become a reality by the time the Gospel was written.

but not now (13:36). After his words about going and preparing a place, Jesus says that the disciples know the way to the place where he is going. Thomas protests, "Lord, we do not know where you are going. How can we know the way?" Jesus answers that he is the way (14:4-6). Jesus says later, "None of you asks me, 'Where are you going?'" (16:5). This statement poses difficulties, for Peter and Thomas ask that very question.[148] Nevertheless, the disciples do not seem to understand where Jesus is going.

Not only does fog cloak where Jesus comes from and where he is going, it also cloaks where he is. Twice Jesus escapes being stoned or arrested (8:59; 10:39). He withdraws from the five thousand when they want to make him king (6:15). The day following the miracle the people do not know how he had gotten to the other side of the sea (6:25). When questioned, the healed blind man does not know where he is (9:12). The Jews do not know if he will come to the Passover feast, and the Pharisees want to know where he is so that they can arrest him (11:56-57).

Not only is Jesus' way unfathomable, so is his message. Even Nicodemus, a teacher of Israel, does not understand it (3:4, 9). The Jews continually misunderstand him (cf. 6:52; 10:6). Even the disciples are unclear about his meaning. In the farewell discourse they show frequent misunderstanding and say, "We do not know what he is talking about" (16:18). When Jesus dismisses Judas at the table, they do not understand (13:38). At the end of the discourse, however, they say, "Yes, now you are speaking plainly, not in any figure of speech! Now we know that you know all things, and do not need to have anyone question you" (16:29-30).[149] Question still remains, though, whether they truly understand, for they will soon be scattered and leave Jesus alone (16:32).

Not only Jesus' message but also his person is shrouded in mystery. The Jews marvel that he has learning when he has never studied (7:15). Later they ask him blankly, "Who are you?" (8:25). They know neither Jesus nor the Father (8:19). Even the disciples do not know him (14:7, 9).[150] John emphasizes that he

---

[148]Cf. Brown, Gospel, XIII-XXI, p. 710, who briefly surveyed a number of opinions.

[149]On 16:30, cf. N. H. Bream, "No Need to Be Asked Questions: A Study of Jn. 16:30," in Search the Scriptures: New Testament Essays in Honor of Raymond T. Stamm, GTS 3 (Leiden: E. J. Brill, 1969), pp. 49-74.

[150]The condition in 14:7 is here understood as contrary to fact, thus making the verse a reproach. Cf. Brown, Gospel, XIII-XXI, p. 621; Bultmann, Gospel, p. 607 n. 3. The condition

98

did not know Jesus prior to the baptism (1:31, 33). Although Jesus comes to reveal the Father, his origin and destiny, his message, and his person are nevertheless hidden.

Jesus, however, invites persons to enter into the mystery. To his first two disciples, he says, "Come and see" (1:39). He invites the Samaritan woman to come and drink the living water he has to give (4:10, 13-14). He offers the crowd the bread of life (6:27). As the hidden revealer, Jesus summons the believer to participate in the mystery of the divine. It is only in this tension between revelation and hiddenness that God can be experienced.[151]

The revelation of God in Wisdom is also hidden. The inaccessibility of Wisdom is portrayed most prominently in the hymn of Job 28. Like a refrain verses 12-13 sound:

But where shall Wisdom be found?
And where is the place of understanding?
Mortals do not know the way to it,
and it is not found in the land of the living.

Wisdom is hidden (cf. v. 21). The only one who knows the way to Wisdom is God (cf. vv. 23-27). Likewise, no one knows Jesus' way (John 7:35-36; 8:22; 14:5), except the Father. Baruch 3:9-4:4 takes up the theme of the inaccessibility of Wisdom from Job 28: "No one knows the way to her, or is concerned about the path to her" (Bar. 3:31). Finally, Sirach, which is primarily characterized by available wisdom, nevertheless takes up something of the theme of hiddenness: "Wisdom is like her name; she is not perceived by many" (6:22).

Because Wisdom is hidden, humanity is exhorted to seek and find her. Wisdom assures those who seek her that they will find her (Prov. 8:17; Wis. 6:12-14). Joy is promised to those who seek her (Sir. 4:11-12); she will become known to those who seek her (Sir. 6:27). Though Wisdom is hidden, her revelation becomes known to those who seek her.

The Gospel employs the theme of hiddenness in the portrayal of Jesus. This revealer is not completely transparent; his way is marked by darkness as well

can also be understood as real, thus making 14:7a a promise. Cf. Schnackenburg, Gospel, III, 67; Barrett, Gospel, pp. 458-459. Cf. also Bruce M. Metzger, A Textual Commentary on the Greek New Testament: A Companion Volume to the United Bible Societies' Greek New Testament (London: United Bible Societies, 1971), p. 243, in which the majority of the committee understood 14:7 as a promise, but Kurt Aland understood it as a reproach.

[151]Cf. Bultmann, Gospel, pp. 161, 296, for a discussion of the hiddenness of revelation.

as light. He is hidden from unbelievers and even from the disciples. Nevertheless, out of the hiddenness, Jesus calls for persons to experience his revelation. Both Wisdom and Jesus are hidden revealers.

It was noted in the previous chapter that a tension exists in the Wisdom material between accessibility and hiddenness.[152] Job 28 and Baruch 3:9-4:4 are perhaps the best representatives of hidden Wisdom, while Proverbs 1-9 and Sirach primarily present available Wisdom. It seems that the Gospel has combined both these traditions in the presentation of Jesus as revealer. The Gospel proclaims that in Jesus the Wisdom of God is available to those who believe, just as Sirach says that in the Law Wisdom is available. But the Gospel also depicts Jesus as hidden and elusive to humanity, much like Wisdom is in Job 28. These two strands of wisdom, hiddenness and availability, are taken up in the Gospel in the presentation of Jesus as revealer.

It is necessary to summarize this section. From his position as intimate with God, Jesus has come as the revealer of God. He calls people to believe not only in God but in himself. In order to communicate the depth of this revelation, Jesus and his ways are enveloped in hiddenness. This characterization of Jesus as revealer matches the characterization of Wisdom as revealer. The style of discourse, the images, and the themes are taken up in the Gospel in its portrayal of Jesus. Wisdom reveals God, as a spirit meeting the believer in every thought, and as the Law meeting the believer in right conduct. Wisdom, however, has now become a person in Jesus of Nazareth; he has made God known.

Acceptance-Rejection

He was in the world, and the world came into being through him, yet the world did not know him. He came to what was his own, and his own people did not accept him. But to all who received him, who believed in his name, he gave power to become children of God, who were born, not of blood or of the will of the flesh or of the will of man, but of God (John 1:10-13).

The revelation which Jesus brings acts as a sword which divides humanity into two camps. This section, then, refers to the soteriological dualism of the Gospel. It combines with the spatial dualism of the world above-below to form the Gospel's unique world-view. The Johannine cosmology is dualistic, and so is the

---

[152]Cf. above, p. 10.

100

anthropology. A person either believes that Jesus is the revealer of God and experiences life or denies it and falls under judgment. There is no middle ground!

This theme appears as early as the prologue and continues throughout the Gospel. Dodd noted that the whole story of the ministry in chapters 2 through 12 is "a story of sifting and selection."[153] This is also the story of Wisdom. This section will delve into the theme of acceptance-rejection and show how it is developed in the Gospel and the Wisdom material. The division which Jesus causes will first be considered, followed by the rejection he meets.

Division

Just as the Johannine spatial dualism is symbolized primarily in terms of the world above and the world below, the soteriological dualism is symbolized primarily in terms of light and darkness. Jesus comes as light of the world (1:4, 9; 8:12; 9:5) and attracts those who would come into his light (3:21; 12:35, 46). These are the children of light (12:36). They have life (1:4; 8:12), and, by implication, truth and spirit. Others, however, reject the light of the world and remain in darkness (3:19-20). Their existence is characterized by aimlessness (12:35), judgment (3:19), death, and falsehood.

The Gospel narrative reaches a crescendo at a number of points when Jesus' person and message results in a division among his hearers. Such points are clustered in chapters 6-8, beginning with a division among the disciples (6:60, 66). Dodd perceptively observed, "The third episode [chap. 6] culminates in a sifting of the early followers of Jesus; and the present, central episode [chaps. 7-8] carries the story forward, by showing how at every stage and at every level of Christ's auditors the process of 'polarization' goes on."[154]

The setting for chapters 7-8 is the Feast of the Tabernacles. Merely the prospect of Jesus' presence provokes controversy: "There was considerable complaining about him among the crowds. While some were saying, 'He is a good man,' others were saying, 'No, he is deceiving the crowd'" (7:12). The division among the disciples is projected upon the people at large.[155] Jesus' appearance

---

[153]Dodd, Interpretation, p. 353.
[154]Ibid.
[155]The affirmative response, "He is a good man" (7:12a) corresponds to Peter's confession, "You are the Holy One of God" (6:69), and the negative response, "He is leading the people

troubles the waters further. Many believe in him, but the leaders send officers to arrest him (7:31-32). On the great day of the feast Jesus speaks again (7:37-38), and a division (σχίσμα) results (7:43). Some believe in him as the Messiah, others acclaim him as the prophet, and still others reject him because of his origin (7:40-42). After Jesus' discourse in 8:12-29, many believe in him (v. 30), but these same "believers" take up stones against him in reaction to his words about his priority to Abraham (8:59). Jesus' statements about his relationship to the Father provoke a division among his hearers.[156]

The appearance of Wisdom also provokes a division among her hearers. A soteriological dualism appears in the Wisdom material. This dualism is symbolized in terms of the "two ways." J. Coert Rylaarsdam summarized this perspective: "The doctrine of the two ways, prominent in later Judaism, postulates two classes of men, each rather immutable, the way of evil and the way of righteousness (Prov. 8:20). The former leads to darkness and death (Prov. 4:19; 20:20; Job 3:4, 5, 6). . . . . The latter leads to light and life (Prov. 2:13, 18)."[157] The two ways are often symbolized in terms of light and darkness.

> But the path of the righteous is like the light of dawn,
> which shines brighter and brighter until full day.
> The way of the wicked is like deep darkness;
> they do not know what they stumble over (Prov. 4:18-19; cf. also 2:13; Wis. 5:6).

This soteriological dualism of "two ways" is well developed in the speeches of Wisdom in Proverbs 1:20-33 and 8:1-36. Her presence divides humanity into two camps, those who listen to her and those who turn away. Both speeches end with this separation:

> For waywardness kills the simple,
> and the complacency of fools destroys them;
> but those who listen to me will be secure
> and will live at ease, without dread of disaster (1:32-33).

> For whoever who finds me finds life
> and obtains favor from the Lord;

---

astray" (7:12b) corresponds to the disciples' response, "This is a hard saying; who can listen to it?" (6:60)

[156]Division also appears in 9:16, because of the blind man healed, in 10:19, because of Jesus' words about being the good shepherd, and in 11:45-46 because of the raising of Lazarus.

[157]J. Coert Rylaarsdam, "The Proverbs," in Peake's Commentary on the Bible, ed. Matthew Black and H. H. Rowley (London: Thomas Nelson & Sons, 1962), p. 446. Cf. also Fennema, "Jesus," pp. 59-62.

but those who miss me injure themselves;
all who hate me love death (8:35-36).

The picture is clear: Persons are separated into two groups based on their response to Wisdom. Those who see in her the revelation of God receive life, security, and ease; those who reject her receive injury, judgment, and death.

This soteriological dualism is sometimes concretized in terms of the contrast between Wisdom and Folly.[158] The contrast is set up most sharply in Proverbs 9, in which both Wisdom and Folly prepare their respective feasts and invite the simple to attend. Participation in Wisdom's feast results in life and insight, but a seat at Folly's table offers only death and Sheol.

The dualism is not as pronounced in other sections of the Wisdom material, for the thought there is more of Wisdom's coming to the faithful, either to the individual as a spirit (Wisdom of Solomon) or to the people of Israel as the Law (Sirach, Baruch, and the Tannaitic literature). Sirach speaks of the discipline of Wisdom, which "seems very harsh to the undisciplined" (6:20); she torments and weighs down the disciple (4:17; 6:21). Yet those who remain faithful receive joy, rest, and protection from her (4:18; 6:28-31), but those who go astray will be forsaken and handed over to ruin (4:19).

The soteriological dualism of the Wisdom material is adapted in the Gospel. Like Wisdom's appearance, Jesus' appearance results in a division between those who accept him as the revelation of God and those who reject. Acceptance leads to eternal life and fellowship with God, while rejection leads to death and separation from God.

Rejection

The majority of respondents reject Jesus. The prologue summarizes the response: "The world did not know him. . . . His own people did not accept him" (John 1:10-11). The Gospel narrative confirms this initial assessment: the way of Jesus in the world is the way of rejection, especially among his own people, the Jews. Their interaction with Jesus is characterized by mounting hostility, beginning with controversy and ending in crucifixion.

Rejection of Jesus is focused in the Jews. They do not receive Jesus (5:43). They seek to kill him (7:19; 8:37). They agree that anyone who confesses

---

[158]Cf. above, p. 13.

Jesus to be the Christ will be put out of the synagogue (9:22). They attempt to stone him for blasphemy (10:31). The chief priests and the Pharisees, a group often indistinguishable from the Jews, seek to arrest Jesus (7:32) and plot to kill him (11:47-53). The Jews and the chief priests conspire to persuade Pilate to crucify Jesus (19:5-16). The Jews are Jesus' chief antagonists in the Gospel.

The Gospel's attitude toward the Jews has been a subject of great scholarly interest.[159] The term can be used in both a neutral and a hostile sense. Urban C. von Wahlde showed that the Jews are spoken of in the neutral sense as either members of a distinct religious-political-cultural grouping or the people of Judea or Jerusalem.[160] He concluded that the hostile use almost always speaks of the Jews as the religious authorities.[161] Kysar suggested, however, a broader meaning: They are "stylized types of those who reject Christ."[162] Similarly, Culpepper saw the Jews as representatives of unbelief in the Gospel: "Through the Jews, John explores the heart and soul of unbelief."[163]

The Jews become identified with the world, which in the Gospel represents humanity in rebellion against God. The world, however, does not always have this meaning. It also appears in the neutral sense, meaning humanity in general. As such, the world is the object of God's love (3:16). Jesus was sent by the Father to save the world (3:17; 10:36; 12:47), to give life to the world (6:33, 51), to be the Savior of the world (4:42). This meaning corresponds to "the world below" (cf. 8:23). The world, however, rejects Jesus (1:10), and as the Gospel progresses the term takes on a hostile sense. Satan is the prince of this world (12:31; 14:30; 16:11), and he summons his followers to oppose Jesus and his followers (7:7; 15:18-19). Jesus, however, judges the world (9:39; 12:31) and, through his death and resurrection, overcomes the world (16:33).

In bringing the revelation of God Wisdom too is rejected. Rejection is the refrain of the Wisdom hymns. Wisdom comes to dwell in Israel, but she is rejected

---

[159]Cf. Brown, Gospel, I-XII, pp. lxx-lxxiii; Kysar, Maverick, pp. 55-58; Culpepper, Anatomy, pp. 125-132, and the bibliography listed on p. 125 n. 53.

[160]Urban C. von Wahlde, "The Johannine 'Jews': A Critical Survey," NTS, 28 (1982), 33-60.

[161]Ibid., p. 44. Two verses, 6:41, 52, however, are exceptions to this rule. He attributed them to the redactor. Cf. also Brown, Gospel, I-XII, p. lxxi.

[162]Kysar, Maverick, pp. 57-58. He maintained that when the evangelist uses the term in a different way he is dependent on traditional materials.

[163]Culpepper, Anatomy, p. 129.

and withdraws her presence. Her speech in Proverbs 1:20-33 is a pronouncement of judgment on those who have refused to listen to Wisdom. She issues the following indictment: "I have called and you refused, have stretched out my hand and no one heeded, and . . . you have ignored all my counsel and would have none of my reproof" (vv. 24-25). Switching to the third person, she continues her drumbeat of accusations: "They hated knowledge and did not choose the fear of the Lord, would have none of my counsel, and despised all my reproof" (vv. 29-30). Like Jesus, Wisdom has been utterly rejected by her hearers. Just as they did not receive Jesus and his revelation, neither did they receive Wisdom and her teaching. Furthermore, just as rejection of Jesus leads to death, so also rejection of Wisdom leads to death: "For waywardness kills the simple, and the complacency of fools destroys them" (v. 32).[164] Wisdom responds to this rejection by withdrawing from the people: "They will call upon me, but I will not answer; they will seek me diligently but will not find me" (v. 28). Likewise, Jesus hides himself when faced with the rejection of the crowds (John 8:59; 10:39; 12:36).

The rejection of Wisdom is also a prominent theme in the poem of Baruch 3:9-4:4.[165] The poet explains the reason for the Babylonian captivity: The Is-raelites have forsaken the fountain of Wisdom (3:12); they have not learned the way to her but have strayed from it (3:20-21, 31). As in Proverbs 1, their rejection of Wisdom results in death (Bar.3:28; 4:1b). Israel is addressed five times (3:9, 10, 24; 4:4). The nation as a whole has refused Wisdom. This blanket indictment is not unlike the Gospel's characterization of the Jews; they too have rejected Jesus.[166]

The withdrawal of Wisdom is portrayed most clearly in 1 Enoch 42:1-2.[167] It is not said specifically that the reason for her withdrawal is rejection, but this can be inferred. It was noted above that the ascent of Wisdom into heaven may have influenced the ascent of Jesus.[168] Jesus' ascent, however, is not a result of rejec-

---

[164]Prov. 8:32, of course, refers to physical death in contrast to the good life, while the Gospel refers to eternal death in contrast to eternal life.

[165]Cf. above, pp. 15-16.

[166]It is not said in the Gospel, however, unlike in Baruch, that Israel rejected Jesus, for Israel is a positive term in the Gospel: John baptizes so that Jesus might be revealed to Israel (John 1:31); Nathanael is a true Israelite because he comes to Jesus (John 1:47).

[167]Cf. above, p. 20.

[168]Cf. above, p. 64.

tion but part of God's predetermined plan for the salvation of humanity (cf. John 3:14; 12:32).

The revelation of God which Wisdom brings is rejected by humanity in general and Israel in particular, just as the revelation of God in Jesus is rejected by the world and by his own people, the Jews. The rejection of Wisdom was a standard element in the Wisdom story. In order to express the hostility Jesus met, the Gospel took up this element and made it part of the story of Jesus, Wisdom incarnate. The message was this: the outreaching love of God in Wisdom-Jesus is continually blunted by rejection.

Intimacy with Disciples

But to all who received him, who believed in his name, he gave power to become children of God; who were born, not of blood nor of the will of the flesh nor of the will of man, but of God (John 1:12-13).

Although the world rejects Wisdom-Word, a few see in this one the revelation of God. They form a community around Wisdom-Word in which they experience love, life, and the spirit. Such is the picture of Jesus and the disciples in the Gospel. He is depicted as forming a community around himself and imparting to that community special revelation. A similar picture is presented of Wisdom and her disciples. This section will give attention to the intimacy which each has with the disciples.

In the first half of the Gospel the way of Jesus is characterized by rejection, principally from the Jews; "his own" have rejected him. All along the way, however, Jesus draws persons to himself; he seeks a new "his own." At the outset of his ministry, Jesus takes the initiative in calling disciples. He bids Andrew and an unnamed disciple, "Come and see" (1:39), an invitation which Philip takes up in calling Nathanael (1:46). Jesus says to Philip, "Follow me" (1:43). To these disciples Jesus imparts the revelation of God. He says to them, "Very truly, I tell you, you will see heaven opened, and the angels of God ascending and descending upon the Son of Man" (1:51). This is partially fulfilled in the Cana miracle, in which Jesus manifests his glory to the disciples (2:11).[169] The disciples have an "insider's view" of the revelation which Jesus brings.

---

[169]Cf. Brown, Gospel, I-XII, p. 105; Barrett, Gospel, p. 190.

In the first half of the Gospel Jesus' intimacy with "his own" receives its most extensive treatment in the Good Shepherd discourse (10:1-18). In contrast to the thieves and robbers (the Pharisees), the good shepherd (Jesus) calls his own sheep by name and leads them out.[170] The sheep follow him, for they know his voice, but they will not follow a stranger, for they do not know his voice (vv. 3-5). Jesus says it explicitly in an "I am" saying: "I am the good shepherd. I know my own and my own know me, just as the Father knows me and I know the Father. And I lay down my life for the sheep" (vv. 14-15). The intimacy that exists between Jesus and the Father is shared with Jesus and the disciples. It is an intimacy of mutual knowledge. As Barrett pointed out, this mutual knowledge is a mutual determination, of the shepherd to his sheep in love and of the sheep to the shepherd in gratitude, faith, and obedience.[171] This intimacy is substantiated by Jesus' laying down his life (cf. also 15:13).

The second half of the Gospel begins appropriately:

> Now before the festival of the Passover, Jesus knew that his hour had come to depart from this world and go to the Father. Having loved his own who were in the world, he loved them to the end (13:1).

Jesus is now "in the circle of his own."[172] While conflict characterizes his ministry in the world, love characterizes his ministry with the disciples. Dodd observed that the key word in chapters 13-17 is $\dot{\alpha}\gamma\dot{\alpha}\pi\eta$.[173] Indeed, even his departure out of the world is an expression of love for the disciples.[174] At this point the Gospel enters a new stage. The first half of the ministry of Jesus is conducted openly, meeting opposition on every front. Chapters 13-17, however, depict Jesus in private with "his own," teaching them how to carry on after his departure. The reader is taken inside this inner circle to observe the close bond between the revealer and his disciples.

---

[170]In the following chapter Jesus calls the name of Lazarus, and he comes out of the tomb (11:43-44).

[171]Barrett, Gospel, p. 376. Cf. also Bultmann, Gospel, 280-282.

[172]Schnackenburg's title for this section, Gospel, III, 1.

[173]Dodd, Interpretation, p. 398.

[174]Brown, Gospel, XIII-XXI, p. 563, noted that the two ideas of love for the disciples and of return to the Father intertwine to form the leitmotif of the second half of the Gospel.

The farewell discourse (13:31-17:26) brings into focus the intimacy shared between Jesus and the disciples.[175] The relationship they have had all along is now clarified. The disciples have been the recipients of Jesus' revelation (cf. 2:11). To them he has revealed the Father (14:9), he has made known all that he has heard from the Father (15:15; 17:8, 14); he has revealed the Father's name (17:6, 26). Yet in the farewell discourse Jesus reveals himself completely. The veil is removed; the disciples are initiated into the divine life. Like the one whom Jesus loved, all the disciples now recline in the bosom of Jesus (13:23).

The farewell discourse contains special revelation which Jesus imparts to the disciples on the eve of his death. First, Jesus interprets for the disciples the significance of his death. It is not a death of humiliation but rather of glorification (13:31). Through it he goes to the Father to prepare a place for the disciples, so that they may be where he is (14:2-3, 28). It is a voluntary laying down of his life out of love for them, his friends (15:13). It results in joy for them (16:22; 17:13). They will experience new power in prayer, for they will receive whatever they ask in Jesus' name (14:13-14; 15:16; 16:23, 26). Jesus' death is for his own.

Furthermore, to his own Jesus promises the Spirit. He assures the disciples that if he does not go, the Spirit will not come (16:7). The Spirit is another Paraclete whom Jesus will send after his departure (14:16).[176] In this way, Jesus will come to his disciples, for the Spirit will remind the disciples of what Jesus said (14:26; 16:14) and bear witness to him (15:26). Through the Spirit, Jesus equips the disciples for the coming conflict with the world (15:18-16:14). The Spirit will be of aid because he will convict the world of sin, righteousness, and judgment (16:8-11).

---

[175]The literature on the farewell discourse is vast. Cf. Brown, Gospel, XIII-XXI, pp. 581-604, esp. the bibliography on pp. 603-604, and now Fernando F. Segovia, The Farewell of the Word: The Johannine Call to Abide (Minneapolis: Fortress Press, 1991). The farewell discourse will here be treated as unit with the recognition that a number of discourses have probably been combined.

[176]Much has been written on the Paraclete sayings. Cf. Brown, Gospel, XIII-XXI, pp. 1135-1144, esp. the bibliography on pp. 1143-1144; Schnackenburg, Gospel, III, 138-154; and now Burge, Anointed, esp. pp. 4-41, 139-143, 203-221. For a good brief treatment of the Paraclete, along with a discussion of the implications for Christology, cf. Robin Scroggs, Christology in Paul and John, Proclamation Commentaries, ed. Gerhard Krodel (Philadelphia: Fortress Press, 1988), pp. 85-91.

Jesus also gives to the disciples the commandment to love one another (13:34-35; 15:12, 17). It is the rule which will guide the community after Jesus' departure. Jesus himself has provided both the source and the standard of love: Even as (καθώς) I have loved you, love one another" (13:34b). As Bultmann observed, καθώς does not describe the degree or intensity of the disciples' love for one another but its basis. Jesus' love finds it fulfillment in the disciples' love for one another.[177] Following the commandment to love authenticates that they are Jesus' disciples (13:35) and friends (15:14).

In their relationship to one another, the disciples are to love; in their relationship to Jesus, they are to abide. This message is vividly pressed home in the allegory of the vine (15:1-11). Abiding in Jesus does not mean a oneness of essence achieved through mystical experience but a oneness of will achieved through obedience to Jesus' commandment to love (v. 10). The disciples abide in Jesus, and Jesus abides in the disciples through their loving one another.

Abiding in Jesus results in bearing fruit (vv. 4-5; cf. v. 16), thus glorifying the Father and proving to be disciples (v. 8). Love and abiding authenticates one's discipleship. Abiding also results in having done whatever one asks (v. 7). Abiding in Jesus is akin to asking in his name (14:13-14; 15:16; 16:23, 26). Again, Jesus presents as the model his love for his disciples, which is grounded in the Father's love for him (vv. 9-10). Love flows from the Father to Jesus to the disciples. The Father loves Jesus; Jesus loves the disciples; the disciples are to respond to this love by loving one another.

Loving one another and abiding in Jesus results in unity in the community and in the Father and the Son.[178] It is for this unity which Jesus prays in chapter 17. This prayer is often called "the High Priestly Prayer,"[179] but it is only a

---

[177]Bultmann, Gospel, p. 525. Cf. also Brown, Gospel. XIII-XXI, p. 612, who contended that Jesus is primarily the source of the disciples' love for one another and only secondarily the standard.

[178]Cf. Brown, Gospel. XIII-XXI, p. 776: "The Johannine statements about unity imply both a horizontal and a vertical dimension. The unity involves the relation of the believers to the Father and the Son (vertical) and the relation of the believers among themselves (horizontal)."

[179]Bultmann, Gospel, p. 489 n. 6, and Brown, Gospel. XIII-XXI, p. 747, traced this designation back to the Lutheran theologian David Chytraus (1531-1600), though Barrett, Gospel, p. 500, noted that was hinted at by Cyril of Alexandria.

priestly prayer in the sense that it is an intercessory prayer.[180] As the Son of the Father, Jesus prays for his own. He prays "that they may be one, as we are one" (17:11, 22, cf. also v. 21). Again, Jesus' relationship to the Father provides the model for the disciples' relationship to one another. Appold wrote, "Ecclesiological oneness in John is a relational quality which receives its intrinsic meaning from the believer's inclusion into the presence of Christ."[181] He continued that the oneness of love between the disciples is a projection of the oneness of love between the Father and the Son.[182] Käsemann observed that the Gospel's ecclesiology is unfolded with its Christology as its point of orientation and departure.[183]

The new place to which Jesus brings the disciples in the farewell discourse is illustrated in the new name he calls them. He calls them servants no longer but friends, because he has revealed to them all that he has heard from the Father (15:15). Yet friendship with Jesus is a task as well as a gift: "You are my friends if you do what I command you" (15:14). Friendship with Jesus is not a status automatically conferred but a response to the revelation of God in Jesus by living out his commandment to love (15:12, 17). Jesus also calls them "little children" (13:33) as he does at the Sea of Galilee during his third resurrection appearance (21:5).[184] Yet there is another level at which Jesus relates to the disciples. At the appearance to Mary Magdalene at the empty tomb, Jesus says, "Go to my brothers and say to them, 'I am ascending to my Father and your Father, to my God and your God'" (20:17). Jesus calls the disciples his brothers and God their Father. In his going to the Father, Jesus opens up his exclusive relationship with the Father to all believers. With Jesus as elder brother, the disciples are taken up into the family of God.

---

[180]Cf. S. Agourides, "The 'High Priestly Prayer' of Jesus," SE (Berlin: Akademie-Verlag, 1968), ed. F. L. Cross, IV, 137-145, who contended that it was a prayer of consolation and admonition, rather than a prayer of consecration, mystagogical instruction, or eucharistic catechism. Cf. also Brown, Gospel, XIII-XXI, p. 747, who compared this perspective to that of the book of Hebrews and Rom. 8:34.

[181]Appold, Oneness, p. 286.

[182]Ibid., p. 40.

[183]Käsemann, Testament, p. 58. It is no surprise that Käsemann supervised Appold's doctoral dissertation Oneness.

[184]The nouns, however, are different: τεκνία in 13:33 and παιδία in 21:5. The author of 1 John addresses his readers as "little children" (τεκνία, 2:1, 12, 28; 3:7, 18; 4:4; 5:21).

In summary, Jesus gathers around himself a community of disciples who exist in an intimate relationship with him. To this community he imparts special revelation. This revelation includes the interpretation of Jesus' death as a going to the Father, the commandment to love, which is related to abiding in Jesus and being one with the community, and the promise of the Paraclete. The intimacy of the disciples have with one another and with Jesus is an intimacy both modeled and stimulated by the intimacy Jesus has with the Father. Johannine ecclesiology is contained within its Christology.

Wisdom too gathers around herself a community. She has her disciples, her children, her school. A number of scholars have noted the similarities between the disciples of Jesus and the disciples of Wisdom.[185] Although Wisdom is responsible for the creation of all humanity (Wis. 9:2a) and has a possession in every people (Sir. 24:6), she stands in a special relationship to the people of Israel. God has given her a dwelling place there (Sir. 24:8-12); she was responsible for the saving acts in Israel's history (Wis. 10:1-11:1). Wisdom, however, has been rejected by Israel (Bar. 3:9-4:4), but she has found that "faithful remnant." Wisdom's disciples are portrayed in different ways, all of which resemble the Gospel's portrait of the disciples.

Proverbs 9:1-6 presents a community gathered around the table, and Wisdom calls the simple to come to her feast. In the same way, the twelve declare their loyalty to Jesus after the Bread of Life discourse (John 6:67-69), and the farewell discourse, in which Jesus reveals himself completely to the disciples, begins at the table (13:4, 21-30). Wisdom of Solomon conceives of Wisdom coming as a spirit creating intimate communion with her disciples: "In every generation she passes into holy souls and makes them friends of God and prophets; for God loves nothing so much as the person who lives with Wisdom" (7:27b-28). Similarly, Jesus will come back to the disciples through the Paraclete (John 14:3, 16-18). After his departure out of the world, the Spirit mediates the presence of Jesus to the disciples. Sirach, however, formalizes this relationship in terms of a school in which the student takes a discipline: "Draw near to me, you who are uneducated, and lodge in the house of instruction" (51:23). The community of Jesus' disciples

---

[185]Cf. Dillon, "Wisdom," p. 277; Feuillet, "Biblical Themes," pp. 89-91; Braun, "S. Jean," pp. 125-128.

resembles a school, for it consists of disciples, children, and friends who keep Jesus' commandments and his word.[186] The relationship between Wisdom and her disciples, both as spirit and as school, has helped shape the Gospel's picture of the relationship between Jesus and his disciples.

In the context of this intimate relationship with those who attach themselves to her, Wisdom makes her revelation known: "She hastens to make herself known to those who desire her . . . and she graciously appears to them in their paths, and meets them in every thought" (Wis. 6:13, 16). She gave to Solomon "unerring knowledge of what exists" (Wis. 7:17-22; cf. also 8:8), as well as good counsel and right judgment (8:9-15). To those who submit to Wisdom's discipline, Wisdom "will reveal her secrets" (Sir. 4:18). She will become known to those who search and seek (Sir. 6:27a); those who reflect on her ways will ponder her secrets (Sir. 6:21); they will be fed with the bread of understanding and the water of wisdom (Sir. 15:3). Wisdom reveals herself to her disciples, whether as the Law in a school or as the Spirit in the mind, just as Jesus reveals himself to his disciples. He manifests himself to those who love him (John 14:21).

The community of Wisdom, like the community of Jesus, is a community of love. Just as love is the key word in John 13-17, so also is love the key word in Wisdom's relationship with her disciples. Numerous references to Wisdom's love for the disciples and the disciples' love for Wisdom appear. Love for Wisdom is defined as seeking her diligently (Prov. 8:17; Sir. 4:12; Wis. 6:12), not forsaking her (Prov. 4:6), and keeping her laws (Wis. 6:17-18). The keeping of the commandments is often equated with the possession of Wisdom (Sir. 1:26; 15:1; 19:20). In the same way, Jesus says, "If you love me, you will keep my commandments" (John 14:15; cf. also 14:21; 15:10). Love, then, in both the Wisdom material and the Gospel is obedience to the commandments.[187] Love of Wisdom results in wealth (Prov. 8:21), immortality (Wis. 6:19), and the revelation of Wis-

---

[186]The hypothesis that the Gospel emerged out of a school has received thorough treatment by R. Alan Culpepper, The Johannine School: An Evaluation of the Johannine-School Hypothesis Based on an Investigation of the Nature of Ancient Schools, SBLDS 26 (Missoula: Mont.: Scholars Press, 1975), pp. 261-290. Cf. below, pp. 135. In keeping with the suggestion of J. Louis Martyn, History and Theology in the Fourth Gospel, rev. ed. (Nashville: Abingdon Press, 1979), pp. 9-10, that the Gospel is written on two levels, the school gathered around the beloved disciple is projected back into the ministry of Jesus as the school gathered around Jesus.

[187]Cf. Forestell, Word, p. 49, who noted that fidelity to the commandments of Jesus is comparable to fidelity to Wisdom.

112

dom (Wis. 6:12). Most of all, she loves those who love her (Prov. 8:17), and God loves those who love her (Sir. 4:14; cf. also Wis. 7:28). Similarly, love of Jesus results in being loved by Jesus and the Father, and it results in special revelation (John 14:21; cf. also 14:23; 16:27; 17:23).

Just as Jesus' disciples are to abide in him (John 15:1-11), so disciples of Wisdom also abide with her. While the Gospel uses the image of the vine to express this idea, the Wisdom material uses a variety of images, such as camping, farming, school, and courtship. In Sirach 14:24-27 the disciple is pictured as a camper, and the author uses a number of metaphors to express the adherence to Wisdom: encamping, fastening a tent peg (v. 24), pitching his tent, lodging (v. 25), camping (v. 26), and sheltering (v. 26). The writer also uses the image of farming, calling the would-be disciple to plow and sow (Sir. 6:19) and take on her yoke (6:24-25; 51:26). He also employs the image of the school in which the untaught lodge (51:23). Wisdom of Solomon uses the image of courtship to express the king's desire for Wisdom: he wanted her to take her as bride to live with him (Wis. 8:2, 9); he called upon God to send her so that she might be with him (9:10). This picture is not unlike that in which Jesus says that he and the Father, presumably through the Spirit, will come and make their home with the one who loves Jesus (John 14:23). The concept of abiding is common to both the Gospel and the wisdom literature, though different images are used.

Abiding, however, is not to be taken lightly. The Gospel makes this point in the allegory of the vine. The Father takes away the fruitless branches and prunes the fruitful; so the disciples have been cleansed by Jesus' word (15:23; cf. 13:10). In much the same way, Wisdom tests her disciples:

For at first she will walk with them on tortuous paths,
she will bring fear and dread upon them,
and will torment them by her discipline
until she trusts them,
and she will test them with her ordinances (Sir. 4:17; cf. 6:20-21, 24-25).

Once the disciple has passed the test, however, Wisdom brings revelation and peace (4:18; 6:28-31).[188]

Jesus promises continued communion with the disciples through the Spirit. Wisdom of Solomon conceives of Wisdom as a spirit (Wis. 1:6; 7:22) who enters

---

[188]Cf. Dillon, "Wisdom," p. 277.

into the souls of her disciples (7:27). Wisdom-Jesus has fellowship with followers through the Spirit.

Jesus models the disciples' relationship to him with his relationship to the Father. As shown above, the Wisdom material does not develop extensively the relationship between God and Wisdom.[189] The intimacy she enjoys with God, therefore, is not held up as a pattern for the intimacy the disciple is to have with Wisdom. The few statements, however, about Wisdom's relationship to God parallel the disciple's relationship with Wisdom. In Wisdom of Solomon the king determines that Wisdom will live with him; she also lives with God (Wis. 8:3, 9). The king loves her; God also loves her (8:2,3). He prays that Wisdom may be with him; she is with God (9:9, 10). Solomon, as a disciple of Wisdom, relates to Wisdom in the same way that she relates to God.

It has been shown that the disciples' relationship to Jesus in the Gospel closely resembles the disciples' relationship to Wisdom in the Wisdom material. Wisdom-Jesus creates a community of believers; in the context of that community, special revelation is imparted in that the believers are commanded to love and to abide; and the relationship of the community to Wisdom-Jesus parallels the relationship of Wisdom-Jesus to God. The evangelist, then, in order to develop further the intimacy of Jesus and the disciples turned to the Wisdom material for inspiration. Jesus is then depicted, not as a mortal teacher gathering around himself a circle of pupils, but as the eternal Wisdom-Word who has intimate fellowship with God and initiates his own into the divine fullness. The Gospel's high ecclesiology, like its Christology, is due not to gnostic influence, as Bultmann had it,[190] but to wisdom influence. In Jesus the disciples experience the Wisdom of God.

Glory and Life

What has come into being in him was life. . . . We have seen his glory, glory as of a father's only son (John 1:3b-4a, 14).

In the presence of Jesus the disciples experience glory and life. This note is first trumpeted in the prologue, and it is sounded throughout the narrative. Jesus glorifies the Father through his signs and ultimately through the hour of his depar-

---

[189]Cf. above, pp. 74, 79.
[190]Cf. Bultmann, Theology, II, 91: "The Johannine terminology pertaining to the Church comes . . . from the area of Gnostic thought." Cf. also Käsemann, Testament, p. 50, who spoke about the "gnosticizing understanding of the Johannine community."

ture from the world; his appearance and his departure bring life for his disciples. Both glory and life are themes which run throughout the Wisdom material. Wisdom too brings glory and life for her followers. This final section will survey the use of these two themes in the Gospel and in the Wisdom material. It will show that the Gospel depended on wisdom for both glory and life.

Glory

The Word-become-flesh possessed glory, "glory as the only Son from the Father" (1:14 RSV). This glory which he has received from the Father he manifests to the disciples (2:11; 17:22) through his signs and ultimately through his death and resurrection. Glory, like love, flows from the Father to the Son to the disciples. Furthermore, it has a soteriological significance, for it results in the disciples participating in Jesus' glory. "I have been glorified in them," Jesus says concerning the disciples (17:10).

As the revelation of God, Wisdom too possesses glory; she is "a pure emanation of the glory of the Almighty" (Wis. 7:25). She too imparts this glory to the disciples. Just as Jesus is glorified in his disciples (John 17:10), Wisdom's disciples obtain glory (Sir. 4:12; cf. also 1:19). Just as Jesus has guarded his disciples, Wisdom guards her disciples with her glory (Wis. 9:11). Wisdom's disciples too participate in her glory.

Jesus' glory is manifested in his signs and in the hour of his death and resurrection. This section will explore these manifestations of glory and show the wisdom influence on each.

Signs. Dodd appropriately entitled the first half of the Gospel "the Book of Signs," for it is dominated by the narrative of Jesus' miracles.[191] These miracles, fewer in number than in the synoptics, also function differently; they are signs which manifest Jesus' glory and lead to faith (John 2:11). Signs, glory, and faith are intertwined. Karl Rengstorf keenly observed, "With the σημεῖον faith arises if the δόξα which shines therein is 'seen,' 1:14."[192] The signs, then, have a

---

[191]Dodd, Interpretation, p. 289; taken over by Brown, Gospel. I-XII, pp. cxxxviii-cxxxix.

[192]Karl Rengstorf, "σημεῖον," TDNT, ed. G. Friedrich and trans. G. W. Bromiley (Grand Rapids: Wm. B. Eerdmans, 1971), VII, 253.

christological and soteriological significance; they point to Jesus as the revealer of God and call for faith in him.[193]

Jesus did many signs that are not recorded in the Gospel (20:30). Indeed, several references are made to signs not described (2:23; 3:2; 6:2 12:37). A number, however, are described in detail. They include the Cana miracle (2:1-11; cf. v. 11: "the first of his signs"), the healing of the official's son (4:46-52; cf. v. 54: "the second sign"), the feeding of the multitude (6:1-14; cf. v. 14), and the raising of Lazarus (11:1-44; cf. 12:18). Also to be included are the healing of the lame man at the pool of Bethzatha (5:1-9) and the healing of a man born blind (9:1-7).[194] The Book of Signs narrates six signs which testify to who Jesus is.

In what sense should the hour of Jesus' death and resurrection be termed a sign? It is not specifically called a sign, but that fact is not decisive.[195] The purpose of the signs is to awaken faith in Jesus as the revealer of God. In two sayings Jesus describes the significance of the hour to the crowds: "When you have lifted up the Son of Man, then you will realize that I am he" (8:28); "I, when I am lifted up from the earth, will draw all people to myself" (12:32). Similarly, when Jesus explains the significance of his death to the disciples, they say, "By this we believe that you came from God" (16:30). The hour of Jesus' departure from the world evokes faith. Furthermore, a number of signs are accompanied by discourses which interpret them.[196] The hour too is accompanied by interpretative material, the farewell discourse, which explains the significance of Jesus' departure for the disciples. As in the first half of the Gospel, narrative and discourse are woven together to proclaim the identity of Jesus.[197]

---

[193]The signs in the Gospel have been another subject of extensive investigation. Cf. Brown, Gospel, I-XII, pp. 525-532; Schnackenburg, Gospel, I, 515-528; Kysar, Maverick, pp. 67-73; Barrett, Gospel, pp. 75-78; Rengstorf, "σημεῖον," pp. 242-257. More recently, cf. Marilyn Meye Thompson, The Humanity of Jesus in the Fourth Gospel (Philadelphia: Fortress Press, 1988), pp. 53-86, where she discusses "Signs, Seeing, and Faith."

[194]It is doubtful that the walking on the water (6:16-21) should be included in this list, for it is linked closely with the feeding miracle; cf. Smalley, Evangelist, pp. 86-87; contra Kysar, Maverick, p. 68.

[195]The healings of the lame man at the pool of Bethzatha (5:1-9) and of the man born blind (9:1-7) are not called signs.

[196]Dodd, Interpretation, p. 290, divided the Book of Signs into seven episodes, "each consisting of one or more narratives of significant acts of Jesus, accompanied by one or more discourses designed to bring out the significance of the narratives." Brown, Gospel, I-XII, p. cxlii, however, noted weaknesses in this scheme.

[197]Cf. Dodd, Interpretation, pp. 270-291; Brown, Gospel, I-XII, p. 581.

The hour of Jesus' death and resurrection, then, is the Gospel's seventh sign.[198] It, however, surpasses the previous six. Indeed, it is the sign to which the others pointed. Brown wrote, "Jesus' death and resurrection break out of the category of sign into the realm of glory; now he makes present and available to men the heavenly realities signified in the miracles of the ministry."[199] The events of the hour comprise Jesus' greatest sign in which he manifested his glory to his disciples.[200]

Wisdom is associated with signs in Wisdom of Solomon 10:15-16:

> A holy people and blameless race
> Wisdom delivered from a nation of oppressors.
> She entered the soul of a servant of the Lord,
> and withstood dread kings with wonders and signs (ἐν τέρασι καὶ σημείοις).

The larger pericope (10:15-21), though connected with chapter 10 as the last historical illustration of the power of Wisdom, also introduces chapters 11-19. These chapters narrate the "wonders and signs" with which Wisdom through Moses withstood the dread kings of Egypt. The Exodus story is retold so that the ten plagues of Exodus 7:8-11:10 become six signs, each consisting of a plague on the Egyptians balanced by a benefit for the Israelites.[201] These six signs lead up to the seventh sign, the drowning of the Egyptians and the crossing of the Israelites at the Red Sea (Wis. 19:1-21), a sign which sums up and surpasses the other six signs. Wisdom of Solomon 11-19 might be known as Wisdom's "Book of Signs."

Georg Ziener and Douglas Clark have both argued that the Gospel narrative of Jesus' signs is patterned upon the narrative of Wisdom's signs in Wisdom of Solomon 11-19.[202] Both demonstrated how the signs in the Gospel correspond to

---

[198] Stephen S. Smalley, "The Sign of John XXI," NTS, 20 (1973-74), 275-288, argued that the miraculous catch of fish (21:1-14) is the seventh sign. Cf. also his Evangelist, pp. 87-88. It functions, however, like the walking on the water, as a subsidiary sign, for it is linked closely to the death and resurrection.

[199] Brown, Gospel, I-XII, p. 581.

[200] Contra Barrett, Gospel, p. 78, who argued that the death and resurrection is not a sign because "it is not merely a token of something other than itself; this event is the thing which it signifies." Yet all the signs participate in the revelation to which they point; the death and resurrection do so more fully, however.

[201] Cf. Maurice Gilbert, La Critique des dieux, AnBib 53 (Rome: Biblical Institute Press, 1973), pp. xvii-xix.

[202] Georg Ziener, "Weisheitsbuch und Johannesevangelium," Bib, 38 (1957), 396-417; Douglas K. Clark, "Signs in Wisdom and John," CBQ, 45 (1983), 201-209. Although the two reached similar conclusions, it is curious that Clark made no reference whatsoever to Ziener.

the signs in the Wisdom of Solomon. Each, however, pursued this matter differently. Ziener grouped them into four categories: the appeasing of hunger, quenching of thirst, illumination of the darkness, and raising of the dead. In each of these four categories, he detected a movement common to both books: miracle, transition from the natural to the spiritual plane, and christological interpretation.[203]

Clark, however, took a bit different tack. He sought a one-to-one correspondence between the signs in the two books. Furthermore, he went beyond Ziener in that he classed Jesus' death and resurrection as the final and greatest sign and demonstrated its correspondence to Wisdom's final and greatest sign, the drowning of the Egyptians and the deliverance of the Israelites at the Red Sea. In both the Wisdom of Solomon and the Gospel the seventh sign sums up and surpasses the other six. Clark's list, then, might be placed in the following form:[204]

Wisdom of Solomon	Gospel
1. Changing of water into blood, giving water from the rock (11:5-14)	1. Changing of water into wine (2:1-11)
2. Sending frogs and quail (11:15; 16:1-4)	2. Healing of official's son (4:46-52)
3. Plague of locusts, setting up bronze serpent (16:5-14)	3. Healing of lame man (5:1-17)
4. Sending of hail and manna (16:5-29)	4. Multiplication of loaves, walking on water (6:1-66)
5. Darkness and light (17:1-18:4)	5. Healing of man born blind (9:1-41)
6. Death of the firstborn, prayer of Aaron (18:5-25)	6. Raising of Lazarus (11:1-44)
7. Drowning and crossing at Red Sea (19:1-9)	7. Death and resurrection (chaps. 18-20)

[203]Ziener, "Weisheitsbuch," pp. 403-415.
[204]Clark, "Signs," pp. 205-208.

118

Although elements in these two arguments seem a bit strained,[205] Ziener and Clark may be said to have proved their point: the Gospel narrative of Jesus' signs is informed by the narrative of Wisdom's signs in Wisdom of Solomon 11-19. In order to tell the story of Jesus as Wisdom Incarnate, the evangelist took up six miracle stories (seven if the death and resurrection is included) from the tradition of Jesus' miracles and shaped them according to the pattern of Wisdom of Solomon 11-19.[206] Thus, they were called signs, from Wisdom of Solomon 10:16. They became, then, not miracles performed by a wonder-worker, but signs performed by the Wisdom of God become flesh, akin to those performed at the Exodus. The Wisdom Christology of the Gospel, then, is joined to the Exodus motif.[207] The signs become acts of liberation, similar to those which effected the liberation of the Israelites from Egypt.[208] Furthermore, glory is a theme linked both with the Exodus[209] and with Wisdom, though not associated in either case with the signs. Under both wisdom and Exodus influence, the Gospel connects glory with the signs. The glory of God, that is, the revelation of God brought to earth by Wisdom-Jesus, is concentrated in these seven events. Through them Jesus manifests his glory, glory as of the only Son from the Father, glory as of Wisdom come from God.

The Hour. The scandal of Christianity has always been the cross (cf. 1 Cor. 1:23). How did the Son of God, the Word become flesh, Wisdom among us,

---

[205]For example, in Clark's scheme, the connections between signs 2 and 3 to their respective counterparts are not obvious, as he admitted. Cf. "Signs," pp. 206-207.

[206]If one assumes a signs source, proposed by Bultmann, Gospel, pp. 6-7, and currently argued by Robert T. Fortna, The Gospel of Signs: A Reconsideration of the Narrative Source Underlying the Fourth Gospel, SNTSMS 11 (Cambridge: Cambridge University Press, 1970), and The Fourth Gospel and Its Predecessor: From Narrative Source to Present Gospel (Philadelphia: Fortress Press, 1988); ; W. Nicol, The Semeia in the Fourth Gospel, NovTSup XXII (Leiden: E. J. Brill, 1972); Urban von Wahdle, The Earliest Version of John's Gospel: Recovering the Gospel of Signs (Wilmington, DE: Michael Glazier, 1989), then it could be said that the wisdom influence occurred at the pre-Johannine level. It is interesting to note that Fortna's suggested signs source includes a passion. Cf. also his "Christology in the Fourth Gospel: Redaction-Critical Perspectives," NTS, 21 (1974-75), 489-504.

[207]This happens to a certain extent in the prologue, where wisdom influence is evident throughout, esp. in the first two stanzas, vv. 1-5 and 6-13; influence from Exodus is evident in the third stanza, vv. 14-19. Cf. above, pp. 40-41.

[208]Rengstorf, "σημεῖον," p. 256, argued that the signs in the Gospel are theologically of fundamentally the same kind as the classical σημεῖα of the OT, the signs in Egypt in the time of Moses." He, however, failed to link them with Wisdom's signs in Wis. 11-19.

[209]For example, in the wilderness wanderings God manifested glory through the miracle of the manna (Exod. 16:7-10), through the cloud (Exod. 16:10), and through the fire (Exod. 24:17).

submit to death on a cross? The majority of the New Testament writers depict the cross as the supreme humiliation, which God reversed at the resurrection. The speeches in Acts testify that people killed Jesus but God raised him up (Acts 2:23-24; 10:39; 13:28-30). The christological hymn in Philippians says that Jesus humbled himself in death but God highly exalted him (Phil. 2:8-11). The synoptic Gospels share much the same perspective (cf. Matt. 27:46; Mark 15:34).

Yet the picture is completely different in the Gospel. The cross and resurrection, rather than split into humiliation and vindication, are joined in the hour, and this hour is the hour of Jesus' glorification. It is the seventh and greatest sign which sums up the other signs as the ultimate manifestation of his glory. Jesus' death and resurrection is the hour in which the Son of man is glorified (John 12:28; 13:31-32); the Father will glorify his name in it (12:28). In it Jesus is lifted up from the earth (3:14; 8:28; 12:32, 34), he gives eternal life to believers (3:14), he draws all people to himself (12:32), and all will know that Jesus is "I am" (8:28). The cross is not humiliation and defeat but victory and glory.

This unique view of the cross has transfigured the Gospel's passion account. Indeed, the same events are narrated as in the synoptics: arrest, trial, death, burial, and resurrection, but these events are looked upon through different lenses in the Gospel. The passion account is not "a mere postscript," as Käsemann had it,[210] but an integral part of the narrative which describes how Jesus returned to the Father and brought glory to the disciples.[211]

The Johannine passion narrative heightens two themes present in the synoptic passion tradition: first, Jesus is king, and second, he is in control of the events of the passion. The kingship theme has been given careful attention elsewhere, and it can only be summarized here.[212] The theme is adumbrated in earlier sections of the Gospel (cf. 1:49; 6:15; 12:13, 15), but in the passion account it surges to the fore. The trial before Pilate is organized around the question, Is Jesus

---

[210]Käsemann, Testament, p. 7.

[211]Cf. Loader, Christology, pp. 102-107, where he discusses Jesus' death as the completion of his task of revelation and judgment. Cf. also Thompson, Humanity, pp. 87-115, where she directly challenges Käsemann's perspective on the Johannine passion.

[212]Cf. Wayne A. Meeks, Prophet-King: Moses Traditions and Johannine Christology, NovTSup XIV (Leiden: E. J. Brill, 1967), pp. 63-99; de Jonge, "Jesus as Prophet and King in the Fourth Gospel," in Jesus, pp. 49-76.

the King of the Jews? (18:33).[213] This title is appropriate only in a nuanced sense: Jesus' kingship is not from the world, and his task is not to rule as king but to bear witness to the truth (18:36-37). Nevertheless, Pilate still refers to Jesus as the king of the Jews, as do the soldiers (18:38; 19:3, 14). Indeed, a crown and robe are placed on him (19:2). The Jews, however, refuse him this royal title, choosing Barabbas the robber instead of Jesus the king (18:39-40) and persisting that their king is Caesar (19:15). Pilate, however, places the title on the cross, over the protests of the chief priests (19:19-22), making Jesus' crucifixion his enthronement.[214] He is given a royal burial, complete with a huge amount of spices and a new tomb (19:39, 41).[215] The theme of kingship in the Gospel parallels that of glory. Glory is evident in Jesus' ministry, but it is fully manifest only in the hour. Likewise, Jesus is king throughout his ministry, but he is truly so, paradoxically, only in crucifixion. Jesus' only crown is of thorns and only throne is a cross.

As king, Jesus is in control of events surrounding him; he directs his destiny even in death and resurrection (cf. 10:17-18).[216] In the hour of the passion Jesus is the calm center in the chaos around him. He sends Judas out to betray him (13:26-30). In the garden Jesus boldly declares that he is the one they are looking for, saying, "I am," and at that the soldiers fall to the ground (18:5, 6). He then negotiates the release of the disciples (18:8-9). Jesus turns his trial before Pilate so that Pilate himself is on trial (18:28-19:16). On the cross he makes arrangements for his mother (19:26-27). He calls for drink in order to fulfill the scripture (19:28-29). His last words are not a cry of dereliction but a triumphant "It is finished" (19:30). Brown summed up the Gospel's perspective: "The passion is not an inevitable fate that overtakes Jesus; he is master of his own fate."[217]

Jesus, then, strides like a colossus through the passion narrative, exercising control and being acclaimed as king. The picture of Jesus in the passion is not unlike the picture throughout the Gospel, for he is always in control and he is recog-

---

[213]Cf. Josef Blank, "Die Verhandlung vor Pilatus: Joh 18,28-29,16 im Lichte johanneischer Theologie," BZ, 3 (1959), 60-81; Ignace de la Potterie, "Jesus King and Judge According to John 19:13," Scr, 13 (1961), 97-111.

[214]Brown, Gospel. XIII-XXI, pp. 912, 919.

[215]Ibid., p. 960.

[216]Cf. Benjamin W. Bacon, The Gospel of the Hellenists, ed. Carl H. Kraeling (New York: Henry Holt and Co., 1933): "Jesus completely dominates the course of events. . . . Clearly a superhuman being, his words and actions are all directed from heaven."

[217]Brown, Gospel. XIII-XXI, p. 818.

nized as king. One would expect, therefore, the same influences on the passion narrative as on the rest of the Gospel. It has been argued in this chapter that the Wisdom material has helped shape the Gospel's rendering of Jesus. This same wisdom has also shaped the Gospel's rendering of Jesus on the cross.

James M. Robinson maintained that wisdom influence explains the absence of a passion narrative in Q. Instead of the death of Jesus, Q speaks of the withdrawal of Jesus, modeled on the withdrawal of Wisdom (cf. Luke 13:35; Matt. 23:38-39; Luke 11:49-50; 13:34; Matt. 23:34-37).[218] In the Gospel, however, the passion narrative is not deleted but transformed. The helpless victim becomes the powerful victor, not only in resurrection but also in crucifixion. The all-powerful Wisdom of God come in the flesh exercises power even in death, so that the cross becomes the ladder to return to the Father. The death and resurrection are joined in the hour of glory. The passion, then, under wisdom influence, is not neglected but rather it is shaped to the theological purposes of the Gospel.

The two prominent themes in the Gospel's passion narrative, kingship and control, are also present in the Wisdom material. Wisdom is associated with the king. She is that which enables the king to govern justly. She says, "By me kings reign, and rulers decree what is just; by me princes rule, and nobles govern the earth" (Prov. 8:15-16). In Wisdom of Solomon 7-9 King Solomon prays for Wisdom. She will enable him to speak with judgment (7:15); she will give self-control and prudence, justice and courage, and good counsel (8:7, 9). Wisdom will guide him in his actions and guard him with her glory (9:11). "Then my works will be acceptable, and I shall judge your people justly, and shall be worthy of the throne of my father" (9:12). The wisdom tradition, then, attributes to the king a high degree of Wisdom which empowered him to reign. The king was full of Wisdom.

This Wisdom is also omnipotent. She is all-powerful and oversees all (two of the 21 attributes of Wisdom listed in Wis. 7:22a-23); she pervades and penetrates all things (7:24); she can do all things and effects all things (7:27; 8:5); evil cannot prevail against her (7:30); she orders all things well (8:1). It is this Wisdom which the Gospel employs in the passion narrative. It possibly came to mind through the question of Pilate, "Are you the king of the Jews?" and the inscription on the cross,

---

[218]James M. Robinson, "Jesus as Sophos and Sophia: Wisdom Tradition and the Gospels," in AWJEC, ed. Robert L. Wilken (Notre Dame: University of Notre Dame Press, 1975), pp. 12-14.

"the King of the Jews," two elements deeply embedded in the passion tradition. Royal Wisdom, as expressed in Wisdom of Solomon 7-9, was ready to hand because of the use the Gospel makes of the Wisdom material in the rest of the narrative. Because of its influence kingship is elaborated and omnipotence is developed. Just as the king governed because he was full of Wisdom, so Jesus as Wisdom incarnate becomes king and exercises complete control in his death and resurrection. The passion narrative brings together these three elements, the cross, Wisdom, and kingship, and this new constellation redefines each. The cross, a symbol of defeat and humiliation, is reinterpreted as a symbol of victory and glorification. Kingship is reinterpreted as something which comes from above and is not of this world. Finally, Wisdom is reinterpreted as an historical person who lived, died, and rose again. It is only at the cross that we know who he is.

Life

The Gospel begins and ends in much the same way: "What has come into being in him was life, and the life was the light of all people" (John 1:3b-4). "These [signs] are written that you may come to believe that Jesus is the Messiah, the Son of God, and that through believing you may have life in his name" (20:31). From the beginning, the Word grants life to those who believe in him. Indeed, this is the purpose of Jesus' coming into the world: "I came that they may have life, and have it abundantly" (10:10). In enacting the Father's will, Jesus gives life to those whom he will (5:21, 24, 26). He is the life (11:25; 14:6). The Gospel presents a soteriological Christology, a Christ for us. As the evangelist tells the Gospel story, Jesus continues to give life to those who have faith (20:31).

Life, ζωή, often appears with the adjective, αἰώνιον (e. g. 3:16, 36; 5:24; 6:40, 47), thus indicating that it is not physical life[219] but eternal life, life infinitely long in duration and infinitely deep in quality. Eternal life is life lived in another dimension. Through faith, the believer partakes of the life of God.[220] This life is present now for the believer. The Gospel, therefore, evidences a realized eschatology.

---

[219]Brown, Gospel, I-XII, p. 506, noted that ψυχή is used for physical life (13:37; 15:13).

[220]Cf. André Feuillet, "Participation in the Life of God According to the Fourth Gospel," in Johannine Studies, pp. 169-180.

Because of its centrality in the Gospel, the theme of life is closely related to two other principal themes, faith and revelation. The Gospel sets up the following sequence: Jesus comes as the revelation of God, a person responds in faith, and Jesus grants life to that person. Revelation is the presupposition of life. Jesus says, "I am the way, and the truth, and the life. No one comes to the Father except through me" (14:6). As the revealer of the Father, Jesus is life. He makes the Father known in order that persons might relate to the Father, and this relationship is eternal life. In order to receive this life one must have faith in Jesus as the revelation of God. Faith is the necessary precondition for eternal life. Over and over, the Gospel repeats the formula that whoever believes in Jesus has eternal life (3:15-16, 36; 6:40, 47; 11:25). Faith is the door by which one enters into eternal life.

Because of the close connection between life and revelation, life is symbolized by many of the images of revelation. Jesus offers the Samaritan woman living water (4:10-14). The revelation which Jesus brings is dynamic, constantly renewing itself like a spring (4:14). Jesus also offers the bread of life, the bread which has come down from heaven and gives life to the world (6:25-29). Just as the one who drinks the living water will never thirst (4:14; 7:37), so also the one who takes the bread of life will never hunger (6:35). The Gospel takes two common images, bread and water, both essential for life, and uses them as vehicles that point to eternal life.[221] If one wants to sustain eternal life, that is, life with God, one must partake of the bread and water which Jesus offers. He presses this message home with a graphic image: "Unless you eat the flesh of the Son of Man and drink his blood, you have no life in you. Those who eat my flesh and drink my blood have eternal life" (6:53-54a).

Life is also expressed by the image of light. The prologue states that the life which came to be in the Word was the light of humanity (1:3b-4). Jesus, the light of the world, gives his followers the light of life (8:12). Life is synonymous with walking in the light (3:21; 9:4; 11:9). Light, then, joins bread and water as an image symbolizing the life Jesus offers. As light, bread, and the source of water, Jesus gives life.

---

[221]This is another example of the evangelist's sacramental perspective; cf. above, pp. 80, 87.

As shown in the previous chapter, life is a central theme in the Wisdom material.[222] Indeed, the revelation of Wisdom, like the revelation of Jesus, is the revelation of life. Like Jesus, Wisdom bestows life upon her followers: "For whoever finds me finds life and obtains favor from the Lord" (Prov. 8:35-36). Just as Jesus is life (John 14:6), it is said of Wisdom, "she is your life" (Prov. 4:13). The revelation of God brought by Wisdom results in life for believers.

The Wisdom material also evidences a kind of realized eschatology. Ziener gave significant attention to this matter in the second part of his study of Wisdom of Solomon and the Gospel.[223] He saw a significant correlation between the realized eschatology of the two books. Eschatological life and death are already actualized. For Wisdom of Solomon, as for the Gospel, immortality is available in this life through the possession of Wisdom (cf. Wis. 5:15; 6:18). It was noted in chapter 1 that life in the bulk of the wisdom literature is the good life here and now filled with many years and prosperity, and to this perspective, the Wisdom of Solomon adds the element of life beyond death, immortality. The good life imparted by Wisdom is the good life in fellowship with God, which cannot be snuffed out by death. The Gospel shares this view.[224] It is interesting to note that ἀθανασία, "immortality," is not used. Perhaps ζωή is retained in order to maintain contact with the older wisdom tradition.

In the Wisdom material life is obtained through the proper response toward Wisdom, just as eternal life comes through proper response to Jesus. The vocabulary of faith, however, is more varied than in the Gospel. Ziener devoted the third section of his study to the similarities between faith in the Gospel and in the Wisdom of Solomon.[225] Eternal life is because of Wisdom-Jesus: The king says, "Because of her (δι' αὐτήν) I shall have immortality" (Wis. 8:13a); Jesus says, "He who eats me will live because of me (δι' ἐμέ; John 6:57). C. Larcher pointed to the conjunction of life and the keeping of the commandments: "Giving heed to [Wisdom's] laws is assurance of immortality" (Wis. 6:18b); Jesus says, "If anyone keeps my word, he will never see death" (John 8:51).[226]

---

[222]Cf, above, p. 35.

[223]Ziener, "Weisheitsbuch," 39 (1958), 37-49.

[224]Forestell, Word, p. 132 n. 111, noted how the phrase in John 6:51, 58 ζήσει εἰς τὸν αἰῶνα recalls Wis. 5:15: δίκαιοι δὲ εἰς τὸν ζῶσιν.

[225]Ziener, "Weisheitsbuch," pp. 49-57.

[226]C. Larcher, Etudes sur le livre de la Sagesse (Paris: Etudes Bibliques, 1969), p. 21.

Many of the same images used to express life in the Gospel are also used in life in the Wisdom material. The water image appears in both places: "Keep your heart with all vigilance; for from it flow springs of life" (Prov. 4:23). This saying parallels Jesus' words about "a spring of water welling up to eternal life" (John 4:14) and "rivers of living water" (John 7:38). Light is also used in conjunction with life: "For the commandment is a lamp and the teaching a light, and the re-proofs of discipline are the way of life" (Prov. 6:23; cf. also Bar. 3:14).

The concept of life in the Gospel is constructed upon the foundation of the Wisdom material. The kerygma of Wisdom, life, becomes the kerygma of the Gospel. Jesus takes up the mantle of Wisdom. Just as she is life, he is life. He stands in the temple offering life to his followers just as Wisdom stood at the gates of the city offering life to her adherents. Jesus is Wisdom incarnate, making Wisdom's appeals to come and experience life, that is, fellowship with God.

This chapter has isolated the wisdom parallels to six themes of the Johannine portrait of Jesus. It is now necessary to summarize briefly those six. Preexistence of Jesus functions in the Gospel much the same way as Wisdom's preexistence in the wisdom literature. The spatial dualism and the sending of the Son by the Father in the Gospel are similar to the spatial dualism and the sending of Wisdom by God in the Wisdom material. Out of his intimacy with the Father, Jesus reveals the Father, just as Wisdom reveals God out of her intimacy with God, though both are depicted as "hidden revealers" The soteriological dualism of the Gospel, which divides people into two camps based on their response to the revealer, resembles the soteriological dualism of the Wisdom material. Those who accept Jesus form a community in which they experience intimacy with her. Glory and life, the primary benefits which the disciples receive from Jesus, are also the benefits which Wisdom gives to her disciples.

In citing these parallels it has not been argued that these themes are exclusively from wisdom. For example, the sending motif in the Gospel has doubtlessly been influenced by the prophetic sending motif as well as by wisdom.[227] Nevertheless, the cumulative value of these parallels is impressive. It leads to the conclusion that the Gospel portrait of Jesus is painted with colors taken from the wis-

---

[227]Cf. above, pp. 55-58.

dom palette. Jesus is depicted as Wisdom incarnate, the outreaching love of God now enfleshed in a man.

Under the influence of other trends such as the prophetic sending motif and the early Christian proclamation, certain wisdom themes are highlighted in the Gospel. For example, the descent from above is moved from the background of the Wisdom material to the foreground of the Gospel. Such an observation does not weaken the argument for wisdom influence on the Gospel; rather it simply notes the creative freedom of the evangelist, who was not bound to apply the colors in the same way previous writers did but could mix them with other colors and brush them on the canvas in new ways. Furthermore, the model standing before the artist was a historical person. Long before the Johannine portrait of Jesus was fashioned, previous sketches had been made, in which Jesus appeared as teacher, miracle-worker, and sufferer. Many of these sketches were incorporated into the Gospel under the rubric of Wisdom.

The Johannine portrait of Jesus is different from the previous portraits of Wisdom because it depicts a man who preached, healed, taught, and died. His history is not obscured, then, but it is painted in luminous colors. Yet this sharpened historical perspective raises numerous questions. How can it be said that a man preexisted creation? How can it be said that a man came down from above? These questions are only answered in terms of Wisdom. The Gospel uses the Wisdom symbol to interpret the significance of Jesus of Nazareth. He is the man Wisdom became. He preexisted creation as God's preexistent Wisdom. He came down from above in that he existed in the divine presence as Wisdom. He revealed God by enfleshing God's Wisdom, the revelation of God. The historical Jesus, then, is clothed in the robes of Wisdom to create the Johannine Christ.

Chapter 3

THE PLACE AND FUNCTION OF WISDOM IN THE FOURTH GOSPEL AND IN THE JOHANNINE COMMUNITY

Wisdom strides through the Gospel in the person of Jesus of Nazareth. He is Wisdom incarnate, God reaching out to humanity to the fullest extent, as a human being. The previous two chapters have demonstrated the dependence of the Gospel prologue and narrative on wisdom. It remains, however, to discuss the place and function which Wisdom has in the Gospel and in the Johannine community. This subject will be approached in this chapter from two directions: literary and socio-historical. The literary section will explore the place of Wisdom in the Gospel, with special consideration of Wisdom as a metaphor and symbol. The socio-historical section will discuss the function of Wisdom in the Johannine community, with particular attention to the community's character and composition at the time the Gospel was written.

Wisdom in the Fourth Gospel: Literary Concerns

In this section the focus will be on the literary function of Wisdom in the Gospel. Attention will first be given to the transformation of Wisdom as a metaphor, myth, and symbol. Then consideration will be given to how this transformed metaphor functions within the Gospel, specifically in the integration of the

128

prologue and narrative. Finally, attention will be given to how Wisdom clarifies the relationship between the Gospel and the biblical and early Jewish literature.

The Transformation of Wisdom

The Gospel expresses the significance of Jesus by applying to him characteristics of Wisdom. He was preexistent with God and assisted in creation. From this preexistent intimacy with God, he was sent in order to reveal God through his words and his works. His discourses, filled with vivid imagery of the revelation he brought, directed the hearer to himself. His miracles were called "signs," for they revealed his glory. Jesus was rejected by most, but a few accepted him, and they formed a community around him, in which they experienced a special relationship with him.

The evangelist, then, has transformed a traditional symbol, concentrating it in Jesus. The symbol carried with it a web of associations, such as preexistence, revelation, and life. Jesus is now placed in the center of that symbolic web, and both Jesus and the associations are transformed. To put it another way, in the biblical and early Jewish literature the vehicle or better-known term of the Wisdom metaphor is woman, but in the Gospel the vehicle is Jesus. Thus, both Jesus and Wisdom are redefined. Jesus is no longer understood merely as a human teacher but as the preexistent revealer of God, Wisdom incarnate. Similarly, Wisdom is now understood as manifested fully not in the Law but in the person of Jesus of Nazareth. Wisdom, then, is the "root metaphor" in the Gospel.

As was noted in chapter 1, Wisdom is a "tensive symbol" rather than a "steno-symbol," that is, it has a multiplicity of meanings rather than a single meaning.[1] Because Wisdom is a tensive symbol, it can be transformed according to the needs of the community, as has been seen in the survey of biblical and early Jewish literature. The evangelist transforms the symbol again, identifying it with Jesus, much as Sirach and Baruch had done in identifying it with the Law. In the Gospel, however, Wisdom is identified with a historical person. Wisdom has become known in this man.

In the biblical and early Jewish literature the Wisdom symbol had become the subject of various stories or myth. The Gospel interprets the story of Jesus through the Wisdom myth. His life, ministry and death is thus placed in a cosmic

[1]Cf. above, p. 25.

context. Indeed, with the help of the Wisdom myth the evangelist constructs a new myth, a Christ myth,[2] one might say, in which the central character is one who came down from above to reveal God. The story of Jesus is told from the perspective of Wisdom in order to create the Christ myth.

Celia Deutsch wrote that the Wisdom myth allowed Jews in the Second Temple era to reflect on issues of cosmogony, revelation, and theodicy, and she showed how Matthew used the Wisdom myth to reflect on these same issues.[3] Indeed, the evangelist used the Wisdom myth in much the same way. He believed that God brought the world into being through the Wisdom-Word, now made known in Jesus. He held that God is known through the person of Jesus, who makes God known to humanity. He also contended that evil has befallen believers because the people have rejected the community in the same way that they rejected Jesus. The Jesus story is seen through the lens of Wisdom.

Prologue and Narrative

Scholars have long debated the relationship between the prologue and the Gospel narrative. The prologue has been considered an introduction for the hellenistic reader,[4] a summary,[5] and an overture or prelude.[6] This study, however, has emphasized the continuity between the prologue and the narrative. Both are significantly influenced by wisdom themes. Both present the same Christology: Jesus is the Wisdom of God come into the world. The prologue expresses this in terms of a hymn to the Word, the Gospel in terms of a narrative about the Son. Wisdom gives content to both these affirmations. Wisdom is the integrating symbol for both prologue and narrative.

---

[2]It is preferable to speak of "myth" here than "mytho-logy" or "reflective mythology." Cf. above, p. 44 and n. 135 listed there.

[3]Celia Deutsch, "Wisdom in Matthew: Transformation of a Symbol," NovT, 32 (1990), 31, 47. Cf. above, p. 26.

[4]Cf. Adolf von Harnack, "Uber das Verhältnis des Prologs des vierten Evangeliums zum ganzen Werk," ZTK, 2 (1892), 230; C. H. Dodd, The Interpretation of the Fourth Gospel (Cambridge: Cambridge University Press, 1953), p. 296; J. A. T. Robinson, "The Relation of the Prologue to the Gospel of St. John," NTS, 9 (1962-63), 127-128.

[5]Cf. Edwyn C. Hoskyns, The Fourth Gospel, ed. F. N. Davey (London: Faber and Faber, Ltd., 1940), p. 137; Heinrich Schlier, "Im Anfang war das Wort: Zum Prolog des Johannesevangeliums," in Die Zeit der Kirche: Exegetische Aufsätze und Vorträge (Freiburg: Herder, 1956), I, 274-284.

[6]Cf. Bultmann, Gospel, p. 13.

130

Brief consideration was given in chapter 1 to the relationship between the prologue and narrative.[7] Warren Carter began to address this question in speaking about the prologue as one symbolic unit in the Johannine cluster of sacred symbols, which has a different literary form from the narrative which follows. As was stated in chapter 1, however, attention must be given to the prologue as hymn or poetry which summoned the emotions of the community in crisis, much as the Wisdom hymns did for the Israelite communities. What results, though, from the combination of poetry and narrative, hymn and story? The prologue sets out symbols, images, and metaphors in poetic form, thus engaging the emotions and imagination of the reader. Attention is centered on this Word-become-flesh, who offers believers light, life, glory, and relationship with God. These symbols and images are further developed in terms of a narrative about a historical figure, Jesus the Son, who taught, performed miracles, met opposition, and died and rose again. The reader's attachment to this figure is strengthened, as the familiar story about Jesus is told in a new way. Wisdom helps integrate prologue and narrative, for it provides the symbols and images for both.

James D. G. Dunn wrote that the evangelist intended his Gospel to be read through the window of the prologue.[8] Such an approach is not unlike the book of Proverbs, where, as Samuel Terrien has shown, Wisdom's appeal to humanity in chapters 1-9 sets the tone for the entire book.[9] Another parallel is found in Wisdom of Solomon, where the various poems in 6:12-9:18 introduce Wisdom, and then chapters 10-19 give her a key role in the narrative of the saving events in Israel's history. Therefore, the reader first becomes acquainted with Wisdom: she assisted in creation, she is the revelation of God, she gives the king the qualities to rule, and she grants immortality. Then the reader learns of Wisdom's participation in the familiar stories about Adam, Abraham, and Moses and Israel in the wilderness, thus solidifying the reader's attachment to Wisdom. In much the same way, the prologue introduces the Wisdom-Word as the preexistent instrument of creation and giver of glory, light, and life, while the narrative presents the familiar

---

[7]Cf. above, pp. 44-47.

[8]James D. G. Dunn, "Let John Be John: A Gospel for Its Time," in Das Evangelium und die Evangelien: Vortäge vom Tübinger Symposium 1982, ed. Peter Stuhlmacher (Tübingen: Mohr-Siebeck, 1983), p. 334.

[9]Samuel Terrien, "The Play of Wisdom: Turning Point in Biblical Theology," HBT, 3 (1981), 133.

stories of the Son as the teacher and miracle-worker, though these stories are told from the perspective of Wisdom. Through the combination of prologue and narrative, the Wisdom-Word acquires a history. The Gospel story gives content to the assertion that the Word "lived among us" (John 1:14). The narrative "fleshes out" the statement of the prologue.

In combining prologue and narrative the Gospel achieves something theologically significant: the Wisdom-Word Christology of the prologue is joined to the Son of God Christology of the narrative.[10] Son of God, the traditional title by which Jesus was known in primitive Christianity, was infused with transcendent meaning through the Word. Jesus Christ, Son of God, was the Wisdom-Word who was with God in the beginning and became flesh. Wisdom-Word was the foundation upon the evangelist built his Son of God Christology.

The Gospel and Jewish Thought

Earlier commentators regarded the Gospel as "one stage in that acute Hellenization" of Christianity.[11] The scholarly pendulum, however, has swung in the opposite direction. The current consensus is that the evangelist is rooted in the biblical and early Jewish literature. Edwin D. Freed demonstrated that the quotations in the Gospel from Hebrew scripture, though fewer than in the synoptics, reveal a thorough training in Jewish tradition and scriptures.[12] F.-M. Braun showed that the Gospel reflects the major streams of Jewish theological thought and expectation.[13] This study has confirmed these findings. It has shown that the Gospel was significantly influenced by the biblical and early Jewish literature, especially the Wisdom material, in its portrayal of Jesus and the salvation he brings. Jewish thought, rather than hellenism, is the rock from which the Gospel is hewn.

---

[10]Cf. James D. G. Dunn, Christology in the Making: A New Testament Inquiry into the Origins of the Doctrine of the Incarnation (Philadelphia: Westminster Press, 1980), pp. 244-245.

[11]Stephen Neill, The Interpretation of the New Testament 1861-1961 (London: Oxford University Press, 1964), p. 315. It is instructive that a significant work on the Gospel of that era was Benjamin W. Bacon, The Gospel of the Hellenists, ed. Carl H. Kraeling (New York: Henry Holt and Company, 1933).

[12]Edwin D. Freed, Old Testament Quotations in the Gospel of John, NovTSup XI (Leiden: E. J. Brill, 1975), p. 175: "There can no longer be any question then that the use of and appeal to the Jewish scriptures is an essential and theologically significant characteristic of John."

[13]F.-M. Braun, Jean le Théologien: Les grandes traditions d'Israel et l'accord des Escritures selon le Quatrième Evangile (Paris: J. Gibalda, 1964), pp. 3-45.

How did the evangelist use the Wisdom material? A. T. Hanson distinguished five ways in which the Hebrew scripture was used in the Gospel.[14] His study, however, was restricted to the use of specific scripture passages in the narrative. In using the Wisdom material, however, the evangelist was more interested in broad themes than in specific passages. Certain Wisdom passages were important to him, such as Proverbs 8, Sirach 24, and Wisdom of Solomon 7:22-8:1, but these passages did not shape the evangelist's terminology as other passages did, perhaps because he did not regard some of these books as inspired scripture. Nevertheless, the evangelist found that this material's portrayal of God's action through Wisdom matched his own conception of God's action through Jesus. At this point, Hanson's list of ways in which the evangelist used Hebrew scripture is helpful. The final two ways are of particular note. First, "Scripture can be detected as the basis of his Christology."[15] In a number of passages, wisdom themes are at the basis of the evangelist's Christology, as the previous chapter has made plain. Second, "Scripture can be shown to have influenced his narrative."[16] The primary example is presented in the signs performed by Jesus, which were influenced by signs of Wisdom in Wisdom of Solomon 11-19.[17] The Wisdom material does more than simply adorn the Gospel narrative, as Hanson had it.[18] Many of its themes are taken over as Gospel themes.

The way that the evangelist used the Wisdom material is significant for biblical theology. The Gospel does not diverge from the Hebrew scripture but emerges out of it. The same God is at work, through Wisdom and then through Jesus. God, who through Wisdom has always gone out from Godself, in creation, in the Exodus, and in the Law, has now extended Godself in Jesus of Nazareth. Yet there is discontinuity as well as continuity, for at no time before has Wisdom become a person. "The Word became flesh"; Wisdom, God moving out from Godself, entered completely the human sphere by becoming a human being. Indeed, this language is mythological, but it is language built upon the Wisdom myth of the biblical and early Jewish literature. The continuity is a continuity of myths; the

---

[14]Anthony Tyrell Hanson, "John's Technique in Using Scripture," in The New Testament Interpretation of Scripture (London: SPCK, 1980), pp. 157-176.

[15]Ibid., pp. 162-166.

[16]Ibid., pp. 166-171.

[17]Cf. above, pp. 106-108.

[18]Hanson, "John's Technique," pp. 171-172.

Johannine Christ myth is built upon the raw material of the Wisdom myth. The discontinuity is the extent to which the mythological has become historical, the personification has become a person. Wisdom is not only the Law read in public worship or private devotion, more than the spirit met in mystical experience; Wisdom is the person encountered in the streets, in the marketplace, by the well, and still encountered through the Spirit. In Jesus Wisdom takes on a human face.

In an important article Terrien proposed Wisdom as an integrating center for a new ecumenical theology of the Bible.[19] Only Wisdom, he argued, not the Word or the Law, is exalted in the Hebrew scriptures to the preexistent status of Proverbs 8. He noted a direct line in form and thought running from Proverbs 8 to Sirach 24 then to John 1 (or better, the whole Gospel). The locus of God's presence shifts from creation to the Law and finally to Jesus Christ. "The theology of cultic presence has moved from the realm of geographical space to that of universal humanity through the mediating mode of wisdom's cosmic praise."[20] Wisdom presents rich possibilities for explorations in biblical theology. This study has done essential groundwork for such forays, for it has shown that the evangelist used Wisdom to place the Christ-event in continuity with what God has been doing all along among God's people.[21]

Wisdom, then, is the root metaphor in the Gospel's presentation of Jesus. She binds closely together the prologue and the narrative, showing the continuity of the Johannine portrait of Jesus. She also binds together the Gospel and Jewish thought, serving as a new center for biblical theology. She unlocks the door to the mysteries of the Gospel.

---

[19]Terrien, "Play of Wisdom," pp. 125-153. It was a further development of material in his Elusive Presence: Toward a New Biblical Theology, Religious Perspectives, Vol. 26 (New York: Harper and Row, 1978), cf. chapter 7, "The Play of Wisdom," pp. 350-389, and his remarks on the future of biblical theology, pp. 471-475.

[20]Terrien, "Play of Wisdom," p. 139.

[21]This approach must be distinguished from the salvation-historical approach to the Gospel taken by Oscar Cullmann, Salvation in History, trans. Sidney G. Sowers, et al. (New York: Harper and Row, 1967), pp. 268-291. He imposed on the Gospel a Lukan perspective in which the life of Jesus is the midpoint of God's saving work linking the history of Israel and the history of the church. Rather than telling the Jesus story in two editions, the evangelist tells it in a two-level drama; cf. below, p. 129. Cf. also the critique in Raymond E. Brown, "The Kerygma of the Gospel According to John," in New Testament Issues, ed. R. Batey (New York: Harper and Row, 1970), pp. 216-219.

Wisdom in the Johannine Community:
Socio-Historical Concerns

Metaphors and symbols do not appear in documents ex nihilo, but they arise out of a community context. The literary, then, necessarily leads to the social; consideration of the place of Wisdom in the Gospel leads to consideration of its function in the Johannine community. What does the Gospel's Wisdom Christology say about the group of believers in which this document originated? Contemporary Johannine scholarship has focused upon the interrelationship between the Gospel's picture of Jesus and the community out of which the Gospel arose.[22] This section will explore the role of Wisdom in the Johannine community. First, the suggestion that the community was a wisdom school will be discussed. Then the hellenistic-Jewish character of the community will be considered. Next, an attempt will be made to locate the use of the wisdom traditions in the history of the community. Finally, roles of men and women in the Johannine community will be explored.

A Wisdom School?

In his study of Johannine Christology in which he allowed a central place for the wisdom background, E. M. Sidebottom wrote, "John undoubtedly belonged to some branch of the Wisdom school."[23] It is unclear exactly what he meant. Did he have in mind that which seems to be in the background of the book of Sirach, in which the author implores the reader to come lodge in his school (Sir. 51:23)? Did Sidebottom use school in the specific sense of an academy or in the general sense of "school of thought"?[24] Johannine studies, however, have advanced significantly in the thirty years since Sidebottom's book. His suggestion can now be evaluated in a formal sense: Can the Johannine community be considered a wisdom school?

---

[22] Cf. the works cited by Robert Kysar in his two articles, "Community and Gospel: Vectors in Fourth Gospel Criticism," in ITG, ed. James Luther Mays (Philadelphia: Fortress Press, 1981), pp. 265-277; and "The Gospel of John in Current Research," RelSR, 9 (1983), 316-317. Cf. also John Painter, "Christology and the History of the Johannine Community in the Prologue of the Fourth Gospel," NTS, 30 (1984), 460-474.

[23] E. M. Sidebottom, The Christ of the Fourth Gospel in the Light of First-Century Judaism (London: SPCK, 1961), p. 19; cf. also his Appendix B, "The Wisdom Background of the Fourth Gospel," pp. 203-207.

[24] The sentences following the above quotation demonstrate that Sidebottom was more interested in the Palestinian Jewish milieu than in the nature of the community: "The point we are making here is that his school was not so divorced from the Palestinian Judaism of the first century as used to be thought" (ibid., pp. 19-20).

First, it must be determined whether or not the community can, properly speaking, be called a school. R. Alan Culpepper gave this subject comprehensive treatment.[25] He isolated nine common characteristics of the ancient schools: groups of disciples emphasizing φιλία and κοινωνία; origins in an exemplary wise or good founder; teachings of the founder and traditions about him; disciples or students of the founder; activities of teaching, learning, studying, and writing; communal meals in memory of the founder; rules or practices of membership; distance or withdrawal from society; and organizational means of ensuring their perpetuity.[26] Culpepper concluded that the Johannine community shared all these characteristics, for it was a community gathered around its founder, the Beloved Disciple.[27]

Of particular interest to this study is the fifth characteristic, activities of teaching, learning, studying, and writing. Culpepper suggested that these activities had a dual focus within the Johannine community: the teachings of Jesus and the scriptures. He envisioned a school in which the scriptures were studied in order to verify and explain Jesus' teachings. Through their study the community found in Jesus the fulfillment of the scriptures.[28]

This study lends support to Culpepper's claims. The evangelist's christological use of wisdom themes suggests the Johannine community was a school in which the Wisdom material was studied. The Johannine community "searched the scriptures" to find its witness to Jesus (John 5:39). This witness they found, among other places, in wisdom. It is appropriate to speak of the Johannine community as a school, but is it also appropriate to speak of it as a wisdom school?

The strong wisdom influence in the Gospel indicates that the evangelist and his community were deeply immersed in the wisdom tradition, as Gunther Reim

---

[25]R. Alan Culpepper, The Johannine School: An Examination of the Johannine-School Hypothesis Based on an Investigation of the Ancient Schools, SBLDS 26 (Missoula, MT: Scholars Press, 1975).

[26]Ibid., pp. 258-259.

[27]Ibid., pp. 287-289. For the Beloved Disciple rather than Jesus as the founder of the Johannine community, cf. pp. 264-267.

[28]Ibid., pp. 274-275. In this he agreed with Barnabas Lindars, New Testament Apologetic: The Doctrinal Significance of the Old Testament Quotations (Philadelphia: Westminster Press, 1961), pp. xi, 129-130; and Peder Borgen, Bread from Heaven: An Exegetical Study of the Concept of Manna in the Gospel of John and the Writings of Philo, NovTSup X (Leiden: E. J. Brill, 1965), p. 3, all of whom held that the Johannine community was an early Christian school in which the Old Testament was studied.

contended in his study of the use of the Hebrew scripture in the Gospel.[29] Certainly the Johannine community was a school in which the wisdom writings were studied, yet it is difficult to label it a wisdom school because other types of literature were studied and used. It was shown in chapter 2 how the prophetic and apocalyptic traditions exerted some influence on the Gospel.[30] The wisdom traditions held a central place, but these traditions were employed inclusively rather than exclusively.[31] Wisdom took the prophet and the Son of Man under her wing.

Hellenistic or Jewish?

As noted above, in former times it was fashionable to consider the Gospel a radically hellenized form of the Jesus story.[32] This study has shown that the determinative influences on the Gospel were not Greek philosophy or Gnosticism, but Jewish themes such as wisdom, propheticism, and apocalypticism. This background places the Gospel squarely in a Jewish milieu. The Johannine community was primarily influenced by Jewish traditions and can be called Jewish Christian.

Placing the Gospel in a Jewish milieu, however, does not rule out hellenistic influence. The important works of Hengel and W.D. Davies have shown that the Palestinian Judaism of the earliest church was thoroughly hellenized.[33] Schnackenburg summarized this issue: "The earlier alternative of Judaism or non-Jewish Hellenism seems to have been left behind, since careful study of the Johannine thought has revealed many connections with both 'worlds' and it has been proved that Judaism and Hellenism were more strongly interwoven than had been thought."[34] The character of the Johannine community should not be expressed as

---

[29]Günther Reim, Studien zum alttestamentlichen Hintergrund des Johannesevangelium, SNTSMS 22 (Cambridge: Cambridge University Press, 1974), esp. pp. 93-96, 188-189, 231-232. Against those noted above in n. 42, however, Reim contended that the evangelist had no written texts of the Old Testament before him but he drew upon tradition.

[30]Cf. above, pp. 60, 65-66.

[31]Cf. George W. MacRae, "The Fourth Gospel and Religionsgeschichte," CBQ, 32 (1970), 22, held that the evangelist drew on a number of religious backgrounds in order to assert the universality of Jesus, although his own background was "primarily in the wisdom tradition."

[32]Cf. above, p. 131.

[33]Martin Hengel, Judaism and Hellenism, 2 vols., trans. John Bowden (London: SCM press, 1975); W. D. Davies, Paul and Rabbinic Judaism: Some Rabbinic Elements in Pauline Theology, 2d ed. (London: SPCK, 1955), esp. pp. vii-xv, 1-16. Cf. also Morton Smith, "Palestinian Judaism in the First Century," in Israel: Its Role in Civilization, ed. M. Davis (New York: The Seminary Israel Institute of the Jewish Theological Seminary, 1956), pp. 67-81; Meeks, "'Am I a Jew?'" pp. 162-169.

[34]Schnackenburg, Gospel, I, 119.

either hellenistic or Jewish but simply hellenistic Jewish. C. K. Barrett wrote, "Even if the Fourth Gospel were exclusively Jewish, one would have to consider it Hellenistic-Jewish."[35]

Furthermore, the use which the evangelist made of the Wisdom material also points to a hellenistic Jewish context. He not only used the early wisdom books such as Job and Proverbs but also the later works such as Wisdom of Solomon and Sirach. These later books display a definite hellenistic influence.[36] Indeed, the Wisdom of Solomon utilizes hellenistic philosophy in its characterization of Wisdom. As this study has shown, the Gospel takes over this picture, though purging it of much of its Platonic terminology and replacing it with more biblical language. The sources which the Gospel uses are hellenistic Jewish.

A number of scholars have attempted to define the character of the Johannine community more closely. Oscar Cullmann contended for heterodox Judaism as the background for the Gospel.[37] John Painter called it "sectarian Judaism of the Hellenistic age."[38] Robert Kysar wrote, "It is the accomplishment of current johannine scholarship that the evidence for the syncretistic, heterodox Jewish milieu of the gospel has become irresistible."[39] He predicted that much of what in the past has been known as Gnosticism will be interpreted as expressions of heterodox Judaism.[40] If the context of the Johannine community is called heterodox Judaism, wisdom must be allowed pride of place.

A word must be said here about the relationship of the Gospel to gnosticism. For a generation or more a determinative place in Johannine studies was occupied by Rudolf Bultmann's suggestion that the "gnostic redeemer myth" was the key to the Gospel.[41] In recent years, however, this hypothesis has fallen into disfavor, for many scholars have pointed out that the myth is an abstraction from later

---

[35]C. K. Barrett, The Gospel of John and Judaism, trans. D. M. Smith (Philadelphia: Fortress Press, 1975), p. 61.

[36]Cf. above, p. 13-15, 16-18.

[37]Oscar Cullmann, The Johannine Circle, trans. John Bowden (Philadelphia: Westminster Press, 1976), p. 32.

[38]John Painter, John: Witness and Theologian (London: SPCK, 1975), p. 19.

[39]Kysar, Fourth Evangelist, p. 270.

[40]Ibid., p. 119.

[41]Cf. the references throughout his The Gospel of John: A Commentary, trans. G. R. Beasley-Murray, et al. (Philadelphia: Westminster Press, 1971). Cf. also his Theology of the New Testament, trans. K. Grobel (New York: Charles Scribner's Sons, 1955), II, 12-14, with a succinct summary of the myth on I, 166-167.

sources.[42] Martin Hengel stated categorically, "In reality there is no gnostic redeemer myth in the sources which can be demonstrated to be pre-Christian."[43]
Furthermore, a number of scholars have pointed out the extensive differences between the thought worlds of the Gospel and the gnostic redeemer myth. Rudolf
Schnackenburg summarized this viewpoint: "The Gnostic redeemer myth and the
Johannine Christology are two different worlds: religious philosophy (in mythical
language) opposed to biblical religion (in the sense of man's being bound to a personal God), myth to history, Gnosis to faith."[44] With the major exception of
Siegfried Schulz,[45] the gnostic redeemer myth is no longer viewed as a viable op-
tion today in Johannine christological studies.[46] Indeed, Wisdom has filled the
void left by the fall of the gnostic redeemer. Reginald Fuller declared boldly, "For
the gnostic redeemer myth we now substitute the Palestinian-Hellenistic-Jewish
wisdom myth."[47] The myth which lies behind the Gospel is not that of the gnostic
redeemer but that of Wisdom. Wisdom is a better matrix from which to understand
Gospel than gnosticism.

A relationship does exist, however, between wisdom, the Gospel, and
gnosticism. Wisdom in the form of Sophia was taken up into the gnostic systems
and given a central role. Ulrich Wilckens wrote, "In almost all Gnostic witnesses
of the most diverse nature and origin the figure of Sophia plays an essential
role."[48] George MacRae concluded that the Jewish Wisdom figure lies at the

---

[42]Cf. above, pp. 24, 32 n. 93.

[43]Martin Hengel, The Son of God: The Origin of Christology and the History of
Jewish-Hellenistic Religion, trans. John Bowden (Philadelphia: Fortress Press, 1976), p. 33. Cf.
also his excursus, "The Gnostic Myth of the Redeemer and the Johannine Christology," in Rudolf
Schnackenburg, The Gospel According to St. John, trans. Kevin Smith (New York: Crossroad,
1982), I, 543-557.

[44]Schnackenburg, Gospel, I, 549.

[45]Siegfried Schulz, Das Evangelium nach Johannes (Göttingen: Vandenhoeck und
Ruprecht, 1972). Cf. above, p. 1 n. 2, p. 32 n. 93.

[46]Cf. Kysar, Fourth Evangelist, p. 271.

[47]Reginald Fuller, "The Incarnation in Historical Perspective," ATR, Supp Series 7
(1976), 64 n. 21. Cf. also Charles H. Talbert, What Is a Gospel? The Genre of the Canonical
Gospels (Philadelphia: Fortress Press, 1977), pp. 53-66, who listed the main problems of Bultmann's thesis and suggested in its place the "Hellenistic-Jewish mythology of a descending-
ascending redeemer" (p. 56), which includes the Wisdom myth.

[48]Ulrich Wilckens, "σοφία," TDNT, ed. Gerhard Friedrich and trans. G. W. Bromiley
(Grand Rapids: Wm. B. Eerdmans, 1971), VII, 500. Cf. also E. Yamauchi, "The Descent of
Ishtar, the Fall of Sophia, and the Jewish roots of Gnosticism," TynBul, 29 (1978), 143, who
wrote, "The Fall of Sophia is one of the most important elements in Gnostic mythology."

source of the gnostic myth.[49] James M. Robinson traced a trajectory from the Wisdom material through gnosticism on which he placed the sayings source Q.[50] The Gospel should also be placed on this trajectory. It was significantly influenced by wisdom, and it exerted influence on the gnostic systems.[51] A Johannine trajectory runs from the Jewish Wisdom material through second-century gnosticism.[52] Yet a trajectory also runs from wisdom through the Gospel into the classical Christology of the early church, as wisdom themes from the Gospel such as preexistence, unity with God, descent, and revelation were taken up in the creeds of the church.[53] Wisdom was a vital movement in Israel, and it launched a number of

---

[49]George MacRae, "The Jewish Background of the Gnostic Sophia Myth, NovT, 12 (1970), 88-94. He listed fifteen parallels between the Jewish Wisdom and the gnostic Sophia as seen in the Sethian-Ophite cosmogonies found in the fourth-century Nag Hammadi texts. These parallels included preexistence, instrumentality in creation, communication of revelation, descent-ascent, and life. Prior to this discussion, he traced briefly the scholarly debate concerning Sophia as a gnostic adaptation of Wisdom. A number of scholars simply assumed this adaptation until Bousset and Wilckens challenged it. Cf. pp. 86-87.

MacRae furthermore discussed the reasons why Wisdom, who is a positive force for good in the Jewish Wisdom material, becomes Sophia, who is both the good revealer and the originator of evil creation in the gnostic systems. MacRae explained this change as a revolt within Judaism, in which a loss of confidence in the created world led the Gnostics to transform the descent of Wisdom into the fall of Sophia by reflection upon the Genesis account of the sin of Eve (pp. 98-99). Yamauchi, "Descent," p. 173, maintained that this loss of confidence took place in the early second century in the wake of the profound disillusionment after the failure of the Bar Kochba revolt.

[50]James M. Robinson, "LOGOI SOPHON: On the Gattung of Q," in James M. Robinson and Helmut Koester, Trajectories through Early Christianity (Philadelphia: Fortress Press, 1971), pp. 71-113.

[51]The first commentary on the Gospel was written by the Gnostic Heracleon. Cf. Elaine H. Pagels, The Johannine Gospel in Gnostic Exegesis, SBLMS 17 (Nashville: Abingdon Press, 1973); and Schnackenburg, Gospel, I, pp. 193-195. In his reconstruction of the history of the Johannine community, Raymond E. Brown held that the secessionists mentioned in 1 John eventually led into gnosticism. Cf. his The Community of the Beloved Disciple: The Life, Loves, and Hates of an Individual Church in New Testament Times (New York: Paulist Press, 1979), pp. 147-155; and The Epistles of John, AB 30 (Garden City, N. Y.: Doubleday and Co., 1982), pp. 104-106.

[52]Stevan L. Davies, The Gospel of Thomas and Christian Wisdom (New York: Seabury Press, 1983), p. 116, also placed the Gospel of Thomas on this trajectory as an earlier formulation of material in the Gospel. Cf. also above, p. 33 n. 99, where it was noted that Robinson contended that the Johannine prologue lies on this trajectory from wisdom to gnosticism.

[53]Cf. the Nicene Creed, which confesses faith in "one Lord Jesus Christ, the only-begotten Son of God, Begotten of the Father before all the ages, Light of Light, true God of true God, begotten not made, of one substance with the Father, through whom all things were made; who for us men and for our salvation came down from the heavens. . ." Cf. Henry Bettenson, ed. Documents of the Christian Church, 2d ed. (London: Oxford University Press, 1963), p. 26. Reginald H. Fuller and Pheme Perkins, Who is This Christ? Gospel Christology and Contemporary Faith (Philadelphia: Fortress Press, 1983), p. 2, wrote, "Christian orthodoxy, Eastern and Western, Catholic and Protestant alike, has in practice taken its basic material for christological reflection from the Gospel of John."

trajectories: one which led directly into gnosticism, another which passed through the Johannine community and then into gnosticism, and a third which passed through the Johannine community and into the early church as represented by the creeds. Both the Gospel and gnosticism were influenced by wisdom.

Place in Community History

The Johannine community might then be called a hellenistic Jewish Christian school in which the wisdom traditions played a central role. How did these traditions function in the community's situation? At what point in the history of the community did wisdom begin to take on such importance? These questions will begin to be answered with the aid of the reconstructions of community history sketched by J. Louis Martyn and Raymond E. Brown.[54]

Scholarly consensus has formed around Martyn's proposal that the situation of the evangelist is best understood in terms of a dialogue with the synagogue.[55] Jewish Christians were being expelled from the synagogues because of their allegiance to Jesus (cf. John 9:22; 12:42; 16:2). In order to meet this crisis the evangelist produced a "two-level drama," the first level containing traditions about the historical Jesus and the second depicting the conflict between the church and the synagogue in the evangelist's own day. The battle was joined over the issue of Christology. Martyn wrote, "It is clear that the issue of Jesus' messiahship stands at the center of the synagogue-church discussion."[56] In pursuing this issue he gave attention to the relationship between Jesus and Moses and Jesus as the Son of Man. Martyn demonstrated how the evangelist leads readers from a confession of Jesus as the Prophet-Messiah like Moses to the confession of Jesus as the Son of Man.[57] It was shown in chapter 2 how the descent of Wisdom from heaven lies behind the descent of the Son of Man.[58] When the believer confessed that Jesus was the Son of Man, this confession also carried the implication that Jesus was Wisdom incarnate.

---

[54]Cf. Brown, Community, App. I: "Recent Reconstructions in Johannine Community History," pp. 171-182, for other proposals.

[55]Cf. J. Louis Martyn, History and Theology in the Fourth Gospel, rev. ed. (Nashville: Abingdon Press, 1979). The first edition was published in 1968.

[56]Ibid., p. 91; cf. also p. 93.

[57]Ibid., pp. 102-151.

[58]Cf. above, pp. 61-63. Martyn, History, p. 141, suggested that the Son of Man motif was influenced by wisdom.

Wisdom was a particularly effective weapon in the battle with the syna-gogue. It was shown in chapter 1 that Sirach and Baruch identified Wisdom and the Law and in the Tannaitic literature this identification was taken up in Wisdom speculation.[59] It is important not to read this latter phenomenon back into the New Testament, because all the sources are later. It is reasonable, however, to suppose that the rabbis had already focused on the identification of Wisdom and the Law by the time of the writing of the Gospel. At the same time that the rabbis identified Wisdom with the Law, the Johannine community identified Wisdom with Jesus. The evangelist employed this identification in polemic with the rabbis. His interest was summarized by Dunn: "The Wisdom of God is present in the Torah, but pre-sent in fulness only in Christ. Christ, not the Torah, is the embodiment of divine Wisdom, the incarnation of God's Word."[60] The question which divided the evangelist and the rabbis, the church and synagogue was, Where shall Wisdom be found? The rabbis found her in the Law, the Johannine Christians in Jesus.

Wisdom Christology was called into service in the conflict with the syna-gogue. At what stage in the history of the Johannine community, however, was it first employed for christological use? Martyn built upon the foundation in his ear-lier work and reconstructed a three-stage community history.[61] In the early period the Johannine community began as a group of Jews in the synagogue who found in Jesus the expected Messiah. In the middle period, however, this group was ex-pelled from the synagogue and some of their preachers were executed. These de-velopments led to new christological formulations in which Jesus was depicted as the Word come from above. In the late period the Johannine community defined its own theology in relationship to the synagogue and other Christian groups in its set-ting, including Christian Jews still in the synagogue and Jewish Christians who had also been expelled.

Wisdom Christology came to the fore in this middle period in which the Johannine Christians were excommunicated from the synagogue. Martyn wrote, "Expelled from the synagogue, the Johannine community was bound to search for a

[59]Cf. above, pp. 13-15, 21-22.
[60]Dunn, "John," p. 333. Cf. also Warren Carter, "The Prologue and John's Gospel: Function, Symbol, and the Definitive Word," JSNT, 39 (1990), p. 47. Cf. above, p. 44-45.
[61]J. Louis Martyn, "Glimpses into the History of the Johannine Community," in The Gospel of John in Christian History: Essays for Interpreters (New York: Paulist Press, 1978), pp. 90-121.

142

mature interpretation of the expulsion, and that search led it to new christological formulations."[62] They found such an interpretation in Wisdom who, though responsible for the creation of the world, was rejected by the world. Her rejection by the world corresponded to their rejection by the Jews. The Jews, the opponents of the Johannine Christians in the evangelist's day, became the opponents of Jesus-Wisdom in the Gospel. The community, however, made up "his own" whom Jesus-Wisdom loved to the end (John 13:1). Wisdom facilitated the move from the Christology of Jesus as the expected Messiah to the Christology of Jesus as the eternal Son of God.

Such a conclusion is in line with the findings of John Ashton and Carter in the articles summarized in chapter 2, for both sought to locate the prologue in the community's excommunication from the synagogue.[63] Yet it has been shown that Wisdom informs not only the prologue but also the narrative. Throughout the Gospel, then, the Wisdom myth is used to interpret the community's experience and assist in self-definition in the wake of excommunication. Wisdom, therefore, once again helped answer questions of theodicy.

Brown offered the most comprehensive history to date of the Johannine community "from the beginning" to "the last hour."[64] His schema consists of four phases, the first two of which are of interest to this study. Phase 1, the period of origins, corresponds roughly to Martyn's first and second periods. Brown agreed with Martyn that the originating group consisted of Jews in the synagogue who accepted Jesus as the Davidic Messiah. He also, however, postulated a second group consisting of Jews of an anti-Temple bias who understood Jesus as the Mosaic Messiah and evangelized in Samaria. The entrance of this second group stimulated the development of a high, preexistence Christology. Such a Christology led the Jewish leaders to expel the Johannine Christians from the synagogue. Also in this period Gentiles were accepted into the community. In Phase 2, the period of the Gospel, the community may have moved to the Diaspora, thus bringing out the

---

[62]Ibid., p. 105.

[63]Cf. John Ashton, "The Transformation of Wisdom: A Study of the Prologue of John's Gospel," NTS, 32 (1986), 181; Carter, "Prologue," pp. 49-50. Cf. above, pp. 44-45.

[64]Cf. primarily his Community. Cf. also his "Johannine Ecclesiology--The Community's Origins," in Mays, ITG, pp. 291-306; "'Other Sheep Not of This Fold': The Johannine Perspective on Christian Diversity in the Late First Century," JBL (1978), 5-22; and Epistles, pp. 69-115.

universalistic strain in Johannine thought. This phase corresponded to Martyn's late period, for the community further defined its relationship to the Jews, Jewish Christians, and Apostolic Christians.

Brown pushed back the entrance of high Christology into the stream of Johannine thought. Rather than a response to expulsion from the synagogue, the shift from low to high Christology occurred as a response to the integration of the second group into the community. Brown's conception of christological development in the Johannine community can be stated in terms of a Hegelian dialectic. The thesis, the original group's royal Davidic Christology, came into contact with the antithesis, the second group's prophetic Moses Christology, resulting in the synthesis, incarnational Wisdom Christology. Again, Wisdom served as an agent of reconciliation, not only in terms of traditions but also in terms of groups within the Johannine community, much as Wisdom had reconciled mainstream Judaism and the sages in an earlier period.

Wisdom Christology, then, was the cause rather than the result of expulsion from the synagogue, according to Brown. He criticized Martyn for failing to explain why the Johannine community developed a Christology that led to their expulsion from the synagogue.[65] In Brown's schema Wisdom Christology was more firmly embedded in the Johannine tradition. It was not a convenient tool which the community found upon excommunication, but it helped shape community identity from the beginning.

Brown perhaps underestimated the cataclysmic nature of the expulsion from the synagogue and its implications for Johannine thought. Wisdom may have served as both cause of and response to excommunication. In the community's emerging Wisdom Christology the rabbis saw a challenge to the supremacy of the Law. The Johannine Christians were expelled because of their initial formulations of Jesus as Wisdom incarnate. Once expelled, the community further developed wisdom themes in polemic against the synagogue. The one who had been agent of reconciliation took up the sword for battle.

Yet Wisdom continued to build bridges as well as walls. Brown suggested that the entrance of Gentiles and a possible geographical move from Palestine to the Diaspora would have brought out the universalistic implications in Johannine

---

[65]Brown, Community, p. 174.

thought. Just as Wisdom facilitated Judaism's contact with the hellenistic world in the Wisdom of Solomon, so she facilitated Christianity's contact with the Diaspora. A reader who was informed by Stoic and Platonic worldviews would have easily understood the prologue and the spatial dualism of the Gospel, though both owe their origin to wisdom. In the Diaspora the evangelist set up Wisdom in the high places to call to all those who would listen.

Wisdom came to the fore in three important episodes in the history of the Johannine community. She helped shape Johannine thought in the originating period of the community, she forged the weapons in the struggle against the synagogue, and she built the bridge to the Diaspora. Wisdom helped the Johannine community define itself and articulate its thought in each new situation.

Perhaps the community's history helps shed light on the Gospel's interesting combination of hidden and available wisdom.[66] Jesus as hidden Wisdom rejected by the Jews gave validation to the community's own experience of rejection by the synagogue. It set up firm boundaries with the synagogue, and it nurtured solidarity within the community. On the other hand, Jesus as available Wisdom calling to all people assisted in the evangelistic task of the community both in its appeal to "secret believers" in the synagogue and to Gentiles in the Diaspora. Wisdom helped guide the community through the vicissitudes of its history.

Gender Roles in the Community

Wisdom was an important tool in the self-definition of the community, both in its polemic against the synagogue and in its evangelization in the hellenistic world. But how did Wisdom function in terms of the internal relations within the community? Like all symbols, Wisdom arose out of social structures and legitimated them.[67] The symbol, then, should tell us something about the structure of the Johannine community. Specifically, the transformation of the female Wisdom into the male Jesus should give us some clue about the roles fulfilled by men and women in the community.

Probably the most thorough treatment of the role of women in early Christianity is that of Elisabeth Schüssler Fiorenza in her ground-breaking study In Memory of Her. She maintained that the Palestinian Jesus movement established a

---

[66]Cf. above, pp. 90-91.
[67]Cf. above, pp. 24-25.

"discipleship of equals," which recognized the full humanity of all persons, including women. The God who initiated this radical equality is depicted as Sophia, and Jesus is presented as a prophet and child of Sophia (cf. Luke 7:35; 11:49; 13:34; Matt. 11:28-30).[68] Fiorenza concluded that "the Sophia-God of Jesus made possible the invitation of women to the discipleship of equals."[69]

Later in her study Schüssler Fiorenza gave attention to the role of women in the Johannine community.[70] She noted that the community was inclusive of both women and men in discipleship and leadership, calling it "astonishing that the evangelist gives such a prominent place to women in the narrative."[71] The public ministry of Jesus begins and ends with a woman, Mary mother of Jesus and Mary of Bethany. At Cana Jesus' mother tells the servants (διάκονοι, perhaps a reference to the leading ministers of the community), "Do whatever he tells you" (John 2:5). The dialogue with the Samaritan woman (4:4-42), which is set alongside the dialogue with the misunderstanding Nicodemus, is based on a tradition that attributed a primary role to a woman missionary in the conversion of the Samaritans. Mary and Martha, along with their brother Lazarus, are said to be beloved by Jesus (11:5), and these "beloved disciples" respond in two different ways: Martha confesses that Jesus is the Christ, the Son of God (11:27), surpassing the confession of Peter in 6:69 and fulfilling the purpose of the Gospel in 20:31; and Mary anoints Jesus, thus fulfilling the role of διάκονος. Four women and a male disciple stand at the cross (19:25-27), thus creating a new family in which they are brothers and sisters. One of these women, Mary Magdalene, is the first to see the empty tomb and to receive an appearance of the Risen Lord (20:1-18), thus making her the primary apostolic witness to the resurrection. Schüssler Fiorenza concluded that the

---

[68]Elisabeth Schüssler Fiorenza, In Memory of Her: A Feminist Theological Reconstruction of Christian Origins (New York: Crossroad, 1984), pp. 130-140. Questions have been raised as to whether the Jesus movement can be accurately described as a "discipleship of equals," since after all, Jesus did choose 12 men as disciples. Cf. John Koenig (and the response by Schüssler Fiorenza) in "Review Symposium. Elisabeth Schüssler Fiorenza, In Memory of Her. Four Perspectives," Horizons, 11 (1984), 144-146, 154-157; Cain Hope Felder, Troubling Biblical Waters: Race, Class, Family (Maryknoll, NY: Orbis, 1989), p. 77.

[69]Schüssler Fiorenza, Memory p. 140.

[70]Ibid., pp. 323-333. Cf. also Raymond E. Brown, "Roles of Women in the Fourth Gospel," TS, 36 (1975), 688-699, reprinted in his Community, pp. 189-198; Sandra M. Schneiders, "Women in the Fourth Gospel and the Role of Women in the Contemporary Church," BTB, 12 (1982), 35-45.

[71]Ibid., p. 326.

146

women disciples "are paradigms of women's apostolic leadership in the Johannine communities. As such they are not just paradigms of faithful discipleship to be imitated by women but by all those who belong to Jesus' 'very own' familial community."[72]

Although Schüssler Fiorenza had made the connection between Wisdom in Q and the "discipleship of equals" in the Palestinian Jesus movement, she made no such connection between Wisdom in the Gospel and the prominence of women in the Johannine community. Nevertheless, such a bond seems to be present. Just as Jesus as the prophet and child of Sophia included all people, especially women, in his movement, so also Jesus as Wisdom incarnate enabled women to exercise key roles in the Johannine community. Indeed, perhaps the prominence of wisdom themes attracted women into the community. Furthermore, the presence of such themes in the Gospel legitimizes their leadership role.

Nevertheless, it must be noted that although women are prominent in the Gospel, they do not have an ongoing role in the narrative. No woman character appears in more than two scenes. For example, the mother of Jesus is at Cana and at the cross; Mary and Martha appear at the raising of Lazarus and at the anointing; Mary Magdalene is present at the cross and at the empty tomb. Women in the Gospel, then, appear and disappear. Men, however, in the form of the disciples, do have continuing roles. The disciples as a whole are said to be the recipients of Jesus' revelation,[73] and individual disciples such as Peter, Thomas, Philip, and Andrew play important parts in the continuing narrative. Pride of place in the Gospel, though, belongs to that disciple whom Jesus loved (13:23; 19:26; 20:2; 21:7, 20). He is the one who reclined in the bosom of Jesus (13:23), who believed in the resurrection solely on the basis of the empty tomb (20:8), who was the first to recognize the Risen Lord on the shore (21:7), and who was already following when Jesus told Peter to follow (21:19-20). The Beloved Disciple, then, is depicted as having a special relationship with Jesus; indeed, his relationship with Jesus is akin to that which Jesus has with God, for just as Jesus is in the bosom of the Father (ϵἰς τὸν κόλπον τοῦ πατρός, 1:18), so the Beloved Disciple is the bosom of Jesus (ϵν τὸν κόλπῳ τῷ 'Ιησοῦ, 13:23). It is the testimony of the

---

[72]Ibid., p. 333.
[73]Cf. above, pp. 105-110, where the intimacy which Jesus has with the disciples is discussed.

Beloved Disciple upon which the Gospel is based (21:24). It seems, then, that Schüssler Fiorenza's position must be amended: although women had important roles in the Johannine community, the key positions were held by males, especially one particular male, the Beloved Disciple.

Furthermore, that disciple continued to have authority in the community through the Paraclete. Culpepper showed that the Beloved Disciple functioned in the Johannine community in the same way that the Gospel predicts that the Paraclete would.[74] Just as the Paraclete would be sent to be with the disciples (14:16-17, 26) and teach them all things and remind them of all that Jesus said (14:26), so also the Beloved Disciple was sent to bear true witness to Jesus' words and deeds. He was the "first Paraclete for the Johannine community,"[75] and after his death the Spirit became "another Paraclete" (14:16). The Spirit, then, affirmed the continuing authority of the Beloved Disciple in the community. It legitimated the authority of those who taught and led the community in his stead.

How did Wisdom function in this development? Deutsch argued that just as Wisdom in the biblical and early Jewish literature had legitimated the male sages, female Wisdom identified with the male Jesus in Matthew legitimated a male teaching class in the Matthean community.[76] Much the same phenomenon occurred in the Johannine community. The Gospel proclaimed that Wisdom was now incarnated in Jesus. This affirmation served to legitimate the authority of the Beloved Disciple and the male teachers who carried on in his stead.[77]

Thus, the presence of Wisdom in the Gospel seems to have had a two-pronged function in the roles which men and women exercised in the Johannine community. On the one hand, Wisdom would have attracted women to the community and legitimated the leadership which they performed. On the other hand, Wisdom becoming flesh in the male Jesus, to whom a male disciple bore witness, would have reinforced the primary leadership positions in the community held by

---

[74]Culpepper, School, pp. 267-270; cf. also his Anatomy of the Fourth Gospel: A Study in Literary Design (Philadelphia: Fortress Press, 1983), pp. 122-123.

[75]Culpepper, School, p. 269.

[76]Celia Deutsch, "Jesus as Wisdom; Metaphor and Social Structure in Matthew's Gospel," paper presented to the Israelite and Early Christian Wisdom Section of the annual meeting of the Society of Biblical Literature, Kansas City, MO, November 23, 1991, pp. 6, 15. Cf. also her "Wisdom," p. 47.

[77]It is unlikely, then, that the evangelist was a woman, a possibility held out by Schüssler Fiorenza, Memory, p. 333.

males. Although women had an important place in the community, men filled the determinative roles.

This chapter has discussed the literary function of Wisdom in the Gospel and its social function in the Johannine community. Wisdom in the Gospel represents the transformation of a traditional symbol, which is now identified in Jesus. This symbol brings the prologue and the narrative into unity. Through this symbol, one also can see the continuity of the Gospel and Jewish thought. The wisdom themes of the Gospel indicate that the community was a hellenistic Jewish Christian school in which the wisdom traditions were intensively studied. Wisdom played an important role in community history, enabling the community to meet new situations in which it found itself. Wisdom both attracted women into the community and legitimated male leadership. Wisdom, therefore, has a significant place both in the Gospel and in the community out of which the Gospel arose.

Chapter 4

CONCLUSION

This study has now come to the end of its journey. It has traveled a long and arduous path in following the way of Wisdom through the biblical and early Jewish literature, through the Gospel prologue, and through the Gospel narrative. Now standing on the summit, it is possible both to look back and survey the road traveled and to look ahead and chart frontiers yet unexplored. A summary of the study will first be presented. Then suggestions for further research will be offered.

Summary

The introduction set out the course to be followed. Chapter 1 surveyed contemporary scholarship in Wisdom in biblical and early Jewish literature and the transformation of Wisdom in the Johannine prologue. The pictures of Wisdom were first traced through the biblical and early Jewish literature, and Wisdom was seen as the preexistent agent of God, who was present at creation and who brings humanity into intimacy with God. Wisdom functioned as a myth, metaphor, and symbol, often expressed in poetic form. She emerged in times of crisis in order to affirm the presence of God and build up community. The prologue of the Gospel of John takes over many of the themes from the Wisdom material. Like Wisdom, the Word participated in creation and redemption, bringing life, light, and glory. Also like Wisdom, the Word is a symbol and myth, placed in the form of a hymn, engaging the community's emotions so that in crisis they might affirm that Wisdom, the presence of God, was now experienced in Jesus.

The heart of the study was chapter 2, in which the wisdom themes in the Johannine portrait of Jesus were examined. Six such themes were discussed: preexistence, descent-ascent, revelation-hiddenness, acceptance-rejection, intimacy with disciples, and glory and life. Preexistence, a consistent characteristic of both Jesus and Wisdom, functions in the same way in both the Gospel and the Wisdom material. The descent-ascent schema of the Gospel is influenced both by the wisdom tradition and the apocalyptic Son of man tradition. Out of his intimacy with the Father, Jesus reveals the Father, and he calls people to believe in him as the revealer. Wisdom too reveals God and points the believer to herself as the bearer of that revelation. They both speak in "I" statements, they use similar images to describe their revelation, and they both appear as "hidden revealers." The appearance of the revealer in the Gospel and in the Wisdom passages results in a division in humanity between those who reject and those who accept. The believers form a community around both Jesus and Wisdom, and that community is imparted special revelation. The community receives glory and life. Jesus' glory is revealed in the signs and in the hour, both of which have come under wisdom influence. Life is the primary gift which both Jesus and Wisdom bestow upon believers. The cumulative value of these parallels leads to the conclusion that the evangelist depicts Jesus as the Wisdom of God incarnate.

Chapter 3 discussed the literary function of Wisdom in the Gospel and its social function in the Johannine community. Wisdom in the Gospel represents the transformation of a traditional symbol, which is now identified in Jesus. This symbol brings the prologue and the narrative into unity. Through this symbol, one also can see the continuity of the Gospel and Jewish thought. The wisdom themes of the Gospel indicate that the community was a hellenistic Jewish Christian school in which the wisdom traditions were intensively studied. Wisdom played an important role in community history, enabling the community to meet new situations in which it found itself. Wisdom both attracted women into the community and legitimated male leadership. Wisdom, therefore, has a significant place both in the Gospel and in the community out of which the Gospel arose.

Suggestions for Further Research

Though this study has carefully explored the territory, many stones have been left unturned. This section will point out a few uncharted paths for future exploration.

This study has considered Wisdom as a symbol, metaphor, and myth, and a few perspectives from literary criticism and cultural anthropology were brought to bear. Nevertheless, a study of Wisdom in the Gospel could be enriched by a cross-disciplinary definition of symbol, metaphor, and myth, which would not only include literary criticism and cultural anthropology but also psychology. The analytical psychology of Carl G. Jung would be particularly helpful because myth and symbol held an important place in Jung's thought.[1] Indeed, in Jung's most explicitly theological work, "Answer to Job," he speaks of Sophia as the feminine principle in Yahweh which affords self-reflection.[2] Joan Chamberlain Engelsman used Jung's theory of the archetypes of the collective unconscious in discussing Sophia as an archetype of the Great Mother. She contended that Sophia was a powerful figure in Judaism, but she was repressed both in Philo, where she was replaced by the masculine Logos, and in early Christianity, where she was replaced by the male Jesus.[3] Perspectives from analytical psychology have much to add to studies of Wisdom in the New Testament and especially in the Gospel.[4] Furthermore, it seems that there is room for dialogue between psychological criti-

---

[1]One of Jung's most important works was Symbols of Transformation, CW 5, trans. R. F. C. Hull, Bollingen Series XX (Princeton, NJ: Princeton University Press, 1952). Cf. also his "Symbols and the Interpretation of Dreams" and "The Symbolic Life" in his Miscellany, CW 18, trans. R. F. C. Hull, Bollingen Series XX (Princeton, NJ: Princeton University Press, 1952), pp. 183-264, 267-290; and the book he wrote with four other analysts Man and His Symbols (Garden City, NY: Doubleday & Co., 1964).

[2]Carl G. Jung, "Answer to Job," in Psychology and Religion: West and East, CW 11, trans. R. F. C. Hull, Bollingen Series XX (Princeton, NJ: Princeton University Press, 19), pp. 355-470.

[3]Joan Chamberlain Engelsman, The Feminine Dimension of the Divine (Philadelphia: Westminster Press, 1979). Cf. also Erich Neumann, The Great Mother: An Analysis of the Archetype, Bollingen Series 47 (Princeton, NJ: Princeton University Press, 1953).

[4]For two preliminary attempts to understand the Gospel through a Jungian perspective, cf. my "Jung and John," Exp, 7 (1988), 77-92; "Again, a Symbolic Reading of the Fourth Gospel," paper presented to the New Testament section of the Central States SBL meeting, Columbia, MO, March 26, 1990. Cf. also Schuyler Brown, "The Beloved Disciple: A Jungian View," in The Conversation Continues: Studies in Paul and John in Honor of J. Louis Martyn, ed. Robert T. Fortna and Beverly R. Gaventa (Nashville: Abingdon Press, 1990), pp. 366-377.

cism and reader-response theory. How does a text engage the emotions and imagination of the reader? Specifically, what role does Wisdom play in the Gospel's engaging the psyche of the reader?[5]

There is also a need for a consistent feminist analysis of Wisdom in early Christianity. Elisabeth Schüssler Fiorenza and Elizabeth A. Johnson have made some good beginnings in this area.[6] The point is often made that Wisdom enables us to see the feminine dimension of the divine.[7] While this is certainly true, the definitive symbol for God in the New Testament is nevertheless a male. Rosemary Radford Ruether has well said, "We need to go beyond the idea of a 'feminine side' of God, whether to be identified with the Spirit or even with the Sophia-Spirit together, and question the assumption that the highest symbol of divine sovereignty still remains exclusively male."[8] More reflection needs to be done on the effect of the replacement of a female Wisdom with a male Jesus. What effect did it have on the roles of women and men in the early church? What effect does it have on readers of the New Testament today?

Yet historical and literary studies also await. For example, the need exists for a comparative study of Wisdom Christology in the New Testament. Wisdom categories are applied to Christ not only in the Gospel but in Paul, Q, and Matthew, as recent studies have shown. How do these Wisdom Christologies compare? What are the similarities and differences between them? How do they function in the documents in which they appear? How did they function in the communities out of which these documents emerged? Given the pervasiveness of Wisdom in the

---

[5]For a reader-response approach to Wisdom in Matthew, cf. Russell Pregeant, "The Wisdom Passages in Matthew's Story," SBLSP, ed. David J. Lull (Atlanta: Scholars Press, 1990), pp. 469-493. The most thoroughgoing treatment of the Gospel from reader-response theory is Jeffrey Lloyd Staley, The Print's First Kiss: A Rhetorical Investigation of the Implied Reader in the Fourth Gospel, SBLDS 82 (Atlanta: Scholars Press, 1988). Cf. also R. Alan Culpepper and Fernando F. Segovia, eds., The Fourth Gospel from a Literary Perspective, Semeia 53 (Atlanta: Scholars Press, 1991). As noted in the introduction (cf. above, p. 6) I am contemplating a study of the Gospel informed both by Jungian psychology and reader-response criticism.

[6]Elisabeth Schüssler Fiorenza, In Memory of Her: A Feminist Theological Reconstruction of Christian Origins (New York: Crossroad, 1984), pp. 130-140, 188-192; Elizabeth A. Johnson, "Jesus the Wisdom of God: A Biblical Basis for Non-Androcentric Christology," ETL, 61 (1985), 261-294.

[7]Cf. Adela Yarbro Collins, "New Testament Perspectives: The Gospel of John," JSOT, 22 (1982), 51. This entire issue of JSOT deals with the feminist interpretation of the Bible.

[8]Rosemary Radford Ruether, Sexism and God-Talk: Toward a Feminist Theology (Boston: Beacon Press, 1983), p. 61.

New Testament, what conclusions can be drawn about its function in early Christianity? Now that numerous studies have been done on Wisdom in individual documents, it is perhaps time for a more comprehensive work discussing the role of Wisdom in the New Testament and the early church.

More work, however, remains to be done in the Gospel. The emphasis in this study has been on Wisdom Christology, but the Gospel also contains a Wisdom pneumatology. Not only is Jesus described in terms of Wisdom but so is the Paraclete.[9] Nevertheless, wisdom themes in the Johannine presentation of the Paraclete deserve the same comprehensive treatment as has been given here to the presentation of Jesus. If the Paraclete is depicted in terms of Wisdom, how does that affect the relationship between Jesus and the Paraclete? Is this one way in which the evangelist brings the two together for the reader? What does this say about Johannine Christology and ecclesiology? Is the evangelist saying that Wisdom, which was present in fullest measure in Jesus, is still present in the community through the Spirit?

Wisdom research, however, must not stop at the limits of the Gospel or of the New Testament, but it must also embrace Hebrew scripture and early Jewish literature. Wisdom Christology, then, can enrich biblical theology. As noted in the previous chapter, Samuel Terrien suggested Wisdom as the new integrating center for biblical theology.[10] At times when "the mighty acts of God" held ascendancy in biblical theology,[11] the wisdom literature was the forgotten stepchild. Wisdom, however, may serve as a bridge between the two testaments. Furthermore, she also can help facilitate Jewish-Christian dialogue. Wisdom has made a significant impact on both Jewish and Christian theology. For Jews, Wisdom is known primarily in the Law, following the tradition initiated by Sirach, Baruch, and the Tannaitic literature. For Christians, however, Wisdom is known in Jesus, as witnessed by such New Testament documents as Matthew and the Gospel. It seems, then, that Wisdom might serve as a basis for dialogue between Jews and Christians. How is the decisive manifestation of Wisdom similar yet different for Jews and Christians?

---

[9]Cf. Raymond E. Brown, The Gospel According to John, XIII-XXI, AB 29A (Garden City, N.Y.: Doubleday and Co., 1970), p. 1139.

[10]Cf. above, pp. 133.

[11]Cf. George Ernest Wright, God Who Acts: Biblical Theology as Recital (Naperville, IL: Alec R. Allenson, 1952).

What has been the impact of the two different revelations upon their respective communities of faith?

Wisdom Christology is a new frontier which scholars have only recently begun to explore. It has already yielded many treasures for New Testament Christology, biblical theology, and contemporary Christology. Yet many more lie buried in the field, their riches waiting to be mined.

BIBLIOGRAPHY

Agourides, S. "The 'High Priestly Prayer' of Jesus." Studia Evangelica, Vol. IV. Ed. F. L. Cross. Berlin: Akademie-Verlag, 1968.

Aland, Kurt. "Eine Untersuchung zu John 1.3-4: über die Bedeutung eines Punktes." Zeitschrift für die neutestamentliche Wissenschaft, 59 (1968), 174-209.

Albright, William F. "The Goddess of Life and Wisdom." American Journal of Semitic Languages and Literatures, 36 (1919-20), 258-294.

_____. "Some Canaanite-Phoenician Sources of Hebrew Wisdom." Supplement Vetus Testamentum, 3 (1955), 1-15.

Aletti, J.-N. "Proverbes 8,22-31. Etude de Structure." Biblica. 57 (1976), 25-37.

Appold, Mark J. The Oneness Motif in the Fourth Gospel: Motif Analysis and Exegetical Probe into the Theology of John. Wissenschaftliche Untersuchungen zum Neuen Testament 2,1. Tübingen: Mohr-Siebeck, 1976.

Argyle, A. W. "Philo and the Fourth Gospel." Expository Times, 63 (1951-52), 385-386.

Ashton, John. "The Transformation of Wisdom: A Study of the Prologue of John's Gospel. New Testament Studies, 32 (1986), 161-186.

Ausejo, Serafin de. "¿Es un himno a Cristo el prologo de San Juan?" Estudios bíblicos, 15 (1956), 223-277, 381-427.

Bacon, Benjamin W. The Gospel of the Hellenists. Ed. Carl H. Kraeling. New York: Henry Holt and Company, 1933.

Ballard, J. M. "The Translation of John xvii.5." Expository Times, 47 (1935-36), 284.

Barr, James. "Hypostatization of Linguistic Phaenomena in Modern Theological Interpretation," Journal of Semitic Studies, 7 (1962), 85-94.

Barrett, C. K. Essays on John. Philadelphia: Westminster Press, 1982.

_____. The Gospel According to St. John: An Introduction with Commentary and Notes on the Greek Text. 2d ed. Philadelphia: Westminster Press, 1978.

_____. The Gospel of John and Judaism. Trans. D. M. Smith. Philadelphia: Fortress Press, 1975.

Bauer, Walter, William F. Arndt, and F. Wilbur Gingrich. A Greek-English Lexicon of the New Testament and Other Early Christian Literature. 4th ed. Chicago: University of Chicago Press, 1957.

Becker, J. "Aufbau, Schichtung und theologieschichtliche Stellung des Gebetes in Johannes 17." Zeitschrift für die neutestamentliche Wissenschaft, 60 (1969), 56-61.

_____. "Beobachtungen zum Dualismus im Johannesevangelium." Zeitschrift für die neutestamentliche Wissenschaft, 65 (1974), 71-87

_____. Das Evangelium des Johannnes. Gutersloh: Mohn, 1979/1981.

_____. "Ich bin die Auferstehung und das Leben. Eine Skizze der johanneischen Christologie." Theologische Zeitschrift, 39 (1983), 138-151.

Berger, Peter. The Sacred Canopy: Elements of a Sociological Theory of Religion. Garden City, NY: Doubleday, 1969.

Bernard, J. H. A Critical and Exegetical Commentary on the Gospel According to St. John. International Critical Commentary. Ed. A. H. McNeile. Edinburgh: T. & T. Clark, 1928.

Bettenson, Henry, ed. Documents of the Christian Church. 2nd ed. London: Oxford University Press, 1963.

Blank, Josef. "Die Verhandlung vor Pilatus: Joh 18,28-19,16 im Lichte johanneischer Theologie." Biblische Zeitschrift, 3 (1959), 60-81.

Blass, F. and A. Debrunner. A Greek Grammar of the New Testament and Other Early Christian Literature. Trans. and rev. Robert W. Funk. Chicago: University of Chicago Press, 1961.

Blenkinsopp, Joseph. Wisdom and Law in the Old Testament: The Ordering of Life in Israel and Early Judaism. Oxford Bible Series. New York: Oxford University Press, 1983.

Boismard, M. E. St. John's Prologue. Trans. Carisbrooke Dominicans. London: Blackfriars Publications, 1957.

Borgen, Peder. Bread from Heaven: An Exegetical Study of the Concept of Manna in the Gospel of John and the Writings of Philo. Novum Testamentum, Supplements X. Leiden: E. J. Brill, 1965.

_____. "God's Agent in the Fourth Gospel." Religions in Antiquity: Essays in Memory of Erwin Ramsdell Goodenough. Ed. Jacob Neusner. Leiden: E. J. Brill, 1968.

_____. "Logos was the True Light: Contributions to the Interpretation of the Prologue of John." Novum Testamentum, 14 (1972), 115-130.

_____. "Observations on the Targumic Character of the Prologue of John." New Testament Studies, 16 (1969-70), 288-295.

Boström, Gustav. Proverbienstudien: Die Weisheit und das fremde Weib in Spruche 1-9. Lund: C. W. K. Gleerup, 1935.

Bowen, R. "The Fourth Gospel as Dramatic Material." Journal of Biblical Literature, 49 (1930), 292-305.

Braun, F.-M. Jean le Théologien: Les grandes traditions d'Israel et l'accord des Escritures selon le Quatrième Evangile. Paris: J. Gabalda, 1964.

_____. "Messie, Logos, et Fils de l'homme." La Venue du Messie. Ed. E. Massaux, et al. Paris: Desclee de Brouwer, 1962.

Bream, N. H. "No Need to Be Asked Questions: A Study of Jn. 16:30." Search the Scriptures: New Testament Essays in Honor of Raymond T. Stamm. Gettysburg Theological Series 3. Leiden: E. J. Brill, 1969.

Brown, Raymond E. The Community of the Beloved Disciple: The Life, Loves, and Hates of an Individual Church in New Testament Times. New York: Paulist Press, 1979.

_____. "Does the New Testament Call Jesus God?" Jesus God and Man. New York: Macmillan Press, 1967.

_____. The Epistles of John. The Anchor Bible, Vol. 30. Garden City, NY: Doubleday and Co., 1982.

_____. The Gospel According to John, I-XII. The Anchor Bible, Vol. 29. Garden City, NY: Doubleday and Co., 1966.

_____. The Gospel According to John, XIII-XXI. The Anchor Bible, Vol. 29A. Garden City, NY: Doubleday and Co., 1970.

_____. "The Kergyma of the Gospel According to John." New Testament Issues. New York: Harper and Row, 1970.

158

_____. "'Other Sheep Not of This Fold': The Johannine Perspective on Christian Diversity in the Late First Century." Journal of Biblical Literature, 97 (1978), 5-22.

_____. "The Qumran Scrolls and the Johannine Gospel and Epistles. New Testament Essays. New York: Paulist Press, 1965.

_____. "Theology of Incarnation in St. John." Contemporary New Testament Studies. Ed. M. Rosalie Ryan. Collegeville, MN: Liturgical Press, 1965.

_____. "Who Do Men Say That I Am?--A Survey of Modern Scholarship on Gospel Christology." Biblical Reflections on Crises Facing the Church. New York: Paulist Press, 1975.

Brown, Schuyler. "The Beloved Disciple: A Jungian View." The Conversation Continues: Studies in Paul and John in Honor of J. Louis Martyn. Ed. Robert T. Fortna and Beverly R. Gaventa. Nashville: Abingdon Press, 1990.

Buchsel, Friedrich. "κρίνω." Theological Dictionary of the New Testament. Vol. III. Ed. Gerhard Kittel. Trans. G. W. Bromiley. Grand Rapids: Wm. B. Eerdmans, 1964.

_____. "μονογενής." Theological Dictionary of the New Testament. Vol. IV. Ed. Gerhard Kittel. Trans. G. W. Bromiley. Grand Rapids: Wm. B. Eerdmans, 1967.

Buhner, J. Der Gesandte und sein Weg im 4. Evangelium. Wissenschaftliche Untersuchungen zum Neuen Testament 2,2. Tübingen: Mohr-Siebeck, 1976.

Bultmann, Rudolf. "ἀλήθεια." Theological Dictionary of the New Testament. Vol. I. Ed. Gerhard Kittel. Trans. G. W. Bromiley. Grand Rapids: Wm. B. Eerdmans, 1964.

_____. "γινώσκω." Theological Dictionary of the New Testament. Vol. I. Ed. Gerhard Kittel. Trans. G. W. Bromiley. Grand Rapids: Wm. B. Eerdmans, 1964.

_____. The Gospel of John: A Commentary. Trans. G. R. Beasley-Murray, et al. Philadelphia: Westminster Press, 1971.

_____. "The History of Religions Background of the Prologue to the Gospel of John." The Interpretation of John. Ed. John Ashton. Issues in Religion and Theology 9. Philadelphia: Fortress Press, 1986. Translation of "Der religionsgeschichtliche Hintergrund des Prologs zum Johannes." ΕΥΧΑΡΙΣΤΗΡΙΟΝ: Festschrift für H. Gunkel. Göttingen: Vandehoeck und Ruprecht, 1923.

_____. Theology of the New Testament. 2 vols. Trans. K. Grobel. New York: Charles Scribner's Sons, 1955.

_____. "ζωή." Theological Dictionary of the New Testament. Vol. II. Ed. Gerhard Kittel. Trans. G. W. Bromiley. Grand Rapids: Wm. B. Eerdmans, 1964.

Burge, Gary M. The Anointed Community: The Holy Spirit in the Johannine Tradition. Grand Rapids: Wm. B. Eerdmans, 1987.

Burkett, Delbert. The Son of Man in the Gospel of John. Journal for the Study of the New Testament Supplement Series 56. Sheffield: JSOT Press, 1991.

Burnett, Fred. The Testament of Jesus-Sophia: A Redaction-critical Study of the Eschatological Discourse in Matthew. Washington, DC: University Press of America, 1981.

Cadman, W. H. The Open Heaven: The Revelation of God in the Johannine Sayings of Jesus. Ed. G. B. Caird. New York: Herder and Herder, 1969.

Cady, Susan, Marian Ronan, and Hal Taussig. Sophia: The Future of Feminist Spirituality. San Francisco: Harper & Row, 1986.

Cahill, P. J. "The Johannine Logos as Center." Catholic Biblical Quarterly, 38 (1976), 54-72.

Camp, Claudia V. Wisdom and the Feminine in the Book of Proverbs. Bible and Literature Series 11. Sheffield: Almond, 1985.

Carter, Warren. "The Prologue and John's Gospel: Function, Symbol, and the Definitive Word." Journal for the Study of the New Testament, 39 (1990), 35-58.

Charlesworth, James H. John and Qumran. London: Geoffrey Chapman, 1972.

_____. The Old Testament Pseudepigrapha. 2 vols. Garden City, NY: Doubleday and Co., 1983, 1985.

Christ, Felix. Jesus Sophia: Die Sophia-Christologie bei den Synoptikern. Abhandlungen zur theologie des Alten und Neuen Testaments 57. Zürich: Zwingli-Verlag, 1970.

Clark, David J. "In Search of Wisdom: Notes on Job 28." Bible Translator, 33 1982), 401-405.

Clark, Douglas K. "Signs in Wisdom and John." Catholic Biblical Quarterly, 45 (1983), 201-209.

Collins, Adela Yarbro. "New Testament Perspectives: The Gospel of John." Journal for the Study of the Old Testament, 22 (1982), 47-53.

Colpe, Carsten. Die religionsgeschichtliche Schule: Darstellung und Kritik ihres Bildes vom gnostichen Erlosermythus. Göttingen: Vandehoeck und Ruprecht, 1961.

Colson, F. H. and G. H. Whitaker, trans. Philo Judaeus. 10 vols. The Loeb Classical Library. New York: Putnam, 1929-1962.

Conzelmann, Hans. "The Mother of Wisdom." The Future of Our Religious Past. Ed. James M. Robinson. London: SCM Press, 1971.

_____. "φῶς." Theological Dictionary of the New Testament. Vol. IX. Ed. Gerhard Friedrich. Trans. G. W. Bromiley. Grand Rapids: Wm. B. Eerdmans, 1974.

_____. "σκότος." Theological Dictionary of the New Testament. Vol. VII. Ed. Gerhard Friedrich. Trans. G. W. Bromiley. Grand Rapids: Wm. B. Eerdmans, 1971.

_____, and Walther Zimmerli. "χαίρω." Theological Dictionary of the New Testament. Vol. IX. Ed. Gerhard Friedrich. Trans. G. W. Bromiley. Grand Rapids: Wm. B. Eerdmans, 1974.

Coppens, Joseph."Le Fils de l'homme dans l'evangile johannique. Ephemerides theologicae lovanienses, 52 (1976), 28-81.

Cory, Catherine. "Docetism and the 'Glorification' of the Johannine Jesus." Paper presented to the Johannine Literature Section of the Annual Meeting of the Society of Biblical Literature, Kansas City, MO, November 23, 1991.

Craddock, Fred B. The Pre-existence of Christ in the New Testament. Nashville: Abingdon Press, 1968.

Crenshaw, James L. Old Testament Wisdom: An Introduction. Atlanta: John Knox Press, 1981.

_____, ed. Studies in Ancient Israelite Wisdom. New York: KTAV, 1976.

Cullmann, Oscar. The Christology of the New Testament. Rev. ed. Trans. Shirley Guthrie and Charles A. M. Hall. Philadelphia: Westminster Press, 1963.

_____. Early Christian Worship. Trans. A. S. Todd and J. B. Torrance. Philadelphia: Westminster, 1953.

_____. The Johannine Circle. Trans. John Bowden. Philadelphia: Westminster Press, 1976.

_____. "Ο ΟΠΙΣΩ ΜΟΥ ΕΡΧΟΜΕΝΟΣ." The Early Church. Ed. A. J. B. Higgins. London: SCM Press, 1956.

_____. Salvation in History. Trans. Sidney G. Sowers, et al. New York: Harper and Row, 1967.

Culpepper, R. Alan. Anatomy of the Fourth Gospel: A Study in Literary Design. Foundations and Facets. Philadelphia: Fortress Press, 1983.

_____. The Johannine School: An Evaluation of the Johannine-School Hypothesis Based on an Investigation of the Nature of Ancient Schools. Society of Biblical Literature Dissertation Series 26. Missoula, MT: Scholars Press, 1975.

_____. "The Pivot of John's Prologue." New Testament Studies, 27 (1980), 1-31.

_____, and Fernando F. Segovia, eds. The Fourth Gospel from a Literary Perspective. Semeia 53. Atlanta: Scholars Press, 1991.

Dahms, John V. "The Johannine Use of Monogenēs Reconsidered." New Testament Studies, 29 (1983), 222-232.

Davey, J. Ernest. The Jesus of St. John: Historical and Christological Studies in the Fourth Gospel. London: Lutterworth Press, 1958.

Davies, Stevan L. The Gospel of Thomas and Christian Wisdom. New York: Seabury Press, 1983.

Davies, W. D. Paul and Rabbinic Judaism: Some Rabbinic Elements of Pauline Theology. 2nd ed. London: SPCK, 1955.

Debrunner, Albert, et al. "λέγω." Theological Dictionary of the New Testament. Vol. IV. Ed. Gerhard Kittel. Trans. G. W. Bromiley. Grand Rapids: Wm. B. Eerdmans, 1967.

Delling, Gerhard. "ἄρχω." Theological Dictionary of the New Testament. Vol. I. Ed. Gerhard Kittel. Trans. G. W. Bromiley. Grand Rapids: Wm. B. Eerdmans, 1964.

_____. "λαμβάνω." Theological Dictionary of the New Testament. Vol. IV. Ed. Gerhard Kittel. Trans. G. W. Bromiley. Grand Rapids: Wm. B. Eerdmans, 1967.

_____. "πλήρης." Theological Dictionary of the New Testament. Vol. VI. Ed. Gerhard Friedrich. Trans. G. W. Bromiley. Grand Rapids: Wm. B. Eerdmans, 1968.

Deutsch, Celia. Hidden Wisdom and the Easy Yoke: Wisdom, Torah and Discipleship in Matthew 11:25-30. Journal for the Study of the New Testament Supplement Series 18. Sheffield: JSOT Press, 1987.

_____. "Jesus as Wisdom; Metaphor and Social Structure in Matthew's Gospel." Paper presented to the Israelite and Early Christian Wisdom Section of the

162

Annual Meeting of the Society of Biblical Literature, Kansas City, MO, November 25, 1991.

_____. "Transformation of Symbols: The New Jerusalem in Rv 21:1-22:5." Zeitschrift für neutestamentliche Wissenschaft, 78 (1987),

_____. "Wisdom in Matthew: Transformation of a Symbol." Novum Testamentum, 32 (1990), 13-47.

Dillistone, F. W. "Wisdom, Word, and Spirit: Revelation in the Wisdom Literature." Interpretation, 2 (1948), 275-287.

Dillon, Richard J. "Wisdom Tradition and Sacramental Retrospect in the Cana Account (Jn 2,1-11)." Catholic Biblical Quarterly, 24 (1962), 268-296.

Dix, Gregory. "The Heavenly Wisdom and the Divine Logos in Jewish Apocalyptic." Journal of Theological Studies, 26 (1924-25), 1-12.

Dodd, C. H. Historical Tradition in the Fourth Gospel. Cambridge: Cambridge University Press, 1963.

_____. The Interpretation of the Fourth Gospel. Cambridge University Press, 1953.

_____. "The Portrait of Jesus in John and in the Synoptics." Christian History and Interpretation: Studies Presented to John Knox. Ed. W. R. Farmer , C. F. D. Moule, and R. R. Niebuhr. Cambridge: Cambridge University Press, 1967.

Drummond, James. Philo Judaeus: The Jewish-Alexandrian Philosophy in His Development and Completion. London: Williams and Norgate, 1888.

Dunn, James D. G. Christology in the Making: A New Testament Inquiry Into the Origins of the Doctrine of the Incarnation. Philadelphia: Westminster Press, 1980.

_____. "Christology Yet Once More: A Further Letter to Professor Wiles." Theology, 85 (1982), 360-361.

_____. "John VI--An Eucharistic Discourse?" New Testament Studies, 17 (1971), 328-338.

_____. "Let John be John: A Gospel for Its Time." Das Evangelium und die Evangelien: Vorträge vom Tübinger Symposium 1982. Ed. Peter Stuhlmacher. Tübingen: Mohr-Siebeck, 1983.

_____. "Some Thoughts on Maurice Wiles's 'Reflections.'" Theology, 85 (1982), 96-98.

_____. "Was Christianity a Monotheistic Faith from the Beginning?" Scottish Journal of Theology, 35 (1982), 303-336.

Dyroff, A. "Zum Prolog des Johannesevangeliums." Pisciculi. Ed. Theodor Klauser. Munster: Aschendorff, 1939.

Edwards, Richard A. A Theology of Q: Eschatology, Prophecy and Wisdom. Philadelphia: Fortress Press, 1976.

Eichrodt, Walther. Theology of the Old Testament. Trans. J. A. Baker. 2 vols. Philadelphia: Westminster Press, 1967.

Eltester, W. "Der Logos und sein Prophet." Apophoreta: Festschrift für E. Haenchen. Beiheft zur Zeitschrift für neutestamentliche Wissenschaft. Berlin: Töpelmann, 1964.

Engelsman, Joan Chamberlain. The Feminine Dimension of the Divine. Philadelphia: Westminster Press, 1979.

Epp, Eldon Jay. "Wisdom, Torah, Word: The Johannine Prologue and the Purpose of the Fourth Gospel." Current Issues in Biblical and Patristic Interpretation: Studies in Honor of Merrill C. Tenney. Ed. G. F. Hawthorne. Grand Rapids: Wm. B. Eerdmans, 1975.

Evans, Craig A. "On the Prologue of John and the Trimorphic Protennoia." New Testament Studies, 27 (1981), 395-401.

Fascher, Erich. "Christologie und Gnosis im vierten Evangelium." Theologische Literaturzeitung, 93 (1968), 721-730.

Felder, Cain Hope. Troubling Biblical Waters: Race, Class, and Family. Bishop Henry McNeal Turner Studies in North American Black Religion 3. Maryknoll, NY: Orbis, 1989.

Fennema, David A. "Jesus and God According to John: An Analysis of the Fourth Gospel's Father/Son Christology," Ph.D. dissertation, Duke University, 1979.

Feuillet, André. Le Christ, Sagesse d'après les Epîtres Pauliennes. Etudes bibliques. Paris: J. Gibalda, 1966.

_____. "Les Ego Eimi christologiques du quatrième Evangile." Recherches de Science Religieuse, 54 (1966), 5-22, 213-240.

_____. Johannine Studies. Trans. Thomas E. Crane. Staten Island, NY: Alba House, 1964.

_____. Le mystere de l'amour divin dans le johannique. Etudes bibliques. Paris: J. Gibalda, 1972.

_____. Le Prologue de quatrième Evangile. Paris: Brouwer, 1968.

_____. "Redemptive Incarnation in the Johannine Writings." Introduction to the New Testament. Ed. André Robert and André Feuillet. Trans. Patrick Skehan, et al. New York: Desclee Co., 1965.

Filson, Floyd V. "The Gospel of Life." Current Issues in New Testament Interpretation. Ed. W. Klassen and G. F. Snyder. New York: Harper, 1962.

Forestell, J. Terence. The Word of the Cross: Salvation as Revelation in the Fourth Gospel. Analecta Biblica 57. Rome: Biblical Institute Press, 1974.

Fortna, Robert T. "Christology in the Fourth Gospel: Redaction-Critical Perspectives." New Testament Studies, 21 (1974-75), 489-504.

_____. "From Christology to Soteriology: A Redaction-critical Study of Salvation in the Fourth Gospel." Interpretation, 27 (1973), 31-47.

_____. The Fourth Gospel and Its Predecessor: From Narrative Source to Present Gospel. Philadelphia: Fortress Press, 1988.

_____. The Gospel of Signs: A Reconstruction of the Narrative Source Underlying the Fourth Gospel. Society for New Testament Studies Monograph Series 11. Cambridge: Cambridge University Press, 1970.

Freed, Edwin D. Old Testament Quotations in the Gospel of John. Novum Testamentum, Supplements XI. Leiden: E. J. Brill, 1965.

_____. "Theological Prelude to the Prologue of John's Gospel." Scottish Journal of Theology, 32 (1979), 257-269.

Fuller, Reginald H. The Foundations of New Testament Christology. New York: Charles Scribner's Sons, 1965.

_____. "The Incarnation in Historical Perspective." Anglican Theological Review, Supplemental Series, 7 (1976), 57-66.

_____, and Pheme Perkins. Who is This Christ? Gospel Christology and Contemporary Faith. Philadelphia: Fortress Press, 1983.

Gaertner, Bertil. John 6 and the Jewish Passover. Coniectanea Neotestamentica 17. Lund: C. W. K. Glerrup, 1959.

Gaffney, James. "Believing and Knowing in the Fourth Gospel." Theological Studies, 26 (1965), 215-241.

Gammie, John G., et al, eds. Israelite Wisdom: Theological and Literary Essays in Honor of Samuel Terrien. Missoula, MT: Scholars Press, 1978.

_____. "Spatial and Ethical Dualism in Jewish Wisdom and Apocalyptic Literature." Journal of Biblical Literature, 93 (1974), 356-385.

Gaster, T. H. "Old Testament Notes: Prov. 8:30." Vetus Testamentum, 4 (1954), 77-78.

Geertz, Clifford. The Interpretation of Cultures: Selected Essays. New York: Basic Books, 1973.

Gench, Frances Taylor. "Wisdom in the Christology of Matthew." Ph. D. dissertation, Union Theological Seminary in Virginia, 1988.

Gese, Harmut. Essays on Biblical Theology. Trans. Keith Crim. Minneapolis: Augsburg, 1981.

_____. "Wisdom, Son of Man, and the Origins of Christology: The Consistent Development of Biblical Theology." Trans. U. Mauser. Horizons in Biblical Theology, 3 (1981), 23-57.

Gilbert, Maurice. La Sagesse de l'Ancien Testament. Gembloux: Duculot, 1979.

Girard, M. "Analyse structurelle de Jn 1, 1-18: l'unité des deux Testaments dans la structure bipolaire du prologue de Jean." Science et Esprit, 35 (1983), 5-31.

Goodenough, Edwin R. By Light, Light: The Mystic Gospel of Hellenistic Judaism. Amsterdam: Philo Press, 1969.

Gordis, R. The Book of God and Man. Chicago: University of Chicago Press, 1965.

Goulder, Michael, ed. Incarnation and Myth: The Debate Continued. Grand Rapids: Wm. B. Eerdmans, 1979.

Green, Michael, ed. The Truth of God Incarnate. Grand Rapids: Wm. B. Eerdmans, 1977.

Grillmeier, A. Christ in Christian Tradition: From the Apostolic Age to Chalcedon (451). Trans. J. S. Bowden. New York: Sheed and Ward, 1965.

Gunton, Colin E. Yesterday and Today: A Study of Continuities in Christology. Grand Rapids: Wm. B. Eerdmans, 1983.

Habel, Norman C. "Of Things Beyond Me: Wisdom in the Book Of Job." Currents in Theology and Mission, 10 (1983), 142-154.

_____. "The Symbolism of Wisdom in Proverbs 1-9." Interpretation, 26 (1972), 131-157.

Haenchen, Ernst. John 1: A Commentary on the Gospel of John Chapters 1-6. Hermeneia. Trans. Robert W. Funk. Ed. Robert W. Funk with Ulrich Busse. Philadelphia: Fortress Press, 1984.

166

_____. John 2: A Commentary on the Gospel of John Chapters 7-21. Hermeneia. Trans. Robert W. Funk. Ed. Robert W. Funk with Ulrich Busse. Philadelphia: Fortress Press, 1984.

Hamerton-Kelly, Robert. "The Idea of Pre-existence in Early Judaism: A Study in the Background of New Testament Theology." Th. D. dissertation, Union Theological Seminary in the City of New York, 1966.

_____. Pre-existence, Wisdom, and the Son of Man: A Study of the Idea of Pre-existence in the New Testament. Society for New Testament Studies Monograph Series 21. Cambridge: Cambridge University Press, 1973.

Hanson, Anthony Tyrell. Grace and Truth: A Study in the Doctrine of the Incarnation. London: SPCK, 1975.

_____. "The Jesus of the Fourth Gospel." New Divinity, 5 (1974), 20-24.

_____. The New Testament Interpretation of Scripture. London: SPCK, 1980.

Hare, Douglas R. A. The Son of Man Tradition. Minneapolis: Fortress Press, 1990.

Harnack, Adolf von. "Uber das Verhältnis des Prologs des vierten Evangeliums zum ganzen Werk." Zeitschrift für Theologie und Kirche, 2 (1892), 189-231.

Harner, P. B. The "I Am" of the Fourth Gospel: A Study of Johannine Usage and Thought. Facet Books. Philadelphia: Fortress Press, 1970.

Harris, J. Rendel. The Origin of the Prologue of St. John's Gospel. Cambridge: Cambridge University Press, 1917.

Hayward, C. T. R. "The Holy Name of the God of Moses and the Prologue of St. John's Gospel." New Testament Studies, 25 (1978-79), 16-32.

Hengel, Martin. Judaism and Hellenism. 2 vols. Trans. John Bowden. London: SCM Press, 1975.

_____. The Son of God: The Origin of Christology and the History of Jewish-Hellenistic Religion. Trans. John Bowden. Philadelphia: Fortress Press, 1976.

Hick, John, ed. The Myth of God Incarnate. Philadelphia: Westminster Press, 1977.

Hoskyns, Edwin C. The Fourth Gospel. Ed. F. N. Davey. London: Faber and Faber, Ltd., 1940.

Hruby, L. "La Torah identifiée à la Sagesse et l'activité du 'Sage' dans la tradition rabbinique." Bible et Vie Chrétienne, 76 (1967), 65-78.

Hurtado, Larry W. One God, One Lord: Early Christian Devotion and Ancient Jewish Monotheism. Philadelphia: Fortress Press, 1988.

Imschoot, P. van. "Sagesse et Espirit dans l'Ancient Testament." Revue Biblique, 47 (1938), 23-49.

Inge, William. Christian Mysticism. London: Charles Scribner's Sons, 1899.

Irwin, W. A. "Where Shall Wisdom Be Found?" Journal of Biblical Literature, 80 (1961), 133-142.

Jacob, Edmond. Theology of the Old Testament. New York: Harper, 1958.

Jendorff, Bernard. Der Logosbegriff. Europaiische Hochschriften, 20/19. Frankfurt: Lang, 1976.

Jeremias, Joachim. "The Revealing Word." The Central Message of the New Testament. Philadelphia: Fortress Press, 1981.

Johnson, Elizabeth A. "Jesus the Wisdom of God: A Biblical Basis for Non-Androcentric Christology." Ephemerides theologicae lovanienses, 61 (1985), 261-294.

Jonge, Marinus de. "Jesus as Prophet and King." Jesus: Stranger from Heaven and Son of God. Ed. and trans. John E. Steeley. Society of Biblical Literature Sources for Biblical Study 11. Missoula, MT: Scholars Press, 1977.

Jung, Carl G. "Answer to Job." Psychology and Religion: West and East. The Collected Works of Carl G. Jung, Vol. 11. Trans. R. F. C. Hull. Bollingen Series 20. Princeton, NJ: Princeton University Press, 1952.

_____. Miscellany. The Collected Works of Carl G. Jung, Vol. 18. Trans. R. F. C. Hull. Bollingen Series 20. Princeton, NJ: Princeton University Press, 1952.

_____. Symbols of Transformation. The Collected Works of Carl G. Jung, Vol. 5. Trans. R. F. C. Hull. Bollingen Series 20. Princeton, NJ: Princeton University Press, 1952.

_____, M.-L. von Franz, Joseph L. Henderson, Jolande Jacobe, and Aniela Jaffé. Man and His Symbols. Garden City, NY: Doubleday and Company, 1964.

Käsemann, Ernst. "The Structure and Purpose of the Prologue to John's Gospel." New Testament Questions of Today. London: SCM Press, 1969.

_____. The Testament of Jesus. Trans. Gerhard Krodel. Philadelphia: Fortress Press, 1968.

Kaufman, Gordon D. The Theological Imagination: Constructing the Concept of God. Philadelphia: Westminster Press, 1981.

168

Kayatz, Christa. Studien zu Proverbien 1-9. Neukirchen Vluyn: Neukirchener, 1966.

Keck, Leander E "Jesus in New Testament Christology." Australian Biblical Review, 28 (1980), 1-15.

_____. "Toward the Renewal of New Testament Christology." New Testament Studies, 32 (1986), 362-377.

King, J. S. "The Prologue to the Fourth Gospel: Some Unresolved Problems." Expository Times, 86 (1974-75), 372-373.

Kittel, Gerhard. "λόγος." Theological Dictionary of the New Testament. Vol. IV. Ed. Gerhard Kittel. Trans. G. W. Bromiley. Grand Rapids: Wm. B. Eerdmans, 1967.

Kleinknecht, Hermann and Walter Gutbrod. "νόμος." Theological Dictionary of the New Testament. Vol. IV. Ed. Gerhard Kittel. Trans. G. W. Bromiley. Grand Rapids: Wm. B. Eerdmans, 1967.

Kloppenborg, John S. The Formation of Q: Trajectories in Ancient Wisdom Collections. Philadelphia: Fortress Press, 1987.

_____. "Isis and Sophia in the Book of Wisdom." Harvard Theological Review, 75 (1982), 57-84.

_____. "Wisdom Christology in Q." Laval théologique et philosophique, 34 (1978), 129-147.

Knibb, M. A. "The Date of the Parables of Enoch: A Critical Review." New Testament Studies, 25 (1978-79), 345-359.

Knox, John. The Humanity and Divinity of Christ: A Study of Pattern in Christology. Cambridge: Cambridge University Press, 1967.

Knox, Wilfred L. "The Divine Wisdom." Journal of Theological Studies, 38 (1937), 230-237.

Koenig, John, et al. "Review Symposium. Elisabeth Schüssler Fiorenza, In Memory of Her. Four Perpectives." Horizons, 11 (1984), 144-157.

Kraemer, Werner. Christ, Lord, Son of God. Trans. Brian Hardy. Studies in Biblical Theology 50. London: SCM Press, 1966.

Kruijk, Th. C. de. "The Glory of the Only Son (John 1:14)." Studies in John Presented to Professor Dr. J. N. Sevenster. Novum Testamentum, Supplements XXIV. Leiden: E. J. Brill, 1970.

Kuhl, Josef. Die Sendung Jesu und der Kirche nach dem Johannes-Evangelium. Studia Instituti Missiologici Societatis Verbi Divini, 11. St. Augustin: Steyler Verlag, 1967.

Kysar, Robert. "The Background of the Prologue of the Fourth Gospel: A Critique of Historical Methods." Canadian Journal of Theology, 16 (1970), 250-255.

_____. The Fourth Evangelist and His Gospel: An Examination of Contemporary Scholarship. Minneapolis: Augsburg Publishing House, 1975.

_____. "The Gospel of John in Current Research." Religious Studies Review, 9 (1983), 314-323.

_____. John the Maverick Gospel. Atlanta: John Knox Press, 1976.

Lang, Bernhard. Frau Weisheit. Düsseldorf: Patmos, 1976.

_____. Wisdom and the Book of Proverbs: An Israelite Goddess Redefined. New York: Pilgrim Press, 1986.

Langkamer, P. Hugolinus. "Zur Herkunft des Logostitels im Johannesprolog." Biblische Zeitschrift, 9 (1965), 91-94.

Larcher, C. Etudes sur le livre de la Sagesse. Paris: Etudes bibliques, 1969.

Lefebure, Leo D. Toward a Contemporary Wisdom Christology: A Study of Karl Rahner and Norman Pittenger. Lanham, MD: University Press of America, 1988.

Lightfoot, R. H. St. John's Gospel: A Commentary. Ed. C. F. Evans. Oxford: Clarendon Press, 1956.

Lindars, Barnabas. The Gospel of John. New Century Bible. Grand Rapids: Wm. B. Eerdmans, 1972.

_____. Jesus Son of Man: A Fresh Examination of the Son of Man Sayings in the Gospels. Grand Rapids: Wm. B. Eerdmans, 1984.

_____. New Testament Apologetic: The Doctrinal Significance of the Old Testament Quotations. Philadelphia: Westminster Press, 1961.

_____, and S. S. Smalley, eds. Christ and Spirit in the New Testament: Studies in Honour of C. F. D. Moule. Cambridge: Cambridge University Press, 1973.

Loader, William. "The Central Structure of Johannine Christology." New Testament Studies, 30 (1984), 188-216.

170

_____. The Christology of the Fourth Gospel: Structure and Issues. Beitrage zur biblischen Exegese und Theologie, Band 23. Frankfurt am Main: Peter Lang, 1989.

McCool, F. J. "Living Water in John." The Bible in Current Catholic Thought. Festschrift for M. Gruenthaner. Ed. J. L. McKenzie. New York: Herder & Herder, 1962.

McDonald, Durstan R., ed. The Myth/Truth of God Incarnate: The Tenth National Conference of Trinity Institute. Wilton, CT: Morehouse-Barlow Co., 1979.

Macgregor, G. H. C. The Gospel of John. Moffatt New Testament Commentary. London: Hodder and Stoughton, 1928.

Mack, Burton Lee. Logos und Sophia: Untersuchungen zur Weisheitstheologie im hellenistichen Judentum. Göttingen: Vandenhoeck und Ruprecht, 1973.

_____. "Wisdom Myth and Mytho-ology." Interpretation, 24 (1970), 46-60.

McKane, William. Proverbs: A New Approach. The Old Testament Library. Philadelphia: Westminster Press, 1970.

McNamara, M. "Logos of the Fourth Gospel and Memra of the Palestinian Targum." Expository Times, 79 (1967-68), 115-117.

Macquarrie, John. Principles of Christian Theology. 2d ed. New York: Charles Scribner's Sons, 1977.

MacRae, George W. "The Fourth Gospel and Religionsgeschichte." Catholic Biblical Quarterly, 32 (1970), 13-24.

_____. "The Jewish Background of the Gnostic Sophia Myth." Novum Testamentum, 13 (1970), 86-101.

Maddox, Robert. "The Function of the Son of Man in the Gospel of John." Reconciliation and Hope: New Testament Essays on Atonement and Eschatology. Festschrift for L. L. Morris. Ed. R. J. Banks. Exeter: Paternoster Press, 1974.

Maher, M. "Some Aspects of Torah in Judaism." Irish Theological Quarterly, 38 (1971), 310-325.

Märbock, J. Weisheit im Wandel: Untersuchungen zur Weisheitstheologie bei ben Sira. Bonn: Peter Hanstein Verlag, 1971.

Marcus, R. "On Biblical Hypostases of Wisdom." Hebrew Union College Annual, 23 (1950-51), 157-171.

Martyn, J. Louis. The Gospel of John in Christian History: Essays for Interpreters. New York: Paulist Press, 1978.

_____. History and Theology in the Fourth Gospel. Rev. ed. Nashville: Abingdon Press, 1979.

_____. "Source Criticism and Religionsgeschichte in the Fourth Gospel." Perspective, 11 (1970), 247-273.

Mastin, B. A. "A Neglected Feature of the Christology of the Fourth Gospel." New Testament Studies, 22 (1975-76), 32-51.

Mattill, A. J. "Johannine Communities behind the Fourth Gospel: Georg Richter's Analysis." Theological Studies, 38 (1977), 294-315.

Mayer, G. Index Philoneus. Berlin: Walter de Gruyter, 1974.

Mays, James Luther, ed. Interpreting the Gospels. Philadelphia: Fortress Press, 1981.

Mealand, David L. "The Christology of the Fourth Gospel." Scottish Journal of Theology, 31 (1978), 449-467.

Mearns, Christopher L. "Dating the Similitudes of Enoch." New Testament Studies, 25 (1978-79), 360-369.

Meeks, Wayne A. "'Am I a Jew?'--Johannine Christianity and Judaism." Christianity, Judaism, and Other Greco-Roman Cults: Studies for Morton Smith. Part 1: New Testament. Ed. J. Neusner. Leiden: E. J. Brill, 1975.

_____. "The Divine Agent and his Counterfeit in Philo and the Fourth Gospel." Aspects of Religious Philosophy in Judiasm and Early Christianity. Ed. Elisabeth Schüssler Fiorenza. Notre Dame: University of Notre Dame Press, 1967.

_____. "Man from Heaven in Johannine Sectarianism." Journal of Biblical Literature, 91 (1972), 44-72.

_____. The Prophet-King: Moses Tradition and the Johannine Christology. Novum Testamentum, Supplements XIV. Leiden: E. J. Brill, 1967.

Metzger, Bruce M. "On the Translation of John 1:1." Expository Times, 63 (1951-52), 125-126.

_____. A Textual Commentary on the Greek New Testament: A Companion Volume to the United Bible Societies' Greek New Testament. London: United Bible Societies, 1971.

Michaelis, Wilhelm. "Joh 1,51, Gen 28,12 und das Menschensohn Problem." Theologische Literaturzeitung, 85 (1960), 561-578.

172

_____. "ὁράω." Theological Dictionary of the New Testament. Vol. V. Ed. Gerhard Friedrich. Trans. G. W. Bromiley. Grand Rapids: Wm. B. Eerdmans, 1967.

_____. "σκηνή." Theological Dictionary of the New Testament. Vol. VII. Ed. Gerhard Friedrich. Trans. G. W. Bromiley. Grand Rapids: Wm. B. Eerdmans, 1971.

Middleton, R. D. "Logos and Shekinah in the Fourth Gospel." Jewish Quarterly Review, 29 (1938-39), 101-133.

Miller, Ed L. "The Logic of the Logos Hymn." New Testament Studies, 29 (1983), 552-561.

_____. "The Logos Was God." Evangelical Quarterly, 53 (1981), 65-77.

Miranda, Juan Peter. Die Sendung Jesu im vierten Evangelium: Religions- und theologiesgeschichtliche Untersuchungen zu den Sendungsformeln. Stuttgart: Verlag Katholisches Bibelwerk, 1977.

_____. Der Vater, der mich gesandt hat: Religionsgeschichtliche Untersuchungen zu den johanneischen Christologie und Ekklesiologie. Frankfurt: Herbert Lang, 1972.

Moeller, Henry R. "Wisdom Motifs and John's Gospel." Bulletin of the Evangelical Theological Society, 6 (1963), 93-98.

Moffatt, James. An Introduction to the Literature of the New Testament. 3rd ed. International Theological Library. New York: Charles Scribner's Sons, 1925.

Moloney, Francis J. The Johannine Son of Man. 2d ed. Biblioteca di Scienze Religiose, 14. Rome: Libraria Ateneo Salesiano, 1979.

Moody, Dale. "God's Only Son: The Translation of John 3:16 in the Revised Standard Version." Journal of Biblical Literature, 72 (1953), 213-219.

Moore, George Foot. Judaism in the First Centuries of the Christian Era: The Age of the Tannaim. 3 vols. Cambridge, MA: Harvard University Press, 1927-30.

Moule, C. F. D. The Origin of Christology. Cambridge: Cambridge University Press, 1977.

Muilenberg, James. "The Son of Man in Daniel and the Ethiopic Apocalypse of Enoch." Journal of Biblical Literature, 79 (1960), 197-209.

Murphy, Roland E. "Assumptions and Problems in Old Testament Wisdom Research." Catholic Biblical Quarterly, 29 (1967), 407-418.

_____. "Hebrew Wisdom." Journal of the American Oriental Society, 101 (1981), 21-34.

_____. "The Incarnational Aspects of Old Testament Wisdom." The Bible To-day, 9 (1963), 560-566.

_____. "Israel's Wisdom: A Biblical Model of Salvation." Studia Missionalia, 30 (1981), 1-43.

_____. "What and Where is Wisdom?" Currents in Theology and Mission, 4 (1977), 283-287.

_____. Wisdom Literature and Psalms. Interpreting Biblical Texts. Ed. L. R. Bailey and V. P. Furnish. Nashville: Abingdon Press, 1983.

Neill, Stephen. The Interpretation of the New Testament 1861-1961. London: Oxford University Press, 1964.

Neumann, Erich. The Great Mother: An Analysis of the Archetype. Bollingen Series 47. Princeton, NJ: Princeton University Press, 1953.

Neyrey, Jerome H. An Ideology of Revolt: John's Christology in Social-Science Perspective. Philadelphia: Fortress Press, 1988.

Nicholson, Godfrey C. Death as Departure: The Johannine Descent-Ascent Schema. Society of Biblical Literature Dissertation Series 63. Chico, CA: Scholars Press, 1983.

Nickelsburg, George W. E. Jewish Literature Between the Bible and the Mishnah: A Historical and Literary Introduction. Philadephia: Fortress Press, 1981.

Nicol, W. The Semeia in the Fourth Gospel. Novum Testamentum, Supplements XXXII. Leiden: E. J. Brill, 1972.

Noth, M. and D. W. Thomas, eds. Wisdom in Israel and the Ancient Near East. Festschrift for H. H. Rowley. Vetus Testamentum, Supplements III. Leiden: E. J. Brill, 1955.

Odeberg, Hugo. The Fourth Gospel. Uppsala: Almquist & Wiksells, 1929.

Oepke, Albrecht. "παῖς." Theological Dictionary of the New Testament. Vol. V. Ed. Gerhard Friedrich. Trans. G. W. Bromiley. Grand Rapids: Wm. B. Eerdmans, 1967.

Oesterley, W. O. E. and G. H. Box. The Religion and Worship of the Synagogue. London: Sir Isaac Pitman and Sons, 1911.

Olsson, Birger. Structure and Meaning in the Fourth Gospel: A Text-Linguistic Analysis of John 2:1-11 and 4:1-42. Trans. J. Gray. Coniectanea biblica, New Testament 6. Lund: C. W. K. Gleerup, 1974.

174

Pagels, Elaine H. The Johannine Gospel in Gnostic Exegesis. Society of Biblical
Literature Monograph Series 17. Nashville: Abingdon Press, 1973.

Painter, John. "Christology and the Fourth Gospel: A Study of the Prologue."
Australian Biblical Review, 31 (1983), 45-62.

_____. "Christology and the History of the Johannine Community in the Pro-
logue of the Fourth Gospel." New Testament Studies, 30 (1984), 460-474.

_____. John: Witness and Theologian. London: SPCK, 1975.

Pamment, Margaret. "The Son of Man in the Fourth Gospel." Journal of Theological Studies, 36 (1985), 56-66.

Pancaro, Severino. The Law in the Fourth Gospel: The Torah and the Gospel,
Moses and Jesus, Judaism and Christianity According to John. Novum Testamentum, Supplements XLII. Leiden: E. J. Brill, 1975.

Pannenberg, Wolfhart. Jesus--God and Man. Trans. Lewis L. Wilkins and Duane
A. Priebe. Philadelphia: Westminster Press, 1968.

Pazdan, Mary Margaret. The Son of Man: A Metaphor for Jesus in the Fourth
Gospel. Zacchaeus Studies: New Testament. Collegeville, MN: Liturgical
Press, 1991.

Pfeiffer, G. Ursprung und Wesen der Hypostasenvorsellungen im Judentum.
Stuttgart: Calver, 1967.

Pinto, Basil de. "Word and Wisdom in St. John." Scripture, 19 (1967), 19-27,
107-122.

Pittenger, W. Norman. Christology Reconsidered. London: SCM Press, 1970.

_____. "The Incarnation in Process Theology." Review and Expositor, 71
(1974), 43-57.

_____. The Word Incarnate: A Study of the Doctrine of the Person of Christ.
New York: Harper and Brothers, 1959.

Pollard, T. E. "Cosmology and the Prologue of the Fourth Gospel." Vigilae
Christianae, 12 (1958), 147-153.

_____. Johannine Christology and the Early Church. Society for New Testament
Studies Monograph Series 13. Cambridge: Cambridge University Press,
1970.

Pope, Marvin H. Job. The Anchor Bible, Vol. 15. Garden City, NY: Doubleday
and Co., 1973.

Potterie, Ignace de la "L'arrière-fond du theme johannique de verité." Studia Evangelica, Vol. I. Ed. Kurt Aland, et al. Berlin: Akademie-Verlag, 1959.

_____. "L'emploi dynamique de eis dans Saint Jean et ses incidences théologiques." Biblica, 43 (1962), 366-387.

_____. "'Je suis la Voie, la Vérité et la Vie' (Jn 14,6)." Nouvelle revue théologique, 88 (1966), 917-926.

_____. "Jesus King and Judge According to John 19:13." Scripture, 13 (1961), 97-111.

_____. "Οἶδα et γινώσκω, les deux modes de la conaissance dans le quatrième évangile." Biblica, 40 (1959), 709-725.

Pregeant, Russell. "The Wisdom Passages in Matthew's Story." Society of Biblical Literature 1990 Seminar Papers. Ed. David J. Lull. Atlanta: Scholars Press, 1990.

Pryor, John W. "Jesus and Israel in the Fourth Gospel--John 1:11." Novum Testamentum, 32 (1990), 201-218.

_____. "The Johannine Son of Man and the Descent-Ascent Motif." Journal of the Evangelical Theological Society, 34 (1991), 341-351.

Quell, Gottfried, Gerhard Kittel, and Rudolf Bultmann. "ἀλήθεια." Theological Dictionary of the New Testament. Vol. I. Ed. Gerhard Kittel. Trans. G. W. Bromiley. Grand Rapids: Wm. B. Eerdmans, 1964.

Rad, Gerhad von. Old Testament Theology. 2 vols. Trans. D. M. G. Stalker. New York: Harper & Brothers, 1962-65.

_____. Wisdom in Israel. Nashville: Abingdon Press, 1972.

_____, Georg Bertram, and Rudolf Bultmann. "ζάω." Theological Dictionary of the New Testament. Vol. II. Ed. Gerhard Kittel. Trans. G. W. Bromiley. Grand Rapids: Wm. B. Eerdmans, 1964.

_____, and Gerhard Kittel. "δοκέω." Theological Dictionary of the New Testament. Vol. II. Ed. Gerhard Kittel. Trans. G. W. Bromiley. Grand Rapids: Wm. B. Eerdmans, 1964.

Rankin, O. S. Israel's Wisdom Literature: Its Bearing on Theology and the History of Religion. Edinburgh: T. & T. Clark, reprinted 1954.

Reese, James M. "Christ as Wisdom Incarnate: Wiser than Solomon, Loftier than Lady Wisdom." Biblical Theology Bulletin, 11 (1981), 44-47.

_____. Hellenistic Influence on the Book of Wisdom and Its Consequences. Rome: Pontifical Institute Press, 1970.

Reim, Gunther. Studien zum alttestamentlichen Hintergrund des Johannesevangelium. Society for the New Testament Studies Monograph Series 22. Cambridge: Cambridge University Press, 1974.

_____. "Targum und Johannesevangelium." Biblische Zeitschrift, 27 (1983), 1-13.

Rengstorf, Karl. "ἀποστέλλω (πέμπω)." Theological Dictionary of the New Testament. Vol. I. Ed. Gerhard Kittel. Trans. G. W. Bromiley. Grand Rapids: Wm. B. Eerdmans, 1964.

_____. "σημεῖον." Theological Dictionary of the New Testament. Vol. VII. Ed. Gerhard Friedrich. Trans. G. W. Bromiley. Grand Rapids: Wm. B. Eerdmans, 1971.

Richardson, Alan. An Introduction to the Theology of the New Testament. London: SCM Press, 1958.

Richter, Georg. "Praesentische und futurische Eschatologie im 4. Evangelium." Gegenwart und kommendes Reich: Schuelergabe Anton Voegtle zum 65. Geburtstag. Ed. P. Fiedler and D. Zeller. Stuttgart: Katholisches Bibelwerk, 1975.

Ridderbos, Hermann. "On the Christology of the Fourth Gospel." Saved by Hope: Essays in Honor of Richard C. Oudersluys. Ed. J. I. Cook. Grand Rapids: Wm. B. Eerdmans, 1978.

_____. "The Structure and Scope of the Prologue to the Gospel of John." Novum Testamentum, 8 (1966), 180-201.

Ringgren, Helmer. Word and Wisdom: Studies in the Hypostatization of Divine Qualities and Functions in the Ancient Near East. Lund: H. Ohlssons Bokr, 1947.

Robertson, A. T. A Grammar of the Greek New Testament in the Light of Historical Research. Nashville: Broadman Press, 1934.

Robinson, James M. "Basic Shifts in German Theology." Interpretation, 16 (1962), 76-97.

_____. "Very Goddess and Very Man: Jesus' Better Self." Encountering Jesus: A Debate on Christology. Ed. Stephen T. Davis. Atlanta: John Knox Press, 1988.

_____, and Helmut Koester. Trajectories through Early Christianity. Philadelphia: Fortress Press, 1971.

Robinson, John A. T. "Dunn on John." Theology, 85 (1982), 332-338.

_____. The Human Face of God. Philadelphia: Westminster Press, 1973.

_____. "The Relation of the Prologue to the Gospel of St. John." New Testament Studies, 9 (1962-63), 120-129.

_____. Twelve New Testament Studies. Studies in Biblical Theology 36. London: SCM Press, 1962.

Rochais, G. "La formation du prologue (Jn 1, 1-18)." Science et Esprit 37 (1985), 5-44, 161-187.

Ruckstuhl, E. "Die johanneische Menschensohnforschung 1957-1969." Theologische Berichte. Ed. J. Pfammatter and F. Furger. Zürich: Zwingli-Verlag, 1972.

Ruether, Rosemary Radford. Sexism and God-Talk: Toward a Feminist Theology. Boston: Beacon Press, 1983.

Rylaarsdam, J. Coert. Revelation in Jewish Wisdom Literature. Chicago: University of Chicago Press, 1946.

Sabourin, Leopold. Christology: Basic Texts in Focus. Staten Island, NY: Alba house, 1984.

Sanders, Jack T. The New Testament Christological Hymns. Society for New Testament Studies Monograph Series 15. Cambridge: Cambridge University Press, 1971.

Sandmel, Samuel. Philo of Alexandria: An Introduction. New York: Oxford University Press, 1979.

Sasse, Hermann. "κοσμέω." Theological Dictionary of the New Testament. Vol. III. Ed. Gerhard Kittel. Trans. G. W. Bromiley. Grand Rapids: Wm. B. Eerdmans, 1965.

Savignac, Jean de. "Note sur le sens du verset VIII 22 de Proverbes." Vetus Testamentum, 4 (1954), 429-432.

Schencke, W. Die Chokma (Sophia) in der judischen Hypostasenspekulation. Kristiana: Jacob Dybwad, 1913.

Schillebeeckx, Edward. Christ: The Experience of Jesus as Lord. Trans. John Bowden. New York: Crossroad, 1981.

_____. Interim Report on the Books "Jesus" and Christ." Trans. John Bowden. New York: Crossroad, 1981.

_____. Jesus: An Experiment in Christology. Trans. Hubert Hoskins. New York: Crossroad, 1979.

Schlatter, F. W. "The Problem of Jn 1:3b-4a." Catholic Biblical Quarterly, 34 (1972), 54-58.

Schlier, Heinrich. "Im Anfang war das Wort: Zum Prolog des Johannesevangeliums." Die Zeit der Kirche: Exegetische Aufsätze und Vorträge, Vol. I. Freiburg: Herder, 1956.

Schmid, Hans Heinrich. Wesen und Geschichte der Weisheit. Beihefte zur Zeitschrift für die alttestamentliche Wissenschaft 101. Berlin: Töpelmann, 1966.

Schnackenburg, Rudolf. The Gospel According to St. John. Vol. 1. Trans. Kevin Smyth. Vol. 2. Trans. Cecily Hastings, et al. Vol. 3. Trans. David Smith and G. A. Kon. New York: Crossroad, 1982.

_____. Logos-Hymnus und johanneischer Prologue." Biblische Zeitschrift, 1 (1957), 69-109.

_____. "Der Menschensohn im Johannesevangelium." New Testament Studies, 11 (1965), 123-137.

Schneider, H. "'The Word Was Made Flesh': An Analysis of the Theology of Revelation in the Fourth Gospel." Catholic Biblical Quarterly, 31 (1969), 344-356.

Schneiders, Sandra M. "Women in the Fourth Gospel and the Role of Women in the Contemporary Church." Biblical Theology Bulletin, 12 (1982), 35-45.

Schoneveld, J. "Die Thora in Person. Eine Lekture des Prologs des Johannesevangeliums als Beitrag zu einer Christologie ohne Antisemitismus." Kirche und Israel, 1 (1991), 40-52.

Schulz, Siegfried. Das Evangelium nach Johannes. Göttingen: Vandenhoeck und Ruprecht, 1972.

_____. Die Stunde der Botschaft: Einfuhrung in der Theologie die vier Evangelisten. Hamburg: Furche, 1967.

Schüssler Fiorenza, Elisabeth. In Memory of Her: A Feminist Theological Reconstruction of Christian Origins. New York: Crossroad, 1984.

Schweizer, Eduard. Ego Eimi. Die religionsgeschichtliche Herkunft und theologische Bedeutung der johanneischen Bildreden, Zugleich ein Beitrag zur Quellenfage des vierten Evangeliums. 2nd ed. Göttingen: Vandenhoeck und Ruprecht, 1965.

_____. Jesus. Trans. David E. Green. Atlanta: John Knox Press, 1971.

_____. Neotestamentica: Deutsche und Englishe Aufsätze 1951-1963. Zürich: Zwingli-Verlag, 1963.

179

_____. "σάρξ." Theological Dictionary of the New Testament. Vol. VIII. Ed. Gerhard Friedrich. Trans. G. W. Bromiley. Grand Rapids: Wm. B. Eerdmans, 1971.

_____. "Zum religionsgeschichtlichen Hintergrund der 'Sendungsformel' Gal 4,4f; Rom 8,3f; Joh 3,16f; 1 Joh 4,9." Beiträge zur Theologie des Neuen Testaments. Zürich: Zwingli Verlag, 1970.

Scott, Ernest F. The Fourth Gospel: Its Purpose and Theology. The Literature of the New Testament. Edinburgh: T. &T. Clark, 1908.

Scott, Martin. Sophia and the Johannine Jesus. Journal for the Study of the New Testament Supplement Series 18. Sheffield: JSOT Press, 1992 (forthcoming).

Scott, R. B. Y. Proverbs, Ecclesiastes. The Anchor Bible, Vol. 18. Garden City, NY: Doubleday and Co., 1965.

_____. "The Study of Wisdom Literature." Interpretation, 24 (1970), 20-45.

_____. The Way of Wisdom in the Old Testament. New York: Macmillan, 1971.

_____. "Wisdom in Creation: the 'âmŏn of Proverbs 8:30." Vetus Testamentum, 10 (1960), 213-223.

Scroggs, Robin. Christology in Paul and John: The Reality and Revelation of God. Proclamation Commentaries. Ed. Gerhard Krodel. Philadelphia: Fortress Press, 1988.

Seesemann, Heinrich. "οἶδα." Theological Dictionary of the New Testament. Vol. V. Ed. Gerhard Friedrich. Trans. G. W. Bromiley. Grand Rapids: Wm. B. Eerdmans, 1967.

Segovia, Fernando F. The Farewell of the Word: The Johannine Call to Abide. Minneapolis: Fortress Press, 1991.

Sidebottom, E. M. The Christ of the Fourth Gospel in the Light of First-Century Judaism. London: SPCK, 1961.

Skehan, Patrick W. "Structures in Poems on Wisdom: Proverbs 8 and Sirach 24." Catholic Biblical Quarterly, 41 (1979), 365-379.

Sloyan, Gerard S. What Are They Saying About John? New York: Paulist Press, 1991.

Smalley, Stephen S. John: Evangelist & Interpreter. Exeter: The Paternoster Press, 1978.

_____. "The Sign in John XXI." New Testament Studies, 20 (1973-74), 275-288.

Smith. David. Wisdom Christology in the Synoptic Gospels. Rome: Pontificia Studiorum Universitas A S. Thoma Aq. in Urbe, 1970.

Smith, Dwight Moody. "Johannine Christianity: Some Reflections on its Character and Delineation." New Testament Studies, 21 (1974-75), 222-248.

Smith, J. Z. "Wisdom and Apocalyptic." Religious Syncretism in Antiquity: Essays in Conversation with George Widengren. Ed. B. Pearson. Missoula, MT: Scholars Press, 1970.

Smith, Morton. "Palestinian Judaism in the First Century." Israel: Its Role in Civilization. Ed. M. Davis. New York: The Seminary Israel Institute of the Jewish Theological Seminary, 1956.

Smith, T. C. "The Christology of the Fourth Gospel." Review and Expositor, 71 (1974), 19-30.

Spicq, Ceslaus. Agápē in the New Testament. 3 vols. Trans. M. A. McNamara and M. H. Richter. St. Louis: B. Herder Book Co., 1966.

_____. "Notes d'exégèse johannique. La charité est amour manifeste." Revue biblique, 65 (1958), 358-370.

_____. "Le Siracide et la structure littéraire du prologue de saint Jean." Memorial Lagrange. Paris: J. Gibalda, 1940.

Staley, Jeffrey Lloyd. The Print's First Kiss: A Rhetorical Investigation of the Implied Reader in the Fourth Gospel. Society of Biblical Literature Dissertation Series 82. Atlanta: Scholars Press, 1988.

_____. "The Structure of John's Prologue: Its Implications for the Gospel's Narrative Structure." Catholic Biblical Quarterly, 48 (1986), 241-264.

Stauffer, Ethelbert. "ἀγαπάω." Theological Dictionary of the New Testament. Vol. I. Ed. Gerhard Kittel. Trans. G. W. Bromiley. Grand Rapids: Wm. B. Eerdmans, 1964.

Stead, G. C. "The Valentinian Myth of Sophia." Journal of Theological Studies, 20 (1969), 75-104.

Strachan, R. H. The Fourth Gospel: Its Significance and Environment. 3rd ed. London: SCM Press, 1941.

Suggs, M. Jack. Wisdom, Christology and Law in Matthew's Gospel. Cambridge, MA: Harvard University Press, 1970.

Sundberg, Albert C., Jr. "Christology in the Fourth Gospel." Biblical Research, 21 (1976), 29-37.

Talbert, Charles H. "The Myth of a Descending-Ascending Redeemer in Mediterranean Antiquity." New Testament Studies, 22 (1976), 418-439.

_____. What is a Gospel? The Genre of the Canonical Gospels. Philadelphia: Fortress Press, 1977.

Terrien, Samuel. The Elusive Presence: Toward a New Biblical Theology. Religious Perspectives, Vol. 26. New York: Harper & Row, 1978.

_____. "The Play of Wisdom: Turning Point in Biblical Theology." Horizons in Biblical Theology, 3 (1981), 125-153.

Thompson, Marilyn Meye. The Humanity of Jesus in the Fourth Gospel. Philadelphia: Fortress Press, 1988.

Tobin, Thomas H. "The Prologue of John and Hellenistic Jewish Speculation." Catholic Biblical Quarterly, 52 (1990), 252-269.

Trench, R. C. Synonyms of the New Testament. 8th ed. London: Macmillan and Co., 1980.

Trible, Phyllis. "Wisdom Builds a Poem: The Architecture of Proverbs 1:20-33." Journal of Biblical Literature, 94 (1975), 509-518.

Vawter, Bruce F. "Prov. 8:22: Wisdom and Creation." Journal of Biblical Literature, 99 (1980), 205-216.

_____. "What Came to Be in Him Was Life, Jn 1,3b-4a." Catholic Biblical Quarterly, 25 (1963), 401-406.

Wahlde, Urban C. von. The Earliest Version of John's Gospel: Recovering the Gospel of Signs. Wilmington, DE: Michael Glazier, 1989.

_____. "The Johannine 'Jews': A Critical Survey." New Testament Studies, 28 (1982), 33-60.333

Walker, Anselm. "Sophiology." Diakonia, 16 (1981), 40-54.

Westcott, B. F. The Gospel According to St. John. London: John Murray, 1892.

Whybray, R. N. "Slippery Words, IV Wisdom." Expository Times, 89 (1977-78), 359-62.

_____. Wisdom in Proverbs. London: SCM Press, 1965.

Wicks, H. J. The Doctrine of God in Jewish Apocryphal and Apocalyptic Literature. London: Hunter & Longhurst, 1915, reissued 1971.

Wilckens, Ulrich and Georg Fohrer. "σοφία." Theological Dictionary of the New Testament. Vol. VII. Ed. Gerhard Friedrich. Trans. G. W. Bromiley. Grand Rapids: Wm. B. Eerdmans, 1971.

Wiles, Maurice F. The Spiritual Gospel: The Interpretation of the Fourth Gospel in the Early Church. Cambridge: Cambridge University Press, 1960.

_____. "Reflections on James D. G. Dunn's Christology in the Making." Theology, 85 (1982), 92-96.

_____, and James D. G. Dunn. "Christology--The Debate Continues." Theology, 85 (1982), 324-332.

Wilken, Robert L. Aspects of Wisdom in Judaism and Early Christianity. Notre Dame: University of Notre Dame Press, 1975.

Willett, Michael E. "Jung and John." Explorations, 7 (1988), 77-92.

_____. "Again, a Symbolic Reading of the Fourth Gospel." Paper presented to the New Testament Section of the Central States meeting of the Society of Biblical Literature, Columbia, MO, March 26, 1990.

_____. "The 'I Am' Sayings and the Speeches of Wisdom." Paper presented to the New Testament Section of the Central States meeting of the Society of Biblical Literature, Columbia, MO, April 7, 1986.

Williamson, R. "Philo and New Testament Christology." Expository Times, 90 (1978-79), 361-365.

Wilson, Robert McL. "Philo and the Fourth Gospel." Expository Times, 65 (1953-54), 47-49.

Wink, Walter. John the Baptist in the Gospel Tradition. Society for New Testament Studies Monograph Series 7. Cambridge: Cambridge University Press, 1968.

Winston, David. The Wisdom of Solomon. The Anchor Bible, Vol. 43. Garden City, NY: Doubleday and Co., 1979.

Winter, Paul. "ΜΟΝΟΓΕΝΗΣ ΠΑΡΑ ΠΑΤΡΟΣ." Zeitschrift für Religions und Geistegeschichte, 5 (1953), 335-363.

Wolfson, H. A. Philo. 2 vols. Cambridge, MA: Harvard University Press, 1947.

Woll, D. Bruce. Johannine Christianity in Conflict: Authority, Rank, and Succession in the First Farewell Discourse. Society of Biblical Literature Dissertation Series 60. Chico, CA: Scholars Press, 1981.

Wood, J. The Wisdom Literature: An Introduction. London: Duckworth, 1967.

Wright, G. Ernest. God Who Acts: Biblical Theology as Recital. Naperville, IL: Alec R. Allenson, 1952.

Yamauchi, E. "The Descent of Ishtar, the Fall of Sophia, and the Jewish Roots of Gnosticism." Tyndale Bulletin, 29 (1978), 143-175.

Yee, Gale A. "An Analysis of Prov. 8:22-31 According to Style and Structure." Zeitschrift für die alttestamentliche Wissenschaft, 94 (1982), 58-66.

Zerafa, P. P. The Wisdom of God in the Book of Job. Rome: Herder, 1978.

Zerwick, Max. Biblical Greek. Trans. Joseph Smith. Rome: Scripta Pontificii Instituti Biblici, 1963.

_____, and Mary Grosvenor. A Grammatical Analysis of the Greek New Testament. Rev. ed. Rome: Biblical Institute Press, 1981.

Zickendraht, Karl. "ΕΓΩ ΕΙΜΙ." Theologische Studien und Kritiken, 94 (1922), 162-168.

Ziener, Georg. "Weisheitsbuch und Johannesevangelium." Biblica, 38 (1957), 396-417; 39 (1958), 37-60.

Zimmerman, H. "Das absolute ἐγὼ εἰμί als die neutestamentliche Offenbarungs-formel." Biblische Zeitschrift, 4 (1960), 54-69, 266-276.

INDEX OF MODERN AUTHORS

188

INDEX OF SUBJECTS

vine   86, 92, 112

water   1, 22, 92, 93, 94, 123, 125
wine   22, 89, 91
Wisdom   2, 5, 6, 9, 10, 11, 12, 13,
     14, 15, 16, 17, 18, 19, 20, 21,
     23, 24, 25, 26, 27, 28, 29, 30,
     33, 35, 36, 38, 39, 40, 41, 42,
     43, 44, 45, 46, 47, 54, 55, 58,
     61, 62, 64, 66, 67, 70, 74, 75,
     78, 79, 84, 85, 89, 90, 91, 94,
     98, 101, 103, 104,   105,   110,
     111, 113, 114, 116, 118, 119,
     121, 122, 124, 125, 126, 127,
     128, 130, 132, 134, 138, 140,
     142, 143, 149, 150, 152, 153
wisdom literature   4, 5, 33, 39, 41,
     58, 74
Wisdom material   2, 40, 42, 46, 47,
     49, 54, 55, 57, 58, 61, 64, 70,
     74, 75, 83, 85, 87, 88, 94, 95,
     102, 112, 113, 121, 124, 125,
     126, 135, 139
wisdom tradition   27, 57, 60, 65,
     66, 67, 88, 95, 121, 140, 148
Wisdom of Solomon   6, 13, 16, 17,
     18, 19, 23, 24, 25, 26, 27, 35,
     36, 37, 38, 39, 40, 41, 42, 43,
     49, 54, 58, 61, 62, 70, 74, 75,
     78, 79, 83, 84, 88, 91, 98, 102,
     110, 111, 112, 113, 114, 116,
     117, 118, 121, 122, 124, 125,
     130, 132, 137, 144
women   30, 146, 147, 148,   150,
     152
Word   17, 31, 33, 34, 35, 36, 37,
     38, 40, 42, 43, 46, 51, 52, 91,
     105, 113, 119, 122, 129, 130,
     131, 132, 141
world 38, 39, 52, 54, 57, 62, 72, 73,
     75, 96, 100, 103, 107, 142

DDS